DYING FOR TRIPLICATE

A TRUE STORY OF ADDICTION, SURVIVAL AND RECOVERY

(www.dyingfortriplicate.com)

By

TODD A. ZALKINS

To my mom. Thank you for believing in me.
Your endless supply of love and laughter is the
greatest gift a son could ever receive.

In loving memory of my father,
Robert Zalkins & Grammy Nel

Dedicated to all of the countless souls who suffer
in the disease of addiction

AUTHOR'S NOTE

This is a work of nonfiction. The events and experiences detailed herein are all true and have been faithfully rendered as I have remembered them, to the best of my ability. There are some names, identities, and situations or circumstances that have been changed in order to protect the anonymity of various individuals involved.

Some of the conversations are not written to represent word for word documentation, for I have retold them in a way that evokes my true personality and the meaning of what was said, in keeping with the true essence of the actual events.

TABLE OF CONTENTS

PART SIX IN TREATMENT   271

INTRODUCTION

From my journal, September 27, 2009, entry titled "My Best Day"

Yesterday was the best day by far that I have had in sobriety. Something happened that had perfect timing for this moment in my life. I was in the middle of proofreading my story, the manuscript I hope will be a book that can help some people, so I thought I was basically done writing. But what happened on this day was something I could never have imagined occurring, and it makes the perfect introduction. So here goes...

I get manicures and pedicures, and I have been getting them for more than 20 years. My mom once told me, "The girls will like that you do this... Plus, no cute girl wants to see your hands and feet looking like they belong to an alligator." So, I took her suggestion seriously and I have been getting them ever since I was 17. That's a lot of years spending time in salons reading the worst gossip columns and back issues of People magazine, but hey, it's worth it I guess.

Anyway, I was at an indigent detox center called Charlie Street in Costa Mesa today, to talk with some other alcoholics and drug addicts. My sponsor took me there when I had about 32 days of sobriety (at which point I had still not slept), and I have been going there ever since, once a week on average.

After I was at Charlie Street I went to Little Saigon in Westminster to buy this Asian coffee I love, and afterwards I figured I would stop to get a manicure/pedicure. I had never been to this place before and I just thought I would give it a try. No one spoke any English, which is not a surprise as most of the businesses there are Vietnamese or Thai-owned.

They put me in that big comfortable "spa" chair and I started to relax as I usually do, but only for a couple of minutes. There was a young girl (early 20's and obviously very pregnant) who worked there, and she was upset and crying. I had no idea what was going on, but a minute or two later what appeared to be her boyfriend or husband came into the nail salon screaming, and obviously really pissed off.

It was one of those things where you feel the person may have a gun on them—there was that type of anger and intensity in his voice, more like rage. This guy was yelling at the girl working on my feet, and it was getting quite uncomfortable. I was thinking, I am not Superman, but I will certainly jump in if this guy starts to beat up on any of these women. That doesn't fly with me—no way.

The owner of the nail salon was screaming at both of them to leave, and as they were walking out the door, the pregnant girl collapsed. She passed out and then started to go into a full-blown seizure. It was really a scary sight to say the least. No one knew what to do and there was total hysteria in the shop. I couldn't understand a thing they were saying due to their speaking in Vietnamese. There was one English speaking customer who was seated to my left, and I yelled, "Call 911 right now!" as my cell phone was in the car.

I raced over to the angry man whose demeanor had changed. He was quiet and obviously very concerned. Unfortunately, he had given her a sip of water, which was a very bad idea—the pregnant girl had now stopped breathing and there was blood in her mouth and no pulse. I was afraid that this poor young thing was going to die right there on the cold nail salon floor. I learned that she was six months into her pregnancy, but don't ask me how I got that information as I could barely understand a word they said.

Now there were other shop owners rallying to help, but no one was doing anything except expressing sheer panic. The ladies who worked in the nail salon were crying and screaming for help. I calmly grabbed the boyfriend or husband, and pushed him towards her feet, looking at him with a face that said, "I am not screwing around with you right now," and he quickly did what I signaled him to do, which was to hold her legs and rub her feet.

It was close to two minutes since the pregnant girl had stopped breathing, and she had no pulse, so I started to perform CPR. It's a whole different ball game with respect to administering CPR when there is a real human being involved, compared to the plastic dummies you learn CPR on. The fact that this girl was pregnant only seemed to add more pressure and intensity to the situation.

I pinched her nose lightly and breathed into her mouth hurriedly, and then pushed gently a few times right by her lower rib cage area, while being very aware that she was carrying a baby. It was really scary trying to do that and my only thought was "God, please help me…please allow me to help this person so she and her baby can survive."

After a minute or so she started to breathe very softly, and her pulse returned. She was alive. The paramedics and firemen showed up and took her directly to the hospital, and one of the fireman said to me, "A baby is going to be born, and a mother will get to raise her child because of what you did."

Tears ran down my face. I am not a hero. I just happened to be there at the right time, and I am not one to get pats on the back for doing a good job. I am conditioned to doing the wrong thing, and for so long I had done the wrong thing. Had I not been sober I never would have been at a nail salon at 6 p.m. on a Saturday night, are you kidding me? I would be locked up in my house drooling, with drugs everywhere, in my cold cave-like home with absolutely no one around.

I am close to 6'4" and it was funny how all of these small Asian men about 5'3" were patting me on the back and saying in broken English, "You a lifesaver," or, "You a hero!"

I walked back to my chair and put my feet in the water and I fell silent. The ladies in the nail salon were crying tears of joy and thanking me by bringing me cold bottled water and warm towels. And all I could think of at that point were all the people in recovery who had reached their hands out to me when I was really sick and shaking, and when I could barely talk or understand people.

I was in this odd state of "gratitude shock" that made me feel really high for a few moments, and then about ten minutes later I must admit I was very uncomfortable. I was thinking, "Man, after what you just did you deserve a drink or some pills—job well done!" That's my head. After all I have been through, it will still tell me things to corner me sometimes, to get me alone and kill me by encouraging me to repeat the bad choices I have made so often in the past.

I was uncomfortable the entire rest of the night. I wasn't saying to myself, "Man, I am some hero, look what I did"—what I was saying was, "Because I am clean and sober, a mom has a chance to give birth to her baby."

That to me has been worth all of the suffering and pain I have been through, all for that little moment in time where I could for once make a difference to someone else with no strings attached. There wasn't some angle or something I was getting in return. Well, actually, there was something I got in return—I got to grow up just a little bit, and that's all I have ever really wanted.

But it has been a very, very long and painful road to get where I am now. I have often heard that only addicts and alcoholics can relate to that true loneliness that we experience in our disease. It's quite profound, especially when we get to the "end of the road," when the stuff we use actually stops working for us. Yes, there comes a point for a lot of us addicts/alcoholics where the stuff we depended upon for so many years for that "relief" and "escape" from life actually stops working.

When that happens, it is a displacement of self that is very difficult to interpret, and I will do my best on that subject matter later on. I still have some periods of my insane existence to cover and it's important to also point out that drugs and alcohol were often fun, but it's also a million times more important for me to emphasize that my abuse was the primary reason for almost every negative thing that happened in my life: loss of jobs, loss of relationships I valued, loss of loved ones, and on and on.

After 24 years of addiction, on my last stint in rehab I was diagnosed as a hopeless case and my doctor indicated it was possible that my brain might never correctly heal as a result of my drug abuse. I didn't sleep for my first 44 days of sobriety while going through a horrific detoxification.

I was suicidal and rendered completely insane. My addiction to Oxycontin, Norco, Vicodin, Fentanyl, and Valium was inescapable and the noose seemed to get tighter and tighter as time dragged on, never letting me go.

I want to be really clear on two things:

1. I drank and used drugs for a really long time, and I did have some good times early on.
2. There came a time when nothing was fun anymore, and yet I carried on in a state of addiction and prolific sickness for many years, and I can tell you with absolute certainty that I had many more years spent in my addiction where life wasn't any fun at all. For me, the bad years far outweigh any good ones I ever had, which were few and far between, and I assure you that you will see plenty of that later in the story.

I am on the other side of that hell today, but it took a lot of pain and suffering to get to this beautiful place that I now call my life. I never lived life before I got clean—I merely survived. I love my life today, but it wasn't that way for a long time.

In order to be rebuilt I had to first tear myself apart. The following is an account of what I went through.

*Already looking for mischief, with no clothes
on of course.*

Part One
Where it Began...

I grew up in a beautiful area called Naples Island in Long Beach, California. It's a small community. I'm not even sure how many people live there, but there couldn't be more than 1,900 people on the island itself. There are canals that run through it just like in Italy, although I've never been there myself. There is a local business that rows gondolas throughout the canals, and this attracts a lot of tourists. It's an experience that is unique unless you have lived there most of your life, which I have.

Seeing a guy in a "gondola outfit" and hearing him try his best to imitate Pavarotti while rowing folks from out of town is a must see if ever visiting the area. If you grew up in this community, you pretty much saw the water every day, something I took for granted like I did a lot of things in my life. The overall beauty of this place is just overwhelming and on a summer day in the evening hours one can feel completely detached from the rest of the world, where everything around you is perfect, or at least that's how I used to feel many years ago.

It was as safe a place for a kid to grow up as I could ever imagine. On the outside I probably appeared to be a really happy child, but inside I often struggled emotionally. My seeking of approval and the need for attention were basically constant. I couldn't seem to be okay by myself unless my head finally got quiet, which for me was at the end of a school day and after long rigorous exercise.

Playing football after school, swimming in the canals, riding bikes, and causing harmless bits of mayhem and chaos were mandatory for me, and I often was the instigator of this type of behavior.

I'm not sure exactly what prompted my incessant desire to let everyone know I existed—maybe it had something to do with the fact that I didn't get any attention from a father whom I loved dearly. My mother always made me feel loved, but the environment I grew up in had fathers steering the way for their children and mine just wasn't even in the picture.

This sounds like I am blaming my dad, but this is probably just one of many things that contributed to my being the ultimate "attention hunter." When I realized I could make others laugh I wanted to do a lot more of that, and so an audience was really important to me; the world became my little stage for my antics.

A neighbor of ours used to have fireworks in the summertime for the Fourth of July, the really good, and of course, illegal ones. You know, M80s, stuff that would really blow things up, and for a kid at the age of nine or so it was fun to blow the shit out of anything.

In order to get the fireworks my neighbor John would dare me to run around half of Naples Island "streaking" (completely naked). That was perfectly acceptable to me. In the summer there is no better way to cool off than to run around naked for a half hour, piss off most of the neighborhood and then jump in the canal for a nice swim.

My other friends wouldn't even consider doing anything like streak for fireworks. Always the instigator, and looking back I'm convinced I would do it again. The fact is I can be talked into doing just about anything, or I can justify doing something in my head, often without considering the consequences.

So, if I get caught running around with my three-inch dick (okay two inches, I lied) flying around on a hot summer day, my parents will be pissed and I will be in trouble for sure. But, free fireworks? Just for racing around with my little pipe flying about? That's a no brainer... it is on! The way I look at it, restriction is a small price to pay in order to later blow some things up.

It didn't take very long for the neighbors in our little community to figure out who was causing the majority of mischief.

It would be perfectly normal to hear the neighbors say something like this:

Jack: "So, hey there, Bill, how is your weekend going?"

Bill: "Oh, it's just another beautiful weekend here in Long Beach. How are the wife and kids?"

Jack: "She's great, the kids are great, but the wife is all pissed. It's that Zalkins kid again."

Bill: "Oh, sure, that little shit Todd Zalkins—ain't he somethin'? Was it the streaking last Saturday"?

Jack: "Well no, that's just one thing. That little shit showed up at our front door naked, singing Christmas carols, while we were having a dinner party."

Bill: "Christmas carols"?

Jack: "Yes, fucking Christmas carols... while naked... in the middle of summer for God's sake."

Bill: "Well, he does what he does, all right."

Jack: "Yeah, I just wish he wouldn't do it in front of my fucking house while my entire family is over for dinner."

Stuff like that was normal for me, in fact it was mandatory. I had this urge to push the buttons of everyone, not really intending to hurt anyone ever, but to push the envelope enough so they really just remembered who I was. I was just a wise ass looking for a good time.

Now, after I had successfully completed my restriction, I had the fireworks and it was time to get busy. Collecting dog shit was easy back in the 70's because no one ever seemed to pick up after their dog when they took a dump. It would be like, "Oh shit, who did this? Looks like one of Sparky's dumps. When I see that fucking guy Carl (the owner of Sparky) I will tell him! In retribution, I will intentionally take my dog to his house and allow him to crap twice in his front yard."

You know, it's like keeping up with the Joneses. If your dog takes a dump in front of my pad, I will have my dog take two dumps in front of your pad. Even if I myself have to drop trousers and take a dump on your lawn. (Yes, that happened more than once. I was only about ten years old so I didn't really find it a problem, but I think our old neighbor Carl was pretty bent out of shape when he caught me crapping on his lawn.)

Back to the fireworks, so some friends of mine (who had no balls) and I would collect a ton of dog shit. I would be the one to place an M80 or two in a grocery bag with all of the dog shit, and place the bag on the front porch of some random asshole in our neighborhood.

I would light the miniature dynamites and kaboooom!!!! The house that used to be white or cream colored now had the look of how should I say it... like an exterior designer specializing in "making houses look like dog shit exploded all over," does a fabulous job of it!

I am not sure if I ever got caught for doing that. Oh, actually, I think I did. You see? I lied again. Lying would become a very significant character trait for me, because lying gave me flexibility in telling the truth. More often than not, you didn't want to hear the truth of what I had done anyway, especially if it involved destroying the outside of your house with dog shit by way of small pipe bombs, which would be the least of my concerns as I got older.

A Beer for the Little Guy!

My father was an alcoholic to the absolute core of his being. He left my mom, my brother Eric, who was three years older, and me when I was about seven. His idea of being married was having a wife at home and several girlfriends away from it. My dad, Robert, was a very good looking guy.

He stood 6'4", strong and lean, and was in the Marine Corps where he took up boxing at a young age. He was tough, and when he drank, no one ever knew which side of his personality would be revealed. From what my mom has told me, it was a roll of the dice when my dad drank. My dad could be one of the nicest and most loving guys in the world, or the meanest prick in North America... it all depended upon what alcohol had planned for his body chemistry on that particular day.

He had a loving heart too, though he often had a hard time showing it. I can remember my father screaming at my mom and how it terrified me to the bones. I would hide underneath my bed and put my fingers in my ears and whisper, "Please stop yelling at Mom," repeating until I could no longer hear it, and I would cry myself to sleep. Some say physical abuse is far worse than emotional abuse—I would beg to differ, as they are both traumatic and harmful to every human being, in my humble opinion.

Dad would pick up Eric and me for a "very short weekend" starting Saturday morning and ending on Sunday morning. I can't remember how many of these weekends we had, but there weren't a lot of them. He was an executive with Catalina Swimwear, a popular swimwear and sportswear manufacturer in the 60s and 70s.

The position was perfect for him as it allowed him to travel and drink unlimited amounts of alcohol with clients, and it was all business expense. I love that term "business expense." They should just call it, "We will reimburse you to take clients out and get demolished off of all the liquor you can drink account." Maybe that's extreme, and a tad bit too long of a title, but it certainly seems more accurate.

But like my dad, I would later come to love the "Business Expense" accounts. I would guess that 80% of all expenses on expense accounts are bullshit. I know—I had one for years. Except my expense reports were more like 110% bullshit as I seldom drank with clients; I drank with my friends and called it a "business expense," and it was business all right... drunk-monkey business.

An expense account was a gateway to take "friends" out to get completely gassed out of our minds off of booze and whatever else I could conjure up. I would later have a life that was based on conjuring up things that would completely destroy my little world and those around me.

Dad would show up in his Lincoln Continental or Cadillac in the mid-70's with a big Schlitz "Tall Boy" of beer between his legs. I thought that was totally normal. I mean, "It's my dad for God sake and it's 9:00 am, time to pick up the kids—you must have a cold brew in hand when going to pick up your children for a 45-minute stay for the weekend!"

People who drank coffee in the morning were soft. Booze is the way you get through the morning, isn't it? Or, that's what I was shown and led to believe as a kid.

I loved the way my dad smelled with the beer on his breath. That probably doesn't make a lot of sense to the average person, but for me it did. I didn't see my dad drink coffee. He drank booze, and alcoholics like booze and a lot of it. I can remember when I would kiss him on the cheek he had this smell that to me wasn't offensive at all... it was just how I knew him.

One of the best parts of the trip was when he would pick us up in Long Beach, and we would stop by our neighborhood liquor store (Morry's of Naples) where my brother and I would be able to stock up on crap to eat, while dad refueled with a few more brews. What's the problem? No problem with me. It was just another Saturday with dad.

We were then off to Huntington Beach, about twenty minutes south of Long Beach. The best part about it was I would get to sip off his brews, and I loved it. I don't really remember feeling different, but I loved the taste of it. I mean, it's what my dad drinks, and I want to be like dad, or so I thought.

A few pulls off of his Schlitz Tall Boy, Coors or Olympia, and the trip to Huntington Beach was magical. I mean I was seven or eight years old, and I had had a long week of school, and I think every kid that age should be able to have some brews to loosen up over the weekend (I am kidding, I just didn't know any other way).

We would get to Huntington Beach, and bam!! Dad would say, "Todd, get me a beer, wouldja?" "Yes, I will dad, absolutely." For some reason I always liked it when dad said, "wouldja," and it made me laugh every time he said it.

I would have enough time to crack the brew open, take a quick sip or two, and he would never even know the difference. If he knew, he didn't give a shit, so long as I was within yelling distance! Then, when he would sip the brew I would say, "Hey Pop, mind if I have a pull of that brew?" And I would get another pull off the brew. The more Pop drank the more Todd got to drink, and like I said, it's important for every eight year old young man to drink with his father!! (I am kidding again. I will be using a lot of sarcasm in this story—for me it's absolutely necessary).

MOM

My mother's name is Cheryle, and she is the best mom and friend I could ever have hoped for. She's a very playful person, and has a wonderful sense of humor. One of the greatest gifts we have always shared was our ability to understand or find humor in just the oddest things, and she is a beautiful lady on the inside and out.

Unlike my father, my mom doesn't possess the addictive behaviors that I do. She was a social drinker—a cocktail or two at a nice dinner or an occasional glass of wine. In fact, I have never seen my mother drunk, ever. I very seldom saw my dad sober, if ever. They were quite the opposite in the drinking department, in fact the two were like night and day in that regard.

My mom is capable of dishing out the most random x-rated comments, and usually at a time when it ended up making someone very uncomfortable. Yet it was always funny. What I am about to share with you is most likely something that you have never heard, nor can you probably imagine your own mother saying. So here we go…(forgive me, Mom):

I was out with my mom, my stepfather Darryl, and my girlfriend at the time (I will call her Valerie). We were having a blast at this killer Chinese restaurant and we had all drunk a few Mai Tais.

What I mean is, I probably had about five doubles and everyone else had two at the max.

I was getting ready to go on a surfing trip to mainland Mexico and Valerie was commenting on how much she was going to miss me. So, Valerie says something like, "Well, I guess absence makes the heart grow fonder"....and my mother replied, "Yes dear... and for someone else the pussy wetter."

Now, that may sound appalling. But if you knew how she said it, and in the funny way she said it, you would be laughing too. The only one not laughing was Valerie, I am pretty sure of that. I know for certain Darryl and I were in hysterics.

Another thing my mom said along the same lines was when we were at Walt's Wharf in Seal Beach (the best seafood around) and we ordered some oysters and my mom just said, "Yeah, let's order a dozen clits on the half shell." That ruined Valerie's dinner for sure. I actually couldn't even speak for about nine minutes because my jaw was somewhere on the floor beneath me, it was definitely one for the books.

But don't think those gestures made by my mom are a regular thing, because they are not. Timed the right way and with the right delivery, those comments are a home run in my book and absolutely necessary in an often very boring world. That's just my opinion. Looking back I think this was an innocent "test" by my mother to see if my girlfriend could laugh at just about anything.

What occurred in the events mentioned above was not everyday language used by my mother, I was just sharing some examples of how funny she could be. If you find it too over the top, let's just say you would have to have been there.

When my father left, my mom took care of Eric and me. It was not a real popular thing to be divorced at that time, at least not where I lived. One of my favorite things to do as a kid was when my mom and I would go to McDonald's together. To this day I just relish those times, which for me are so special to have in a mother–son relationship.

We would sit in the car after we got our food at the McDonald's on Anaheim Street in Long Beach, which is now a Tommy's Burger I believe. This was a time when my father had left and it was just my brother and me, and Mom of course. It was just cool not having our drunk dad around the house.

This will sound silly, but it's something that I will never forget because it was one of those times when I was young and unaffected, full of life and imagination. Anyway, my mom really liked the French fries, but only the soft ones. She was never interested in a crisp French fry, ever. So I would hunt through the bag and the little cardboard holder of fries, and when I found a soft fry I would get all excited and say, "Found one!" and I would just pass it to my mom. I was the "Soft French fry hunter," and upon receiving the soft fry my mom would reveal her beautiful smile.

Nothing could hurt us. There was no alcoholic father offering verbal abuse; we were just safe. We were at McDonald's for God's sake! No one gets hurt at McDonald's, except of course at the one in San Ysidro in the 80's where some crackpot rolled in there and killed dozens. (I don't find that funny in the least by the way. In fact, a buddy of mine and I had stopped at that same McDonald's five days before on our way back from surfing in Northern Baja, Mexico. That can still send chills down my spine thinking about how heavy that was.)

My mom was and still is a wonderful mother; she worked hard and took really good care of us. I didn't really know what was going on, but my brother was really affected by their getting divorced. He was about ten or eleven when Dad split, and I think it affected him going forward and even to this very day. My brother has always been saddened by our dad divorcing Mom, and the reason I say this is because I think in many ways our dad was my brother's hero.

I Demand Your Attention

For me, I was all about the attention. My mom would give it to me, and I loved every bit of it—she was very attentive and fun. If mom wasn't around I would get the attention from anyone in the neighborhood, and it usually involved some form of joke, or random acts of exposing myself (BA's, or "bare ass" activities were big back then). I would just drop trousers and bend over with butt cheeks blazing, and anything else to score some attention. "Hey... fucking look at me—I am naked and you are not... and your dog sucks"!!

I craved any form of reaction, and in looking back I think I needed that kind of validation, whether it was in a positive form or negative, it made no difference to me.

I wasn't hell-bent 24/7 on ruining our neighborhood. It's just when the urge came for something outrageous, or if life was just a bit too perfect and predictable, it was time for some chaos and I was the perfect individual to dispense it.

I always did well in school, in my early years that is. I loved my teachers for the most part, and even though I was always the "class clown" I did well in my studies and excelled on almost every level. I had this wanting or desire to be liked by everyone, and I would go out of my way for that feeling or impression of being liked.

One thing that came naturally to me was a soft spot in my heart and compassion for those with handicaps or physical disabilities. I would completely lose my mind if another kid made fun of a fellow student with a learning disability or physical shortcoming. I wasn't a violent kid, but I would make it apparent that I would somehow manage to kick the crap out of you or get over on you for demeaning someone who was struggling to begin with. I will get to more of that later, as I had random moments of outburst as a result of witnessing someone causing harm to others, often inflicting serious injury as a result of my actions.

Never did I plan or intend to directly hurt anyone. In fact, I haven't been one to run around and just say to myself, "I want to really fuck someone over today"...not in the least. I always wanted to be some character, and make others laugh without caring about the consequences—having to be that center of attention is what seemed to drive me, and often it would race through my head that I was doing something wrong, but the word "refrain" would just not filter through my brain fast enough.

Laughter was and still is really good medicine for me. Extracting laughs from others has always made me feel good and glow just a little bit inside.

When I really think about it, the fact is that I could never slow my head down. I was disruptive in class, and I would act out and do crazy shit for attention. Like in fifth grade I took a dump in the stand-up urinal, and some sick part of me still finds that funny. I swear the guys who directed the Woody Harrelson movie *Kingpin* ripped that scene off from me when that Amish guy did the same thing. Where are my fucking royalties!!!

My grandmother Nellie Mae was probably the sweetest person I have ever known, next to my mom, and to this day she makes me smile inside just by the mere thought of her. She had a kind heart and beautiful way about her, and she cared deeply for my brother Eric and me. She would spoil us rotten, and one of my favorite things she would do with us was to take Eric and me to Hof's Hut on the weekends, where every time I would get "pigs in a blanket."

I have no idea what kids eat nowadays, but in the 70's "pigs in blankets" ruled.

My Grammy Nel, as Eric and I called her, was our grandmother on our mom's side. She would always take time for us when she wasn't working her tail off at McDonnell-Douglas, the old airplane maker in Long Beach.

Grammy Nel would write down some of the crazy things I would say and put them on index cards, and place all of them in a little silver box as a keepsake. She would later pass away from cancer in 1987 and it was devastating for all of us.

Even as a little boy without drugs and alcohol I was nuts. The following is an example of one of the index cards she wrote on. It's September 7, 1973, and I am a whopping six years old. Grammy Nel and a girlfriend of hers named Marie were taking us to Busch Gardens in Los Angeles, and here's the conversation I had in the car with Marie's son Tony, who was thirteen at the time:

Me: We are going to Busch Gardens today—they serve beer there!

Tony: I drink beer.

Me: I like liquor.

Tony: I like wine.

Me: I like liquor. It makes you drive a car really fast, and you go zoooom!!!

I am six years old for goodness sake, and I am talking about enjoying liquor and the pleasure of drinking and driving. The seed of my insanity had been planted long before I even drank alcohol; it was just waiting to be discovered.

FATHER FIGURE

I guess our family was a bit dysfunctional. It was without a father for a while and then my mom remarried a few years later to a very good man named Darryl. He was a wonderful dad to me, especially as a young boy who so desperately needed a male figure around.

Darryl was tough, very athletic and solid as a rock. That's what young boys like to look up to, someone who can take care of business, and believe me, Darryl took care of business.

He was the sweetest guy in the world, but if some drunk, random asshole wanted to get it on at a ball game or in traffic, he was doomed. If the other guy wanted to start something up, he would get it. Darryl would not hesitate, and this was during a time where you could get away with stuff like this. Nowadays, if you so much as slap a guy who deserves it he ends up owning your house, your automobiles, and most likely steals your wife because of the jail time handed down.

Darryl would light a guy up and then say, "Let's go grab a pizza and throw the football around." He was my kind of guy, and definitely not one to trifle with. He was a social drinker like my mom and he never touched drugs, and he despised people who used drugs.

There were a few buddies of his from his college days at Long Beach State who were alcoholic, and I thought they were fun to be around, but Darryl didn't think that way at all, go figure. I already had the mind of an alcoholic, so I liked the behavior of his hammered cronies at football and basketball games and was a big fan of their outlandish behavior.

Darryl worked hard and provided a very comfortable lifestyle for all of us, and he was funny too. I always loved it when people could make me laugh without trying too hard, and he didn't have to do that. Some people try too hard to be funny and fall flat on their faces. (Here's a hint, if you are not funny, don't try to be funny. But if you are funny, don't ever stop.) A great sense of humor and spreading laughter is a great healer, at least for me.

I often would say or do funny shit because deep down I had some type of pain I didn't want revealed, and I sure as hell didn't want to share it with anyone. Personally, I feel I was blessed with a decent sense of humor, and when in the right frame of mind there is nothing better to me than making someone else smile and get a good belly laugh going due to some offbeat, knucklehead bullshit comment or scenario that came out of my mouth.

Often, Darryl would be an emcee at local charity events or at Long Beach State athletic fund raisers. No one could tell a joke the way he could; he was very animated, and I loved that way about him. But he was also very strict, and that's something I had a hard time with. I thought he was just being a hard ass, but now I know he was just being a hell of a good dad and trying to mold a pain-in-the-ass kid into a decent human being.

That's me on the far left, my brother next to me, and our neighbor Shauna. I am pretty sure I was up to no good on this particular day...I was five years old.

BUTTON PUSHING WISE ASS

I loved pushing people's buttons, mainly my brother's because it was so fucking easy to do. One of my favorite torture methods for my older brother was to race past him on my bike on the way home from school. This gets funnier, I assure you—Eric always had to take a leak the moment he got home. It used to make me think to myself, "You know, Eric, they have rest rooms in our public school systems...You should ask your teachers about where they are located."

So I would beat him home, crash my bike in the front yard, and lock the front door. We didn't have house keys on us then, so he would be close to pissing his pants. I swear it would turn into the opening scene of the Flintstones, where Fred is beating down the door and screaming "Wilma!!!!!" That was my brother, Fred Flintstone, having to take an enormous leak while his smartass brother had locked the door on him.

I would be in tears laughing until I was almost peeing myself. Fred—I mean, Eric would be blue in the face, and then I would unlock the door and run up to my room.

Eric would race to the bathroom and relieve himself, and I would be out of breath from laughing hysterically, and then he would beat the shit out of me. It's just like my addiction though;

for that temporary rush and good feeling, I will endure a lot of pain afterwards. No matter how hard my brother "Fred" would beat on me, I repeatedly found it worth the joy of pissing him off, just to see his reactions.

One of my favorite "button pushing" stories involves a buddy of mine named Greg. I think we were in the eighth grade and sometimes we would find a way to leave school early and go to Lucky's market where we would steal cold beer. It wasn't as though we looked like hoodlums, but then again not too many folks were suspecting that two fourteen year old kids were on a mission to cram Michelob or Miller High Life into their backpacks. (A safe guess would be that I owe Lucky's in the neighborhood of $600, at least.)

Anyway, Greg and I were in the habit for a while of drinking cold frosties (beer) and shooting birds in his backyard with a pellet gun I had taken from my brother. We weren't very good shots, especially after a few brews in us. However, Greg nailed a bird and it landed in his neighbor's yard. The problem is that the bird dropped right where the owner of the home was standing, and this is where Todd the "wise ass button pusher" emerged.

The neighbor was irate and charged next door to confront Greg and me, and I must admit we were both a bit scared, but it's the neighbor's actions that put me into comedic hysterics.

This guy must have been 6'2" and real thin with thick, black glasses, he looked like he was a nerdy type, an engineer or something involving intelligence I couldn't comprehend. So the guy is screaming at the top of his lungs, "What is wrong with you kids!!! Did you just shoot that bird that landed in my yard?"

As he was cursing Greg and me, his head started to make this odd gesture, it was like one of those "bobble head" dolls you see on the dashboards of cars. His neck was all contorted and red, and moving furiously up and down like he was analyzing us from head to toe. His head must have done this about eleven times and I could not stand it any longer.

That's when I took a fresh sip off of the Michelob and looked right at the man as I imitated his head gestures and simply said, "What are you, a fucking pigeon?"

Greg collapsed onto the concrete not able to control the laughter, and went from being stone cold scared to a young kid in a comedy club having heard the funniest thing in his life.

The remark I made found its way back to my parents by sundown, and let's just say that was the last time I shot birds with Greg in his backyard. However, it's important to note that the gentleman would forever be known as "Pigeon" to Greg and me.

*Note: I don't recommend shooting pigeons or any other birds for that matter. But, if you see someone who reminds you of a pigeon, be sure to take it upon yourself to let them know it.

COME OUT AND PLAY

I was always athletic, having been blessed with good hand-eye coordination and stuff like that. I loved sports as a kid, to the point of just plain overkill, because anything I like—I like a lot of. If you can sense where this is going, stick with me. When I say "overkill" I am talking extremes like the following…

We started playing street hockey when I was about ten years old, in 1977. This was a sport that Darryl didn't play with me; it was more something I did with my friends. We were playing hockey way before Wayne Gretzky came to the LA Kings, which is when street hockey really took off in Southern California.

In '77, the Kings still had purple-and-gold uniforms, and the asshole Mighty Ducks weren't even a thought. (I still have a resentment towards the fucking Ducks. They won a Stanley Cup just a few years ago—what year they won it I forget already—but they won it, and the Kings never have, and they are a team named after a Disney Movie!! That just ruins me…)

Okay, back to street hockey. We had all the equipment, helmets, goalie masks, Roller Derby skates, real hockey gloves—the works. I was so into it I used to give my allowance money to my friends in the neighborhood just to sit their asses in the goal so I could work on my wrist shots and slap shots.

I mean, it could be raining, and I have got my poor friend Chad stuck in goal catching fucking pneumonia because I wanted to improve my game, but he did get my allowance money for his efforts. It doesn't even snow in Long Beach and no one played ice hockey, but I had a true love for the game and I wanted to be really good at it, plus my obsessive behavior wouldn't leave me alone.

What Darryl did teach me was football, and I loved football and still do. He played offensive and defensive tackle at Long Beach State in the 60s when they had a decent football team, and for a big guy he was really fast, strong, and old-school tough.

His idols were guys like Jerry Kraemer and Fuzzy Thurston from the golden era of the Green Bay Packers when Vince Lombardi coached them in the 60s. Darryl liked the militant type of discipline a guy like Lombardi handed down, and he would do that with me; the problem was that authority would always be something I would ferociously contend with.

Anyway, Darryl would throw the ball to me, organize games, and play quarterback while all the neighborhood kids competed against each other. I just had a knack for being able to catch any ball thrown near me, and I could run like the wind.

My biggest problem, though, was taking instruction or any type of coaching—in all the sports I played. I had more athletic ability than most, but no discipline to be quiet and listen. I always wanted to joke around and do something to ruffle the feathers of the coach, which is why organized sports really weren't good for me. I thought I had all the skills necessary, but the coaches never thought it was a good idea to put me on most teams. They always said I possessed more talent than most, but I "could not be coached," so they would just pass on me.

This is something that would affect me for most of my life. I never could really see the fact that I was disruptive. Instead, I would focus on the fact that I was good enough athletically and I thought that should be enough. Well, it wasn't.

Looking back on it, they had a good point, and they made the decisions that were best for the team, and probably for their own sanity, but it would take many years for me to understand that. I wasn't verbally abusive to others and didn't call the coach bad names or use poor language, I simply needed more attention, and for me to obtain attention meant acting out and being funny, always at the expense of my not being picked to be on the team.

These failures on my part would bring me much heartache and disappointment later on, but the discovery of drugs would help me compartmentalize and hide just about every bit of it.

BLACK SHEEP

ebellion started to become a healthy alternative for me, at
least that's what I felt. Once I developed the pattern of not
being let onto a team, I sensed I simply didn't belong. This
really jump-started my alcoholic head into thinking that maybe
I was just different. I wanted to be like everyone else, I wanted
to get along with everyone else, and I really wanted to be a part
of something—anything that didn't render me that alone feeling
which I had always possessed.

This feeling drew me inward, and I started to drift apart from
some of my long-time friends. I had many friends I had grown up
with since my early childhood, but I was getting bored. It was time
for a change—because, you know, at the age of thirteen it's time to
get the ball rolling, and that's exactly what I did.

I discovered porn at a young age, and so at the age of thirteen
my impression of what girls really liked or wanted was sex, which
is ironic, because I did too! When video first came out, the tapes
were really expensive, and there was no way a kid of my age could
procure adult films at a retail store.

So, a friend of mine and I did what we thought was the best
thing, we stole some pornos from a neighbor's house, and it didn't
seem to be a big deal. But having our own copy of "Tangerine" was

a very big deal to us, and when I saw Mr. Peckerman bang this hot little redhead, I couldn't stop thinking about how fun sex must be.

I wanted to get involved in this type of activity immediately! I would share these porn tapes with "newly acquired friends," and what I got in return was instant hero status. Finally, I was getting some positive affirmation; porn meant getting more cool friends. I can remember all of us having a look on our faces that was pure astonishment, and I thought to myself, "This chick is so hot, and look how much she is enjoying what Mr. Peckerman is doing to her." In hindsight I know it's just a ridiculous adult film. But for me, the sight of the gorgeous girl getting nailed and loving it was like a new drug for me, and I will obsess incessantly over anything that I can derive pleasure from.

Thirteen is also the age I went to my first keg beer party. Some older guys from our neighborhood, probably seventeen or eighteen, were having this get-together at the handball courts at Wilson High School. A friend and I had stumbled upon it after we finished a baseball game one early Saturday afternoon.

I will never forget one of the older guys saying, "Hey...you little shit...you want a beer?"

My face lit up, "Are you kidding me? Do I want a beer? Heck yeah I want a beer...I want to have a lot of beers!"

I took that sip of keg brew and my buddy George took a few pulls from his big red cup, and the lights just came on. This was my first experience of being able to drink beer without a limit, or without adults around to catch me.

For me, alcohol made the world a very happy place. I instantly fit in, completely. Any rough edges I felt in my heart, in my head, or deep in my soul just vanished with the alcohol racing through me.

We were the youngest ones there, but we were made to feel quite welcome by the older guys. We looked up to all of these characters in many ways as kids today admire their favorite sports stars or musicians. They all surfed really well and they were always with the cutest girls. And of course, they all partied hard. I know that when I was drinking I was a part of something so much bigger than me, or maybe it was just the warm blanket of "acceptance" the alcohol provided.

George and I drank as much as we could until we could drink no more. We were both getting quite dizzy from all the beers, so we decided to bail from the party. We could barely ride our bikes, and we wobbled all over the place like drunk little soldiers too young for the draft.

Our destination was the first open grass spot we could find, about 800 yards away from the party in a place called Recreation Park. We crashed our bikes on the grass, threw up, passed out, blacked out, woke up three hours later, and said, "Fuck man... that was killer!"

Two young kids completely hammered after a little league baseball game. While most of the other kids went home to either do their homework or hang out with their family, George and I were hanging out and repeating language that if heard by our parents would have us on house arrest for a year. We were so impressed by the older crowd, and even more impressed by what alcohol did for us.

The switch was officially turned on for me. I liked alcohol, and we became instant friends—the type of friend that you want to spend a lot more time with, and I would come to find that I could rely on this new friend time and time again.

*9th Grade Photo, after suffering major
disappointment from being stripped of becoming
student body class president.*

QUAALUDES ON CAMPUS

In junior high school I enjoyed causing a ruckus frequently, and sharing my entertainment skills was something I highly valued, as it was imperative for me and my friends to laugh on a regular basis. It was in eighth grade where I had this epiphany: I would run for ninth grade Class President. I was fiercely opposed to the structure of the existing student body government, so some changes needed to take place, and damn it I was the one who was going to sort this shit out!

While drinking some beers with some friends, it dawned on me that all drinking fountains at school needed to be replaced with cold beer taps. I felt it was time that we got rid of that stuff known as "water"! and install some frosty brew taps so we could wet our whistles between classes. This idea really impressed my friends, and the joke spread by word of mouth.

The assholes that I was running against for this prestigious student body title really were assholes. They would have these lame-ass signs and posters that said things like, "Vote for Jennifer, She Can Get the Job Done." Yeah right, in my mind I felt the only "job" Jennifer should have had was giving blow jobs, and she probably was already giving them at that advanced age of thirteen or fourteen. I can't say for sure, as I was never asked to participate.

The other guy, Jeff, was also an asshole, and he did the same shit as Jennifer by utilizing typical and boring campaign signs such as, "Vote for Jeff" which were posted everywhere. I wanted to post campaign signs that just said, "Fuck You Jeff!!!" and "Jennifer Sucks Ass!!!"

I am not kidding—those were the things I thought of as a kid and I still find a lot of it funny. My campaign was to form a "false promise campaign," just like all of the lying, asshole-criminal politicians we have in our country today.

So this was what I believed to be the perfect campaign slogan: "Quaaludes on Campus." I didn't even know what a Quaalude was at the time. But it sounded funny and it was a drug, and I thought that drugs were pretty cool even though I wasn't the master druggie (not yet, anyway).

Running around our small campus, I talked with anyone who would listen. I was your regular lying, hard-working politician, telling classmates, "I will get Quaaludes dispensed to all who desire them, and cold beer will be put into the drinking fountains to wash the 'ludes down with."

I ran with this, and it became a widespread joke (which it was), but people demanded change! The word was out about my political dreams of grandeur and I was called into the office of the Vice Principal, Mr. Anderson, where he said, "Mr. Zalkins, are you running around talking about putting beer taps in the drinking fountains and supplying pills as part of your campaign strategy?"

I was on the immediate defensive, "That's an outrage! Drinking is bad for you, and I hear drugs are bad for you as well… Shame on the individuals responsible for this cheap, petty gossip… I will sue everyone! Get my attorneys on the phone immediately!"

Mr. Anderson, shaking his head, said in the most frustrated voice, "Get out of my office now, Mr. Zalkins… like right this instant!!!"

I was quite capable of pushing the buttons of any of our hard-working faculty members, and I could quickly become "adult-like" in conversation just to ruffle the feathers of the person I was inter-acting with. Always in good spirited fun, my antics were along the lines of the hit movie *Ferris Bueller's Day Off*, but I thought Ferris Bueller was a pussy because he wasn't drinking hard enough, but I still loved the movie.

With my campaign strategy firmly in place and the gossip working its way through the student body, I seriously proceeded to change my act in the classroom—no bullshit. In the early 80's when I was in junior high school we had both "academics" and "conduct" as the two components to our grading system. I generally did really well academically, but my conduct grades were pretty lousy. The grades for conduct were as follows:

E: Excellent (I never saw one of these damned grades on my report card.)

S: Satisfactory (I saw some of these, just not a whole lot.)

N: Non-Satisfactory (Now we are getting somewhere, I saw a bunch of these.)

U: Unsatisfactory (I procured a shit load of these bad boys.)

In order to be successfully placed in the role of student body president, there was a rule that stipulated: "All conduct grades for the previous semester must be Excellent or Satisfactory. A grade of Non-Satisfactory or Unsatisfactory automatically disqualifies the student from the presidency."

If I got one "N" or a "U" I was screwed in the event I won the election. All kidding aside, everyone knew I was a "pleasant" wise-ass, but for the first time I was very serious and determined to become the class president, and without using lame campaign slogans like, "Vote for Todd." We were a young society of beer-drinking pill-takers, and we demanded change! I wanted to win the election on the completely ludicrous pretense of false promises of alcohol and drugs on campus.

It was my ploy of ultimately getting over on everyone, once again pushing the envelope to see how far I could go. During the "semester of judgment," I was very quiet in all of my classes, to the point where others were genuinely concerned.

My fellow classmates thought I was actually under the influence of Quaaludes or Valium. I wasn't disruptive, nor was I the class clown anymore. I was focused for the first time in my life, and I honestly wanted to prove that I could change, and do it honestly while running a dishonest political campaign. After all... people were depending upon me!

The fact is I was so motivated to win the election and get the good conduct grades that I changed for the better almost overnight. I did not want there to be any room for a teacher to give me an "N" or a "U" in conduct. This was the most serious I had ever been in class. There was no sufficient reason for anyone to believe that I could change my behaviors. But I did (at least for that semester), and my reputation was such that I was considered totally out of control, extremely disruptive, and frequently acted out, which was the truth.

But after the semester was over there was not one classmate—even the kids I was running against—who would have said I deserved an" N" or a U, and it's because I put forth the genuine effort for a change in my behavior.

I ended up winning the class election in a landslide, and I was so excited—all that I needed now was proof of my good conduct. The moment of truth finally arrived with the receipt of my report card and all my friends wondering what the results were. I nervously opened the envelope, and I had all "S's" and ONE "N"!! How could that be? That's impossible, who gave me this fucking "N"?

It was that cocksucker, Mr. Novaks Shiner. He was this bald, asshole science teacher who used to have the cutest of our female classmates sit on his lap—ask any of my classmates and they would attest to this. And we used to joke that he was probably molesting his student "aides" behind closed doors. This type of behavior would land his ass in jail these days with the parents suing the Long Beach School District for millions. I knew Mr. Shiner never liked me, so I was exceptionally good in his class during the semester, and my grade should have been an "E" because I was so quiet and well mannered.

But that isn't what happened. I was stuck with the "N" in conduct and stripped of the presidency. It was like the LBPD had beaten the crap out of me emotionally with nightsticks. I couldn't breathe, and it was one of the most devastating moments of my childhood. This may seem ridiculous to a lot of people, but for me, I was really doing the best I could to prove others wrong, and in the end no matter how much I did right, it still was not enough.

This was nuclear for this teenaged boy. No joke. Friends of mine wanted to bum rush Mr. Shiner and physically assault his ass, but I didn't want to be mean like that—I just wanted to light his fucking house on fire with him in it. My stepdad Darryl was beyond livid. He knew that I had mellowed out that semester, and he witnessed the temporary change as well. I found out later he paid Mr. Shiner a visit, and from what I hear it took every fiber within Darryl's being to not beat the shit out of the teacher without a conscience.

If you are out there, Mr. Shiner, be thankful Darryl showed restraint. There's no doubt God was on your side, because I'm not sure you would have been so lucky on other occasions. When I was young, smaller, and weak, I would think how cool it would be for just a few minutes to be strong and tough like my stepdad. I would have been this big dude breaking down Mr. Shiner's classroom door and shoving a glass beaker in his mouth, smacking him a few times, and maybe doing a few science experiments on his eyes and ears. Damn it, Mr. Shiner! We could have all been enjoying cold beer and Quaaludes on campus... even you!

This incident that happened at the age of fourteen drew me completely inward, and from that moment of failure and disappointment I was always looked upon as that kid who "could be successful in life or anything he did if he just toned it down a little." Or, "If that Zalkins kid could just not be so disruptive in class, all of this would not have happened."

I take full responsibility for my actions in school. I often made my bed and had to lie in it. This experience for me, though, was lifechanging and as much as I was an anarchist at heart, and rebellious in my nature, this grew tenfold after this debacle. I proceeded to put on my subliminal "Fuck You" hat, which I would continue to wear for many years to come. It was the final straw for me, and along with the disappointments of not making the sports teams and the feeling of not being liked enough or accepted enough by people, it served to increase my festering insecurities.

Emotionally I turned a corner from which I don't think I ever quite recovered until a few years ago. I'm not saying I would bitch and whine about not being able to be class president, that wasn't the case at all. It just did something to my psyche that perpetuated my resentment and anger towards organized authoritative figures of any kind and anyone who wielded power to control me, including my own parents.

Withdrawing from life became very easy for me from that point on. Alcohol (and not too far away, cocaine) enabled me to put all the negative stuff in my life into tiny little compartments which would remain locked for years. Like a personal "Self Storage for Emotional Turmoil" with no monthly fees required—only the consistent deposit of alcohol and drugs into my system guaranteed me a numb existence that would allow me to operate in the present tense, and not fixate or dwell in my past.

I was now free to be a knucklehead to the fullest degree, and for a long time I enjoyed the type of misery that came with it. But that would all change later, when no enjoyment or fun was attainable and the only thing left was just the maintenance of my addictions, and all the misery and sickness that came along with it.

Part Two
Alcohol Training

It was at age thirteen that alcohol warmed my heart, made things tolerable, and definitely made me feel like I could adapt to anything. The sense of loneliness I had felt for so long just vanished. Now, drinking every day wasn't my deal at all at that age. Drinking was something we could really only pull off on the weekends when my friends and I would "pimp" beer or steal it.

Yes, there is or was such a thing. I think nowadays kids don't have to pimp shit. They act like they are pimps, or wanna-be pimps, but really it's just because of too much shitty rap, and the most fucked up form of medium in history—MTV. They actually have a show called the "Real World" and people actually watch this shit. They put twelve stuck-up little assholes in a house, all of them generally too good looking. The girls all bitch about which dick they are going to suck, and that hopefully their boyfriends won't find out, and the dudes are a bunch of phony lightweights that probably shave each other's balls before going to the clubs.

It's the "real world" all right, in their fucking real imaginary brains. Good old MTV, what a joke. They don't even show Beavis and Butthead anymore. Now that show was genius, and certainly more real world than the "Real World" on MTV. Drop those spoiled little college pricks off in the middle of Compton (that's north Long Beach) and they can see the real world while the Crips are blasting away as they take a "real dump" in their real world pants.

Okay, I got a bit carried away. Actually, I used to love MTV when they played the killer raw videos that were just the camera and the band, not too much fluff. If you pull up the Guns N' Roses video for "Welcome to the Jungle" there are certain angles of the crowd where you can tell it was a mostly empty venue, but the footage was just sick.

I had seen Guns N' Roses at Bogart's in Long Beach way before they were a household name, and that band could bring it like no other. I just now find MTV completely unwatchable; it's all just game shows and really bad "reality" crap.

Where was I? Oh yes, drinking alcohol.

We would drink beers occasionally at lunchtime at Will Rogers Junior High School, and drink booze on the weekends. Mix it, match it, drink it straight, throw up, and do it again. I didn't see any problem with this behavior at all.

Now, weed was also around but it was never really my deal, maybe because of what it did to me, which is simple, in the following order:

1. Take a bong hit, drink a brew, take another bong hit, and drink two or three more brews.
2. Oh shit, I feel like I'm turning Japanese for some reason and my eyes are closing... I can't focus....my eyes are really small and bloodshot.
3. Time to order a big pizza with everything on it! Now!
4. Eat the pizza, every bit of it, as the bong-hit-induced coma sets in, and it's "Say goodnight, everybody."

I didn't like the downward feeling I got from weed, and I never understood friends of mine who "burned" on a daily basis. If I had hit the bong daily, I would have had to drop out of school and work at Pizza Hut full time just for the benefits of having free pizza. And damn it, I will not call it "chronic" either. We didn't have that fucking death weed when I was a kid. You just smoked what you were given, didn't whine like a bitch about it, and proceeded to act silly and eat pizza.

We knew some guys who harvested the good shit in Northern Cal but it was hard to get and really expensive. The hydroponic weed they make today is just ridiculous—one hit and it's possible you might be retarded for thirty days.

Another thing for sure: I did not want to hang around anyone who wasn't "down for the cause," the drinking cause that is. If your idea of fun is rolling with the parents to some lame-ass get together, take me off the list, please! I like being the black sheep, and I don't want to participate in some meaningless event where I will be exposed to some random asshole uncle or third cousin who will piss me off enough to want to start drinking.

So, me and my crew drank and became relatively good at it for being the little shits that we were. We would stuff beer in our backpacks after school at our local markets. You know, because we had a long night of homework ahead of us, and we needed to have a few brews or cocktails to start the night off just the right way.

We had to loosen up after a really hectic day of school and all the traffic we encountered riding our bikes home in our little beach town. It was tough, but we dealt with it the best we could. It was mandatory that we ingested a lot of fucking alcohol!!!

With the fuse of booze being lit full-on, we carried the habit of alcohol consumption into Woodrow Wilson High School. Things would change here for certain, and the stage would then be assembled for future acts of insanity, risk-taking, drug-taking, life-changing, and flat out addiction.

In high school I was even more awkward inside. First off, everyone seemed so much bigger than me. Not that I was small—I guess I was average size, I think like 5'10" and 170, but my perception was that everyone had facial hair and they were all shaving, I thought to myself, "Shit yeah, I wanna grow a beard and look old and pissed off like these assholes."

I am talking about the seniors at Wilson. I call them assholes because the moment we got to 10th grade, all of the girls our age were suddenly all over the older dudes and that just pissed me off. That was a great reason for me to drink. (Not that I couldn't get a chick—I absolutely loved the girls in high school and especially sex with girls. But that's a whole different subject matter for a different place and time.)

I guess what I am trying to say is that from the way I viewed the world, I just didn't measure up. I wished I was smarter and better looking, and I was wanting what someone else had, always comparing myself to others and finding ways to judge and take them down internally. Because I simply didn't feel comfortable in my own skin, but alcohol and drugs would help me tailor a new suit of skin—or armor, depending on what type of day it was.

Drinking at lunchtime was always a lot of fun for me and my friends. Eating was for people who needed to eat. I needed to drink, because I could give a flying fuck about my next class. The only things that interested me were booze, drugs, surfing, and what was under all of that clothing a cute girl was wearing. Those were the real motivators in my life, and I surrounded myself with only those who were involved in the same things as me: getting fucked up, fucking chicks, you know, the good life, at least that's what my impression of the good life was. I didn't know anything really. As the non-addicts and non-alcoholics were growing up, my friends and I were remaining the nice mature age of about ten or eleven for years to come.

I was always behind the curve for sure. Looking back I can see how immature I really was. I didn't want to be that way, it's just who I was. I can now completely see how unfit I was for life, but I didn't really care because drugs and alcohol were my life, my protective shield. Basically every form of entertainment for me involved alcohol and/or drugs.

Even going to the movies we had to sneak in beers, smoke some weed, and try to watch whatever was playing. If I smoked weed at the movies my friends would crack up at me because I would eat three huge packs of Milk Duds and that large tub of popcorn they serve the size of a jacuzzi.

Later I would have butter stains all over my shirt, and my face was all glazed with butter taint. I was a real piece of work.

THE SPOT

After surfing, either after school or on weekends, we would drink. If the surf wasn't any good, we would go straight to this area my friend Eric and I called "the Spot." This little hidden gem was on Treasure Island, a tiny spot on Naples Island that is accessible by one little bridge over one of the canals.

Unless you have lived there or spent time with someone who lived there, you would never be able to find Treasure Island. That's one of the cool things about where we grew up, we had access to some pretty neat areas where no one really cared we were there. As long as we picked up after ourselves and didn't break anything, we had full run of the place—not once were the police called to ruin our day. We probably drank there more than 200 times, now that's a reliable place for a sixteen-year-old to drink, in my opinion.

Eric was a long-time buddy of mine whom I had known since preschool (we weren't quite ready to drink brews in preschool), and we would see each other at school and in passing. If there were no waves or the weather was crummy we would just say, "See you at the Spot," and it didn't even require planning. We just showed up with brews in hand, and we would drink and take a stab at the world's problems.

I think the biggest problem we both had during that time was which girl we could possibly bang, or wondering if she was banging anyone we knew, or would she even be open to the prospect of banging one of us. As the real deep thinkers and philosophers we were, we would analyze this for about four minutes, then move on to the next chick we could possibly bang. Just kidding—sex is not all we thought about, it was just all we talked about.

LARRY FLYNT FOR PRESIDENT

Speaking of getting banged, in high school I fell totally in love with HUSTLER Magazine. Now, I know you are probably thinking "So he liked to jerk off to porno mags," well... no shit. What teenager doesn't like to throw a fresh jack to some hottie in Larry Flynt's masterful publication known as HUSTLER?

Yes, I loved the nudity, but as much if not even more I loved the cartoons in HUSTLER. I mean they were just perfect, nothing tame in the least but completely out-of-control funny.

I would bring the latest copy to school and post the best cartoons in my locker, so between classes twelve to twenty dudes would roll up, wanting to see which comics Todd Zalkins had posted in his locker for the month.

I even subscribed to HUSTLER Humor for many years, a quarterly publication that had—you guessed it—nothing but the sickest, gnarliest cartoon humor imaginable: drugs, racism, hookers, gambling, booze, fucking with politics, ruining the evangelists, it went on and on. I couldn't get enough of it, because I find humor in the totally ridiculous and absurd.

There was also a section at the beginning that was one of my favorites called "Asshole of the Month." (This was in 1984 and

1985, and I believe it carries on to this day. I stopped subscribing to HUSTLER a few years ago, don't ask me why.)

So, I would take the "Asshole of the Month" page out of the magazine, and instead of taping up Jerry Falwell who was appearing in the mag, I would paste a photo of whoever I thought deserved the title of asshole of the month. Sometimes it would be one of our female classmates—as much as I love girls I am a firm believer that a lot of chicks can be assholes!

So, I like to push the envelope, and if I like something, I like it a lot. I have a disease that says to me, "I want more of this, I like this. Please let me have a lot more of this!"

Even as a young kid, I would go way overboard. Whether it was candy, bubble gum, or whatever it was, I had to have more, and eat it or chew it until I would go into a major sugar seizure. One time in first grade I learned from our teacher that carrots were good for your eyesight. It just so happens that upon getting home from school my mom was making a big stew and there was this pile of carrots.

I'm not sure how many were there, but I can tell you I ate every carrot that was there, all because I wanted to make sure I could see better! I also can tell you that I believe I pissed the color of Orange Crush for a day and a half and did not require any more vitamins from the vegetable group for several more years.

My mom was looking around, like, "Where in the hell are all of the carrots"?

I proudly replied, "Probably that brother of mine... You had better speak to Eric immediately." I could go into that "adult" type of talk right away, because not only was I a wise-ass in training, I also took pride in being able to deliver a smartass remark at any given moment.

It's important to point out that I don't remember a lot of my childhood. I just don't. I am not sure if it's because of all the chemicals I put into my body for 24 years, but I am going to take a wild guess and say that all my alcohol and drug abuse certainly has contributed to my lack of memory with respect to my childhood and adult years.

I can remember a lot of specific situations, but I can't say what in the hell I was doing on Christmas Day when I was nine or ten. I was probably playing hockey in the street, eating too much candy, throwing in a few pounds of carrots so I could see better and trying to find some stash of HUSTLER mags!!

TAKING CHANCES

In 1982 I was a sophomore in high school, and like I mentioned earlier I was really uncomfortable and anxious within. The seniors in school were for the most part a bunch of bullying cocksuckers that made me just say to myself, "There will come a day when I will be bigger and stronger than you, and at that point I will track all of you motherfuckers down, tie you all up, drink a bunch of whiskey, smoke some PCP, and treat each of you beard-wearing pricks to a good old-fashioned beating."

I was really intimidated by people bigger and hairier; some disposition made me feel younger and weaker than the guys my own age, trapped in this immature mind. Drinking was such an easy thing to do for many reasons: all my friends drank (although I tended to push the envelope a bit more than most), alcohol was everywhere and at all the fun parties, and it was the key to my missing link, the part of DNA that I needed to put in me to make me feel better about everything around me.

As a sophomore and a scared little kid, I started taking more risks. Here's an example of a risk that was really quite heavy at the time in 1982:

We were living in Belmont Shore, just across the bay from Naples Island. To this day I still find that community one of the most special and unique places. Beautiful beach-style homes loaded with character and taste (for the most part), then just outside of Belmont Shore is Belmont Heights, which has some of the neatest homes.

I always loved a big Spanish-style home, and the Heights have tons of them. Really classic architecture and so well built, most of them constructed in the 20's and 30's. When I think of the area it warms my heart, but I am also quite certain the community as a whole is much happier with me living outside of it now and several miles away.

Across the street from us and two doors down lived a kid my age, Matt, whom I had just recently gotten to know. We got along great and I enjoyed hanging out with him. He and his dad had just moved in about a year before. His dad always had some interesting folks over, and I smelled the weed burning from time to time and I thought, "Right on, your dad rocks, Matt, and his friends rock too."

They would be drinking brews and were just all around pretty cool people. My parents rarely drank and sure as hell weren't lighting the bong or firing up a nice THC fire log. My parents were anti-drug, and I was anti-parents, so go figure where my head was at.

One day in October my friend Matt asked me to come over and check something out. I went over to his house, and in his room there were several of these little sealed plastic bags that were usually for holding jewelry or watch components. I had never seen these little baggies filled with white powder. And I asked him, "What the hell is that?"

Matt just replied, "I think it's cocaine." I had never done cocaine, never bought it, didn't know where to buy it, but I sure as hell wanted to know more. My curiosity was blazing, and my mind was racing, saying things in my head like, "How do you do it? I know you snort it, but how much do you snort?" and on and on...

I didn't have any idea what the effect was like from cocaine, but I was determined to find out. "Let's do some of that, Matt, your dad won't know it's gone."

"No way. I am going to call my aunt and tell her my dad is doing this crap," Matt responded, undoubtedly upset over finding the drugs.

I replied, "Oh, come on, he won't even know it's missing—let's just dabble a bit."

"No way, I am calling my aunt," he insisted.

Here I am, fifteen years old, maybe sixteen, and I am already talking like doing blow is no big thing. "Let's just dabble with some of it." What the fuck did I know? I had no clue whatsoever as to how one does coke, not that it's rocket science, but it just scared me and intrigued me all at once.

The very next day my friend Trent and I broke in to find the stash and steal it. We looked everywhere, and we eventually found it hidden in Matt's dresser drawers. Now I was scared out of my fucking mind. I wasn't a house robber—I didn't break into people's pads and rip off their drugs, but we did, and it was something that I have always regretted doing.

We took the stash to this guy John's house. John was a senior at Wilson and knew all about drugs and how to do them, how to score them and all that jazz. His eyes lit up like a little kid at Christmas upon seeing the little bags of blow. It was like he was being rescued on some deserted island after many years stranded and someone saved his life—he was all smiles with respect to our little score.

He broke out a mirror, chopped the powder up with a razor blade, and then rolled up a dollar bill and snorted the big white rail, and my friend Trent and I went next. All I can tell you is that I got this huge gagging drip at the back of my throat, I swallowed like I was choking, and then, bam! Total euphoria.

It was pure bliss. Everything that was wrong was immediately correct and perfect. My lips and teeth were numb, and I wanted more of the mysterious white powder. "I demand more of that stolen cocaine!" my head rang out.

I didn't become immediately addicted. Snorting it is not like smoking crack or freebasing cocaine, where you can instantly become a fiend for it. But it did stick out in my mind that I wanted to do it again, and sooner rather than later.

The next day at school it was a very, very dark day for me. I was in my algebra class and I saw a guy I knew who was passing out notes and reports to teachers. I saw him through the window of the classroom door, and I will never so long as I live forget the gesture he made. Through this little square window he did the index finger dragging along his throat, indicating, "You are totally fucked."

I had no idea what to think, but I had a really good idea what it was involving. It was involving my crazy, stupid ass breaking into somebody's home and ripping off their drugs. That's what was going on. The gentleman we had robbed actually went to speak to my mom, telling her what we had done.

Later on I thought, how fucking stupid can one be? "Ummm, excuse me, ma'am? I would like to inform you that I have a very strong suspicion that your son has stolen several baggies of my high quality cocaine."

Of course I am exaggerating, but at the time of this debacle my stepdad was in Europe on business, and had he been home there is no doubt I would have gotten the shit beat out of me for doing it, and my neighbor would have gotten the shit beaten out of him just because... well... just fucking because.

I denied it. I stuck to my guns and said, "I don't know what you are talking about." I had no drugs in the house. I had no history of being caught with drugs or really using them (this was going to change real quick with the introduction of blow into my world), so I ended up not being punished because no one could prove anything.

It was so embarrassing for me going forward because every time I would see Matt's dad he would give me a stink eye that made me realize how much of a sack of shit I really was. It really bothered me that I had done this, and years later I actually apologized to Matt's dad and told him I was sorry for what I had done.

This act bothered me for many years, and at times I think about it, and I realize now how "uncool" it was, and even more so, how "uncool" I was.

COCAINE, I THINK I LOVE YOU

Once the "cocaine fuse" was lit for me, I wanted to do it as much as I could. I loved it. When I drank lots of booze, a few nice rails of blow would straighten everything out. The world was just dandy, and I could talk like some philosopher, but I didn't know jack shit.

Anyone who has done coke has experienced "coke talk." I am positive that if I had a playback of even one long night of me and my friends talking out of our ass I would want to find the nearest cliff and jump off of it... immediately.

The things we say on that shit, the bullshit lies, the false promises, the kissing of asses—it's one big pile of bullshit and nonsense looking back on it, yet my world was going to take on a lot more of this type of behavior, and the scene would be repeated over and over for many years.

I wasn't much of a blackout drinker, especially once I discovered the magic of cocaine. Doing blow is the ultimate equalizer when you are partying, and it allowed me to drink a lot more. I would make a lot less sense the later the nights got.

It's normal to not have one meaningful conversation from like 10 p.m. until 4 a.m. By that time I need sex, and chances are I cannot perform, so it's time to watch lots of porn and wish I was the guy on the screen administering the fucking to some real "bright chick" who is probably just doing porn while she finishes law school at night.

Okay, that's a stretch, but I like to give all hard-working porn stars the benefit of the doubt. They are people too, and they have provided me with way too much raging lust, enough to last me for many years. It's not that I wanted to hang out or spend time with a porn star. It's just that when you are high or coming down from the coke, the wanting for that person becomes psychologically and physically unattainable, yet the desire and thirst for the act itself is uncontrollable.

My head would just spin out of control, studying the woman's body as the guy fucking her seems to be the luckiest guy on the planet. Yet when it's all said and done, it seems like it's probably a pretty lonely profession at the end of the day, kind of like my addiction.

Okay, I got lost there for a second, sorry about the tangent. I was talking about not being so much of a blackout drinker due to the aid of cocaine. There was a time in high school, though, that qualified as a legitimate blackout. True alcoholics won't even bat an eye about the following episode, while non-alcoholics will be saying, "I am really glad my daughter never knew you."

SLEEPWALKER

We lived on Santa Ana Avenue in Belmont Shore for many years, just two houses from the corner going towards the ocean from First Street. Locals will know this, non-locals, be patient. We have a street in Belmont Shore—it's the main drag, and it's called Second Street.

All the bars, restaurants, and shops line this mile and a half or so of total character. I love Second Street, and I loved it a lot more in the 70s and 80s when corporate America had not one store there. (Now there are two fucking Starbucks within two or three blocks of each other. That still scares the hell out of me when I think about it.)

There was a liquor store just off the corner of Santa Ana on Second Street, and I think it's long gone now. I am not sure—I don't live there, I don't drink anymore, so what the hell do I care? I am being completely honest when I say, "I think" it's gone. If it's not, please don't take legal action against me.

A local guy I had come to know, Adam, worked there for years. Good guy, really solid and fun to talk with. He would let me hang out in there, and I would look at some good clean filth (aka porno mags, aka periodicals that mattered to me) and just shoot the shit.

What Adam was really cool about was selling me brews and liquor. I fucking loved beer in my early teens, and he had no problem selling it to me, God bless him to this very day—wherever you are Adam, you are still a gem in my eyes.

So on a Friday afternoon I walk into the liquor store and it goes something like this:

Todd: What's up, Adam?

Adam: What do you mean "What's up," Todd?

Todd: Umm, well okay, hello Adam, how are you?

Adam: How am I? Don't you fucking remember last night? (He's shaking his head and trying not to laugh.)

Todd: I haven't given it much thought actually, Adam. I know I drank last night with some friends and went home. What's the problem here? I feel we now have some kind of "negative rapport" brewing.

Adam: Negative rapport? You came in last night, and it was late, and you wanted to use the rest room and buy more beer.

Todd: Adam, that is shocking me. You mean I actually came into your store, which sells beer and liquor which I buy from you regularly, and I actually wanted to make a purchase? Jesus... You should have called the Press-Telegram immediately and asked for front page material on this one. The headline could read, "Zalkins Enters Liquor Store, Wants More Beer....No Shit."

Adam: Yes, you were here like at 10 last night. The problem is you were completely fucking naked, and wanting more beer— that's the problem we have here.

Todd: Okay, now we have a topic of discussion on our hands. Are you saying I was butthoused (drunk) and naked in your store?

Adam: Yes. I am saying that... And yes, you were naked in the fucking store, wanting more alcohol.

Todd: Well.....ummmm.

Adam: Well fucking what?

Todd: Did you give me the beers?

Adam: No! You fool. I told you to get your ass home. You were completely naked walking around Second Street... The mere fact you weren't arrested is a miracle.

Todd: Well, thank you for sharing that with me, Adam, and you know I meant no disrespect... I apologize.

Adam: It's okay, bro... but I think you may have a drinking problem.

Todd: That is a possibility and I am going to look into that right away... Ring me up for a case of Coors.

Adam: You got it.

Todd: Glad we are still friends, Adam.

Like I said, most alcoholics would respond with something like, "I don't see what the problem is with that picture, however, just because you were nude doesn't mean your friend should have denied you that alcohol!"

So, what happened with the aforementioned story is fairly insane, but for me it was just an occurrence. It wasn't a wake up call to stop drinking or even consider stopping. Why the hell would I? Alcohol and drugs gave me everything I needed, and more. It was my friend, lover (when I didn't have one with me), and it never, ever let me down.

Drugs and booze always delivered, and right on time—similar to Federal Express. I like it when I can depend upon something. I like consistency, and I consistently liked the effect that all that stuff did for me. It stripped down complications, revealed what was true, told me what was right and never, ever lied to me. I could depend on alcohol and drugs! Now, where is the fucking party? I have things to do!

My buddies, Eric & Bubba. I am on the far right.
Bubba's car would be destroyed just hours later.

A Tour of Pleasures

Here's another fine example of me and my friends doing something really normal...I mean, abnormal.

Two friends of mine, Bubba and Eric (guys I had known since five years of age), decided it was important to take the day off of school and drive down to Rosarito Beach for the day to drink as much alcohol as possible. School could function well without us, but we could not function well without a good "alcohol mission" to sign up for.

We were all on board. One of the beautiful things about Eric and Bubba is they were as dependable partiers as mankind has ever known. I am grateful they have been in my life, especially during the days when all the booze and drugs worked so well. These are the kind of characters that literally do not have the word "no" in their vocabulary when it comes to getting it on.

There could be some big family commitment, school test, or some other bullshit obligation the next day, and the light was always "green," meaning... "Shit yes, let's get this thing rolling!"

Wherever we ended up, it was perfect. The three of us together were the equivalent of three Navy Seals, but we were the "Special Drinking Ops Unit." We were very dependable, never leaving a brother behind, all for one and one for all, and when we sat down for drinks the most important words said were to the bartender were three simple words, "Keep 'em comin'."

I have a tremendous amount of love for those two brothers of mine; in fact, we almost lost Eric about fifteen years ago when a balcony railing collapsed at one of Bubba's house parties. Eric fell—I mean, he fell on his fucking head and should have died.

Without question he shouldn't be here. He survived, though, and had to take a year off from drinking, and he had to take these anti-seizure medications. The funny thing is he would drink 12 to 24 of those O'Doul's non-alcoholic beers almost every day, for an entire year. So to say Eric missed his beer would be a gross understatement.

We charged down to Mexico first thing on a Friday morning. Bubba had this white, four-door Audi that was pretty comfortable, and it was even more comfortable because he was driving and I could then drink as much as I wanted to. This is no bullshit: three guys like Eric, Bubba, and me going to Mexico to drink 50-cent Coronas and other mixed satanic drinks was kind of like giving us the keys to Fort Knox. We were going to pillage, cause a lot of scenes, and someone will take off their pants and ask some chick if she is available—it will not stop until, well... it just won't stop.

We were all fired up, and we hit a shitload of dive bars in Rosarito. That's all they had anyway at the time (this was in 1984), and we liked that kind of environment. Dirty, smelly, fat dudes are playing that shitty Mexican music which is fun to listen to when you are fucking butthoused out of your mind, the beer is ice cold and tastes like frosty perfection, and they go down as easy as a fat guy at Raging Waters... nice and easy.

Rosarito nowadays should be fucking blown up. What a joke. Bars and nightclubs that look like something from Miami Vice are everywhere, and not that I now give a shit, but getting loaded down there is just as expensive as it is here in Southern California.

Bubba, Eric, and I were just wrecking bars and ourselves, and had easily drunk a case of brews each and many satanic mixed cocktails. I was never one of those assholes who counted or would say like some cheesy fraternity donkey, "I can drink more than you, bro, let's go shot for shot." That was never my bag. I drank a lot, and used a lot of drugs, and to tell you how much I did was nonsense, mainly because I didn't give a shit and also because everyone knew I drank and used way too much as well.

We were absolutely out of our minds, and it was time to get back to Long Beach. This was a time when there was only a few minutes wait at the border; it takes so long now to get across that a pregnant woman in her second trimester can approach the wait at the border and have a healthy, brand-new baby boy by the time she gets through customs. It just takes forever these days.

There was a party for us to get back to in Long Beach, so we were making record time. We had started drinking at about 9 or 10 a.m., and it was now around 4 p.m. We bought a shitload of alcohol to take home with us because it was fun to play the hero and roll up to a party back home with ice-cold Mexican frosties and tequila—the girls loved it and so did we.

Bubba had no business driving, but we were determined to get home. Both Eric and I were just twisted out of our skulls, so we required a nap. I was riding shotgun and Eric was behind me. We were probably asleep for about 30 minutes when there was this thunderous crashing sound and we were awakened and scared shitless. As Eric and I came to, we were blown away at the scene around us.

I am pretty sure that Bubba found it necessary to take a nap while driving, and expected that his Audi would just drive itself back to Long Beach. I awoke to about 50 yards of center divider bushes everywhere, and thank God we did not hit anyone else or hurt anyone else, and lastly, that we weren't hurt either. We all should have died if life were fair.

So there we were on the 5 Freeway, and the CHP pulled up—and mind you Bubba had to have smelled like a representative for Cuervo Tequila who had been on a sea cruise for a week—and the most unbelievable thing happened. The CHP gave Bubba a ticket and took off, knowing that AAA (the auto club) was on the way. In

1984 we caught a break that day, because today Bubba would have been in San Quentin serving bad meatloaf to lifers for driving that drunk.

The tow truck arrived and put Bubba's Audi on its big flatbed, safe and sound. The car was totally bashed in, almost totaled, with landscape strewn over half the 5 Freeway, but we had a house party to get to in Long Beach! We needed to celebrate our new lease on life, and we had a trunk load of brews and liquor.

There was just one problem—there was only enough room in the tow truck for three people. Don't ask me how this happened, but the driver, Bubba, and Eric got into the tow truck, and the AAA driver allowed me to sit in the totally fucked Audi front passenger seat, while on the flatbed of the truck. The best part was I had plenty of cold beer to drink and no one to bitch about the music I was cranking. I had it all going on, and I felt like a king for a few hours.

I had the blessing of cold beer and a great Alpine stereo system in the Audi (and it played wonderfully). I got to enjoy some of the finest punk rock music ever recorded, all Long Beach bands of course: The Falling Idols, The Vandals, and a little TSOL never hurt anybody! Blazing in a tow truck owned by AAA, beer in hand, a raging party ahead of us, and the sound of David Quackenbush of the Falling Idols singing what really mattered to me. I still love that fucking band.

When we pulled up in the hell ride (that being the AAA truck), the driver started unhooking the Audi, and I was just butthoused to the point where everything was funny to me. Bubba was funny, Eric was funny, the tow truck driver was really funny, the fact that I got to drink on a flatbed tow truck for two hours was funny...and the day ain't even over yet! Where's the beer, damn it?!

Then Armageddon occurred. Bubba's mom saw and heard the tow truck from the house, and she was just livid. Eric and I wanted nothing to do with explaining what happened, because I would have gone into straight up Eddie Haskell mode: "Aww, Mrs. Anderson, Bubba saved our lives. Yeah, you should have seen him dodge the pack of wild deer on the highway—we are lucky to be alive. Now I suggest you kiss your son!"

Eric and I dug out of there and ran like hell, but we first feverishly taxed the load of alcohol and made a run to Eric's house, which was literally right behind Bubba's house. We liked to keep things close in proximity in our little world. I am pretty sure to this day that if it were quiet enough, Eric could have easily heard one of Bubba's epic beer farts from across the alley, but they no longer live with their parents—at least, I don't think they do.

That night was golden, we were alive, we had a lot of good alcohol, and we had a great story to tell. But Bubba couldn't make it for some reason, it may have had something to do with the day's events... I'm not too sure.

All my behavior was starting to really wear thin with my mom and Darryl. I was out of control, and I couldn't seem to tell them the truth very much. See, when you live in a household that doesn't tolerate drinking and drugs, and you are an alcoholic and a drug addict, it is a prerequisite that you must lie on a regular basis.

I never enjoyed lying, but it was necessary so I could coexist with my parents and not get caught with all of my bullshit, etc. But they knew I was drinking, the "theft of cocaine" story which never stuck really bothered them, and I had been stealing money from them for my habits, and enough was enough.

Leaving Long Beach...

It was a miserable day when I was told I had to go live with my father in Anaheim Hills. For a young man who had grown up by the beach his whole life and couldn't stand "inlanders" (but they do have the hottest chicks), and who was in the middle of his first year of high school, it was totally devastating. On top of that, I had to leave all of my close friends whom I had known my whole life.

I had no relationship whatsoever with my father—he was really absent from the lives of my brother Eric and me. The thought of moving to Anaheim Hills was like a death sentence to me, and I ramped up my anarchistic ways to completely new levels as a result of this "verdict" handed down by my parents.

It was officially me against the fucking world—no one is sending me inland without paying for it! I moved out to Anaheim Hills, which is about 45 minutes northeast of Newport Beach, just before Christmas of 1983. Things were about to get a whole lot more interesting; Ferris Bueller was an amateur compared to what I had in store for my new neighborhood.

My dad (Robert) was a successful executive and he loved what he did for a living. He loved to work, loved to drink, and loved women, lots of them. He was remarried to a successful woman (Jean) who had done well in the real estate business. Jean had a daughter, Jill, who was my age and was a straight-A student, a wonderful girl, and a great stepsister to me. I would eventually corrupt her to a point where she barely graduated high school, though she originally had her sights set on Stanford University to play volleyball.

We also had a "live-in maid" named Mary. Now, when I think of a maid I think of someone who actually cleans and gets shit done around the house. I am not sure where they found her—maybe from the "Laziest Fucking Maid in the World Service"—because all she did was walk around the house and cook for herself.

I think years before she may have worked for Jean in that capacity, but I never saw her do jack shit. She just seemed to live there, watch TV in her room, and get paid for that. Damn it, I wanted that job! I would have gladly put on those fuzzy slippers and bumped around the house and acted all cranky for a paycheck.

Mary was on all sorts of different medications, God only knows for what, probably Advanced Laziness. But, I made damn sure I taxed some of her pill supply. It probably wasn't a good idea, because I later found out they were blood pressure pills and pills for irritable bowel syndrome. No wonder my heart would race like crazy and I had trouble taking a dump. I caught on after a while and left her pills alone.

My drinking and using took off once I was in the environment of Anaheim Hills, and for good reason. My dad was an alcoholic, and he would buy cases of beer for me and put them into the garage fridge for me and my friends to drink while we played ping pong. He always bought that shit beer Schaeffer, too. He made good money, but he figured it was cheap and I didn't know the difference. Heinekens were out—we were a Schaeffer house, with a lazy fucking maid living there!

I had always wished we had one of those "porno" maids, you know, the maids that wear the skimpy French outfit and as they are dusting they bend over, and then all of a sudden start getting wildly fucked. But that wasn't Mary. In fact, fucking Mary was something that on my horniest of days, ripped off acid and mushrooms and cocaine, would never dream of routing her, and plus I think she was like 80 years old, which pretty much guaranteed a big "no" on that whole deal.

I lived in Anaheim Hills until the end of my junior year of high school (about a year and a half total). I was kicked out of that house, and probably for good reason—mainly my lifestyle and all the little "fuck you's" I would get around to doing, and there were plenty of those for sure.

My dad and stepmom were gone all the time, whether it was travel or late nights with clients. They were hammered all the time, and often I would hide on the floor in between the bed and the wall just trying to drown out the horrible verbal exchanges they would have. It was very unpleasant, and as I mentioned earlier my father was a big guy, 6'4" and strong, and it didn't help my cause given the fact that he boxed in the Marine Corps.

I always knew when a shitstorm was about to hit. The garage door would open, and one or both of the cars arriving would kind of come to a screeching halt. You know that sound—we've all heard it before when we're pissed off and to put an exclamation point to the end of our drive we pull up and slam on the brakes.

Those sounds were normal in our abnormal household. It was always followed with either complete silence (meaning an average shitty night out) or raging screaming (which was a good night for Dad and stepmom). Some people just thrive on that stuff, call them co-dependent, call them whatever. I call them, "You guys should never have tied the knot type people," but that's just me.

I would cover up my fears by drinking more, and more. The worse they fought, the more I withdrew and rebelled. It's not that I rebelled for attention; I rebelled because I enjoyed the chaos, and more often than not my little stunts were quite funny. Someone, somewhere right now may very well be saying, "Remember that time that crazy ass Zalkins kid from Long Beach did such and such?"

The most common drunk things I would hear my dad say are the following three things:

1. "Oh, I see...." (And I am saying to myself, "See what? I don't see a damn thing!")
2. "What do you want from me?"
3. "God damn it, Todd, stop fucking around!"

Those would be used as fuel to the fire, to make my pissed-off stepmom even more livid than she already was. In a way I kind of enjoyed it, because that meant there was some quality chaos that I could stand on the sidelines and check out. We didn't have any family dinners except maybe once a quarter, kind of like what a big corporation does, only during certain holidays did we eat as a family.

We didn't have "dinnertime" at our house—we had "fend for your fucking self time." Usually my stepsister Jill and I would make something together, and often there was nothing in the house to even cook. From the outside the house looked like everything else in the neighborhood, white upper-middle-class bullshit suburb living the American Dream, but for me it was just a nightmare.

I had plenty to do with the nightmare part of my existence, too. I will not blame it on my alcoholic father and stepmother. I had more than my share of issues, and I would only develop more and more chronic issues as time wore on.

ENTERTAINING MYSELF

ere's a snapshot of some of the bullshit that I pulled off, which to me was quite funny and some of it still is. Hell, I was sixteen for God's sake, and alcohol and cocaine were the co-pilots for my sitcom.

I hadn't studied for a test for my History class, and the best way for me to get a postponement was to drink some beers and let off a bunch of these "glass fart-bombs" I bought at a novelty/joke store. These things unleashed napalm type odor. I had no idea a tiny little glass tube could emit that much stink, but they did. Before class I raced in when no one was there, and crushed about six fart bombs and bailed.

These things just destroyed people—fellow classmates were coming out tearing from their eyes and dry heaving. I was crying from the laughter, but the joke was ultimately on me; our teacher ended up just giving us the test on these benches in the outdoors. My fart bombing backfired on me, and I was caught for it and given a suspension.

But that wasn't really punishment for me. It was more like a "free day" to stay home with my school's permission to get high and drunk. The so-called friends I had didn't seem to have a problem with it either, and most of them created a "self-imposed suspension" as well, and came over to help empty out the liquor cabinet. I always had the pure academic crowd in my crew.

I will never forget one particular night while my dad was in New York on business. It was a Sunday because my stepmom was drinking wine in her room watching 60 Minutes—that was a big family night for us! Anyway, I drank some cocktails and beers, and decided it was time to take a drive. I was not licensed to drive at the time, although I was of legal driving age.

I had not completed driver's education at school and I hadn't taken the test at the DMV (which I actually failed twice before eventually passing!). But I really wanted to see how their Cadillacs drove—they had matching Eldorados, those two-door ones that were popular back in the 80s. One was rust-colored and the other black.

I took the rust-colored one first, and about six miles away I drove it through a ranch fence. I hauled ass back home but wasn't finished yet, my step-sister wanted to come for the second ride in the black Caddy.

Being the genius I am, I drove the same route as before, and a few minutes later we were being followed by about six Anaheim police units with their lights blazing. Did I pull over? Shit, no. I drove calmly about four miles until Jill and I arrived at our house. The cops were going shit nuts. This was before cell phones, so they radioed dispatch who then called our house to verify our identities.

I will never forget my stepmom's screams from the house. I wasn't even cited for drunk or reckless driving, and I should have received both as well as a ride to jail. When the cops bailed, my stepmom started throwing potted plants at me from the second story. I found this hilarious, mainly because my dad wasn't around.

She called my father back in New York and he was asleep, but now he was pissed and awake. I remember this well and here's how the conversation went:

Dad: God damn it, Todd! What the hell were you thinking?

Todd: (Nothing but silence)

Dad: Do you hear me, you little shit?

Todd: Yes Dad... I hear you.

Dad: Well, when I get home we are going to have a big talk about this.

Todd: Yeah, wuteva....(click)

Dad: (Calling back right away) Did you just hang up on me you little shit?

Todd: Oh yeah, wuteva....(click)

Dad: (Calling back after my hanging up on him twice in a row) You little asshole!!! When I get home....

Todd: (I interrupted him) Oh yeah, wuteva!!!!! (click)

I was fucked. Let's just say I received more than a big talk—I received a big ass kicking, and it wasn't pleasant. After Dad beat the shit out of me, I just went to the fridge and cracked open a Schaefer beer to help heal my wounds. Isn't that what most kids do after their drunk dad beats the shit out of them?

For me it made sense and then some. Drinking eased the pain, and after a few left hooks to my face, I needed some pain relief. I found that relief in the form of alcohol.

I had a stepbrother as well, but he didn't live with us. His name was Charlie and he was pretty cool, he liked good music and I respect that. Well, he got married, and when he did, I of course drank more than the wedding party put together.

After their wedding, the top part of the cake was put in the freezer to eat later when they had their one-year anniversary. I swear I had no idea that was a tradition, no clue. Well, one night after smoking a bunch of weed and drinking my share of brews, I was hungry.

I mentioned earlier how weed always made me order a pizza and pass out. Well, there was never any food in our house, so I opened the freezer and found the cake. I devoured three quarters of it. I recently discovered that long after I had left Anaheim Hills, they had a big party to celebrate their anniversary. When it was cake time, they went just fucking ballistic. I hear they cursed me for years after that. They are now divorced—maybe it's because I ate the cake... I have no idea on that one either.

All of these things occurred while under the influence of drugs and alcohol. Lying and cheating to get what I wanted or needed was a big part of the equation as well. You know you are a really sick person when you start to believe your own lies. That became something real familiar. I lived in a world of illusion based on drinking and using, so how would I know what was true or false?

My perception of what was right or wrong was so skewed, it's not even funny. But that's how I would live most of my life; I constantly needed affirmation, and the booze and drugs fed it to me.

Señor Heimlich

I have mentioned how authority jaded me quite a bit, and I found myself adding new layers to my detestation of all "powers that be" all the time. When I got angry with authority I fixed it quite easily by chopping up some fat lines of cocaine and drinking as much as possible.

I was working at the Fireside restaurant in Anaheim Hills as a busboy. It was a decent place, and my stepmom helped me get the job. I was trying my best, showing up on time and not getting loaded on the job. My employment stint was short-lived, but for something I never envisioned happening.

It was a busy night on a Friday or Saturday, and the place was packed. The section I was working had this one table of eight, and they were laughing, drinking, and seemed to be having a great time. Then all hell broke loose, and people were screaming for help and I was an earshot away.

What happened was this gentleman choking, and he was going away for the long haul real fast. He was a really big guy, bordering on obese. He was flailing his arms and he was turning different colors in his face. As he stood up I was right behind him, and I gave him the Heimlich maneuver. When I administered this he coughed up this huge piece of bread that flew across the room. I was a hero, and they told me I had saved his life.

Today this would not happen, but I was actually fired that night. I was let go because they said I should have waited for paramedics to arrive. Yeah right—if I had waited any longer the paramedics would not have been necessary, and the coroner would have been the right one to be handling the situation. The manager of the restaurant (Mr. Asshole) said that I could have broken one of the customer's ribs while doing it, in turn creating a lawsuit. Yeah, and I guess a fat dude perishing in the middle of the restaurant on a packed Friday night is the better alternative than trying to save his life.

I was dumbfounded over the whole thing. I later found out that the gentleman I had helped dropped by an envelope the next day addressed to, "Todd the busboy." There was a note in it that just said "Thank you," and in it was a $100 dollar bill. I never saw the money, and I found this out through friends of mine who worked there.

The manager kept the money. I would have loved to have at least had the note. It made me feel good that I had helped someone, but it just was one of those things where maybe I wasn't good enough, and I thought I had done the right thing in a severely panicked atmosphere.

This deal really bummed me out, and I had no recourse. All I wanted was my crummy job, but that wasn't going to happen. I continued to drink more and score cocaine as much as I could, but I never really had much money for it. I loved to drink and snort, but you must have dough to snort blow.

I made a pact with myself that there would be a day that I would not have to worry about the money issue—I would make enough money to buy as much coke or whatever else I could possibly ingest, and the rest of the world could just get fucked.

I would make good on my pact about eight years later, and the game would get much more out of control, and the levels of my addiction would make the stuff I have already talked about look and sound like going to Disneyland.

I spent my remaining days in Anaheim Hills isolated, getting further away from the friends I couldn't even really call friends. I didn't grow up with them, most of them were full of shit, and they wanted nothing to do with me unless I could offer them something.

Then again, I was no different. I think I always wanted to have that feeling that I was part of a crew or a group. I had that in Long Beach, and I didn't have it in Anaheim Hills. I fought with that internally on a daily basis, and my pathetic head would once again tell me I was doing something wrong, and I had no idea what it was.

Drinking at home alone in my bedroom was pretty much a daily thing. I was safe for the most part, because no one was ever really around to check on me. I just did what I wanted, and my stepsister was falling into the same patterns as I had, except she had a lot more to lose than I did.

I was no longer a good student academically because you have to attend class to get decent grades. Attendance was something I didn't give a shit about—I just wanted to follow the party, create a party, be the party, or party alone. I did that well.

School no longer interested me whatsoever, but I felt bad for Jill. She was a really good person, a pretty girl with a lot going for her in all facets of her life. Then her stepbrother, myself that is, introduced her to drinking and everything else, and she just fell prey to it. I was never proud of that at all, and for a long time after I had moved back to Long Beach I beat myself up over the fact I had this negative influence over a really beautiful human being with a very bright future.

I know today she is doing well, she's been married forever and has three children and is living in Houston, Texas. I will never forget how kind she was to me, and how we were very good friends to one another. We had no one else but us, and we had some very scary scenes at home, and those things can form a bond that is hard to break.

MY KIND OF PARTY

One of the last straws for me and my stint of my "Tour de Anaheim Hills" was when my dad was having this really extravagant company Christmas party at our house. Even the CEO was in town from New York, and he arrived in a limo with his wife. It was a really nice party with bartenders and the whole nine yards.

For a guy like me, having open bars, unlimited booze, unreal-looking girls/models (my dad's company specialized in women's swimwear, so follow me here) was like the pinnacle of life for me at the time. And I would take full advantage of this evening... I was not going to fuck around, and I meant business.

The party was going strong when I took a bottle of champagne from the bar and strolled out to the limousine to say "hello" to the driver, this black guy named Reggie. He was absolutely wonderful. We hit it off instantly and we just sat in the limo, and yes, we drank a shitload of booze and watched the Lakers game on the little bullshit limo TV.

I could party with Reggie, so I took it upon myself to offer him some fine powdered cocaine. He didn't even blink an eye—the answer was a resounding "Fuck yes, let's get it on." He was my kind of partier for sure. The holiday gathering wasn't ending early, so we had the time to get blasted out of our minds.

We packed our beaks with blow for a few hours (also known as snorting cocaine for you folks not familiar with my wacky terminology) and toasted the Lakers and the holidays. I could barely even talk after a few hours, which happened a lot to me when on blow, and then I went back in the house.

I proceeded to go through people's belongings and found this beautiful, full-length mink coat that belonged to the CEO's gorgeous wife. Well, I needed to try that on, which I did, and then paraded around the house gassed out of my mind and talking it up with the guests, mainly the models, of which there were plenty.

They thought I was cute, and they would hug me and kiss me on the cheek, and I was like, "Merry Christmas baby, wanna come upstairs and let Santa show you his North Pole?" They would just laugh at me, and it was all fun until Pops heard of this nonsense.

The party was officially over for me, and I was told to go to my room. I said, "Sure" and then completely dismissed what I was told and went back outside to see Reggie. Now he could barely talk because he was so high and drunk, so I packed his beak some more and the game was back on in our world. When it was time to leave, Reggie was so butthoused he couldn't drive the CEO and his wife to their hotel. Everyone was blasted and knew I had been partying with Reggie. My dad was just fucking livid, and later on exclaimed, "My God-damned son got the limo driver hammered!"

This did not go over really well with my dad, not well at all. I received an ass kicking the next day that was fit for a king, because it was a king-sized ass kicking. It didn't matter, because I was so hung over that I couldn't possibly feel worse. It was one of those hangovers that was so heavy your temples feel like they are in a vice and you have no idea what day it is or where you were born—actually, wishing you had never been born is more like it. Champagne + beer + cocaine = a really terrible following day.

That was pretty much it for me residing in Anaheim. I sealed my fate a few months later when I stole money from a retail swimwear and lingerie store that my stepmom and dad had opened. They would later have a nice chain of these stores, but I would not be any part of it. Who in the hell would want me handling any of their hard-earned dollars?

I was kicked out towards the end of the semester, and I was basically homeless. I was sleeping in my car in this canyon back in the hills and it would get wickedly cold at night, somewhere in the low thirties. The bitter cold and shivering felt as though it would never end, and I barely slept for days. In the morning I would get ready for school in the boys' locker room, and all I could do was dream about being back at home in Long Beach.

After word got back home to my mom that I was homeless and had nowhere to go, she asked me to come back. It was one of the happiest days of my life and I cried tears of joy the whole way back to Long Beach, while cranking Generation X's "Promises, Promises" and "Clampdown" by the Clash. If you haven't heard "Clampdown," you should—the song just rocks and it really amps you up. I am pretty sure that several of my friends and I destroyed many pieces of furniture listening to that full blast.

I was coming home, and I had never been happier in my life, although I'm not sure if Long Beach felt the same way.

BACK IN BLACK

My return to Long Beach was something that was too good to be true. I remember listening to songs like, "Back in Black" by AC-DC, being so jacked up about life, and having a new chance to be among the ones I loved so much again. I did not want to fuck this up, so I really toed the line—for a while, that is.

One of the first things my mom and stepdad did was lay down the law. I had to be more accountable than before, which was a tough pill to swallow because I was arriving back in Belmont Shore at the start of the summer before my senior year of high school.

But I was willing to fall in line and do things like be home by 10 p.m. on the weekends—on the fucking weekends! I was seventeen years old, for goodness sake, and I have to be home at 10 p.m.? But I had no choice in the matter, I just loved being back in my hometown of Long Beach.

Going back to Long Beach for me at that time was like a soldier returning home from a war. When I was living in Anaheim Hills I was in a "foreign land" where people, places, and things were all very unfamiliar to me.

But I would find all sorts of ways to bend and break rules. I am an expert at that and well qualified to speak on the subject of breaking rules. Whoever coined the phrase, "Rules were made to be broken" must be a distant relative of mine.

You want to discuss or lay down your rules with me? Fuck your rules. In fact, rules were created just so wise asses like me can push your buttons and force you to develop prison systems! Okay, that's a stretch. Criminal behavior wasn't my specialty. However, driving under the influence, selling cocaine and Oxycontin, and regularly jumping off bridges naked qualify as criminal behavior.

It was a fairly uneventful summer with the exception of my drinking and using. We would drink beers and surf during the day, and drink more beers and hopefully snort some blow at night. I found a good connection for blow during this time, a woman who lived in Seal Beach and had no shortage of the stuff. The quality was good and the price was right.

Don't ask me how, but I have only been arrested once in my life. I was placed in a holding cell in Huntington Beach for an old traffic ticket and I was released a few hours later, so I wouldn't really consider that being arrested. But I was handcuffed, so I guess I was fucking arrested!

A good friend of mine, John, posted the $500 bail. Had he not posted, I would have been shipped off to Orange County Jail where I hear you get to wear really neat orange jumpsuits. I am grateful that didn't happen.

Had I ever been pulled over and searched a few years later, it wouldn't have been Orange County Jail as my destination. It would have been more like San Quentin prison due to what I was carrying. Later on, as a general rule I would have at least two eight balls and upwards to an ounce of blow as well as big grips of pills at any given time. I never ran out of drugs—that was just unacceptable to me!!!

The summer days were wonderful. After surfing in the morning and drinking some brews we would go "free boarding" in the afternoon. Free boarding is surfing behind a motorboat—my buddy had a Boston Whaler and we would use it religiously for our outings.

Nowadays, they call it wakeboarding and you are strapped into the board. It's an entirely different sport now.

For me and my friends, going free boarding in the back-bay near the Edison plant was a great way to drink and plan the evening's events—which never really took much planning, I might add. All we had to figure out was where we were going to party that night and how many girls would be in attendance.

Most people will never go into the water where the Edison plant is, back behind the bay that runs along Studebaker Road in Long Beach. It may look nice, but the water is almost nuclear, about 84 degrees and loaded with God only knows what. It's amazing that none of us ever woke up with a third eye or some strange unknown parasitic disorder that made your balls turn multiple shades of green, yellow, and purple. I do not recommend taking your kids there to swim.

Most things we did involved the water, especially in the summer. Whether it was surfing, free boarding, swimming, chasing girls, riding our beach cruisers—all of it was done by the water. There was no need to go anywhere else. The mere thought of having to go out of town (unless to surf) in the summertime was ridiculous.

NUDITY IS WHERE IT'S AT

When free boarding behind my friend's Boston Whaler, I would frequently do it naked. I liked to expose myself whenever possible and I found it necessary to do this especially around 5 p.m.

The traffic on Studebaker would be heavy with folks getting off work, and there I was sliding on a surfboard with a beer in hand and my dick getting some fresh air. I cannot tell you how many times people would say, "Jesus Christ, was that Zalkins again behind the boat with his pud flying around?" Yes, it was.

Bridge jumping was another hobby of ours, and our friend Brett happened to live on the bay front right by the Appian Way Bridge. Once again, this was my opportunity to shine. It was again important to drink as much as possible and jump off that bridge naked. I of course would time it just perfectly for when the parents of people we knew were driving by. I swear, at times I was the son of Eddie Haskell from "Leave It to Beaver."

My mom would get calls and they would go something like this:

Caller: Well, he did it again!

Mom: Did what?

Caller: Your son was on that bridge again... naked of course.

Mom: This does not surprise me.

Anytime my mom got a call, it was not about my brother Eric—he wasn't the troublemaker. It was about me, and how much crap I had gotten myself into, and would anyone require therapy as a result of it.

I managed to stay out of major trouble in the summer, and it was time for my senior year of high school. Woodrow Wilson High School was pretty cool then, as opposed to what it looks like now. These days it resembles more of a maximum security prison. If Folsom or Pelican Bay ever runs out of room they could just ship some inmates down to Woodrow Wilson High, because no one is getting out of that place during business hours, not even the teachers.

In my last year there in 1984–85, it was quite harmless. My classmates were for the most part pretty cool overall and we had some really cute girls. Nothing like Lakewood or Millikan High School, though—those two always had the most smoking-hot girls, and we could never understand why. Maybe because all the hottest girls are inlanders, as I mentioned a while ago.

We had our share of very, very pretty girls though. And when you have grown up with them, you just don't see it as much. I knew most of the girls from as far back as elementary school, and I looked at them as more like sisters to me. I was probably just a maniac to them, but every now and then I see a girl I grew up with from the old days and they don't run the other way—maybe they want to, though.

I don't want to spend too much time on the high school trip because, quite frankly, I wasn't much a part of it. My reason for going was because by law I had to, and it was a good place to see friends, cause some harmless trouble, and work on my alcoholism. My dreams of going to a good college had faded. I told myself that after high school I would go to Long Beach City College for two years, get good grades, and transfer to UC Santa Barbara or UCLA.

That's what I wanted, but that's not what happened—one has to apply oneself in order to go to the next level. I wasn't going to any level that reflected progress, it was more of a rapid digress or spiral downward.

Steven Spielberg, Jr.

One of the best moments in high school occurred in a film class. Our teacher was Mrs. Townley, and she could flip out at any given moment—she was very volatile. My pushing her buttons may have had something to do with that.

This is way before digital cameras, and all of the high-tech stuff we have today. We used those little 8 mm cameras. We had to get in groups and create and film some stupid movie. My buddy Chris was the director of my group and he thought it would be good to have me play a teacher who murders his students. I believe the character's name was Mr. Lipps, that's right, Mr. Verne Lipps, and we had fun making it for sure.

As we were finishing our film assignment there was one day left until the project was due. I "borrowed" one of the cameras from another group of girls I had known forever and I grabbed some friends of mine. I think there were five of us, and we went into the rest room and filmed four of my friends dropping their shorts and doing a big "bare ass." I was laughing in tears over this. A friend of ours, Scott (aka Cowballs) had these huge nuts, and he pulled them down and slapped them around and we are all just dying. Little did I realize, when I was laughing uncontrollably, that I had filmed myself in one of the mirrors of the rest room.

I figured it all went well, but it didn't end well when Mrs. Townley saw Cowballs slapping his nuts around—they were so big it was like five packs of Big League Chew all wadded up. I hope you find that funny, because I still do to this day.

When Mrs. Townley saw my image holding the camera, I was screwed. A suspension was in order, and I gladly did my time drinking beer at "The Spot" on Treasure Island with my good buddy Eric.

When it was getting close to graduation, all the seniors submitted what their goals and aspirations were.

For example:

Jennifer Rogers wrote: "I'm going to Stanford and plan on being a lawyer like my father."

Bill Thomas wrote: "Going to Long Beach State, going to play water polo and become a nuclear physicist."

And of course, Todd Zalkins had to write: "I want to marry a blonde, nymphomaniac coke dealer who owns a Ferrari dealership."

That was my submission verbatim, and I think someone changed it or deleted it before it was published—but my peers would expect nothing less from me. I can vividly recall just how empty I felt that most people I knew were off to college and actually growing up.

There was a softball size knot I could get in the middle of my chest from all the anxiety I felt, because deep down I wanted to be moving forward like them, I was just incapable of doing what was right. Drugs and alcohol were the only things that allowed me to put up with who I really was, and I know that I was just a very conflicted and often sad kid inside.

Event Planning 101

Both the prom and graduation night had only one theme for me: Booze and Cocaine.

The day before our prom I couldn't get any blow, so I did what I had to do. I contacted my cousin in La Jolla and he started to make some phone calls on my behalf. I would do whatever it required to score and I would not be denied the feeling cocaine gave me on our prom night. I drove down that evening with one of my buddies and we met up with my cousin who was staying at a killer condo he owned on the oceanfront of Pacific Beach.

We started to drink immediately, and my craving for "space coke" kicked in within about 45 minutes. I call it "space coke" because I always got high-grade quality cocaine, the kind of blow that would make you feel numb from the floor up and like you were floating in outer space. I generally hated other people's coke. Because it wasn't space coke! It was just plain, fucking shitty coke.

The deal for scoring coke for the prom was one of those situations where we had to get it from a "friend of a friend," and we all know what that means: Shitty Coke!! However, I trusted my cousin and we proceeded to get ruined off beers and cocktails. Not long after being there, my buddy Eric and I met these girls from Arizona who were staying next door. This was a huge bonus to go along with our search for coke.

In a matter of a few hours, my friend and I convinced these girls we didn't have girlfriends (which we technically had—they were just located in Long Beach at the time), and I managed to have some amazing sex in the hot tub with a girl I had known for about an hour. All road trips should work out like this! But just as I was getting worried we weren't going to score the blow, at around 10:30 we got dialed in with 10 grams of just unbelievably high-grade coke, definitely qualified from outer space.

It's not common to get really great coke when it's the "friend of a friend." What that usually means is a "friend of some guy who's going to screw you," but that did not happen this time. We snorted some big fat rails, and we made the drive back to Long Beach in great shape. I had some "junior porn star" sex with a stranger, and scored the good blow to ensure a great evening for our senior prom. Life was wonderful.

At the prom, more of my time was spent in the bathrooms with friends of mine chopping lines and talking about how much fun we were having. We probably did have some fun, but I was keenly aware that the next day would be horrifying. The next day was always a nightmare after drinking and packing my beak with the white powder. Nothing good ever resulted from doing that type of mixed combination, but I did it anyway... a lot.

When I drank, a bell went off in my head. Like Pavlov's dog, I would basically start to salivate over the thought of cocaine. I knew it would straighten me out and allow me to drink a lot more and keep the party going. Once I ingested alcohol, it was pretty much a guarantee that cocaine use would follow. There were times I just wouldn't even go out at night because I knew we couldn't get the drugs, so why go out?

More often than not I would venture into the most wretched places imaginable looking for the lift that coke gave me. I never had a shortage of friends who wanted to join me for the ride. As time went on, I couldn't tell who my real friends were. Everything was distorted by the heavy using of drugs and alcohol.

That's just the kind of guy I was at the time. I couldn't take anything seriously because I always thought I would just wait until the last minute. Like Kirk Gibson of the Dodgers in the World Series against the Oakland A's, I would just come up to bat at the bottom of the ninth with two out and hit a home run.

Like everything would be all okay, I would stumble upon some opportunity that would just pay off in spades, I didn't need college, and I would just get by on my wits—but it's hard to get by on your wits when you are losing your mind. And slowly but surely, that's what was happening to me.

BUBBA PART 1

I grew up with Bubba on Naples Island, and he's one of the kindest guys you will ever meet. He's also one of the gnarliest, heavy-duty partiers on this planet. This is a man who can take a one-night affair and wind up in Las Vegas with eight friends, of whom most return home divorced and a complete shell of their former selves. I have a great deal of affection for Bubba, as he was there to help me out at many of my low points of desperation while at Long Beach City College.

I was incapable of holding down a job due to my drinking and packing my beak, which was the only job I felt suited me. It didn't pay very well, but I was getting good at it.

Bubba is one of those guys who love you unconditionally when you are his friend, and we have a lot of history between us. To show you the type of guy he is, I will share one of many examples of his generosity: I was really broke and quite hungry during the holidays of 1985 shortly after we graduated from high school. I was living on my own, but most people would not consider it living. Most people ran the other way from me, it was common to hear, "Holy shit, it's that really drunk beak-packing guy. Let's get the hell out of here."

Bubba was making a run to the Price Club (now Costco) for his mother's annual Christmas party. I will never forget how he stopped by my pad unexpectedly to fill up my refrigerator with food to last a week or two. I did not ask him to do this—he just showed up. Never was he one to say, "Okay, you owe me $89.56 for that grub." It was in his nature to do for others, and it's a common thread we have shared for many years. It's a quality not found in a lot of people I know; he's indeed a very special friend.

We were both quite the entrepreneurs at a very young age. In 1979 through 1984 Bubba and I would string up Christmas lights for a lot of folks on Naples Island. Not for free by the way—we were givers for sure, but we weren't fucking stupid, except of course when we drank.

We were in the Christmas Light Service business at the age of twelve, long before these criminals of today who charge $75 to $100 an hour and make a serious job out of it. The money made today would blow doors on what we made, but hey, it was fun and it put a few bucks in our pockets. Plus, it was always fun to see the random "hot Naples wife" strutting around the house.

I was so pathetic as a teenager, very much turned on by the opposite sex, and my mind was full of "insane wishful thinking" that coincided with my not living in reality. It was perfectly normal to have the following dialogue with Bubba:

Me: Hey Bubba, did you see that?

Bubba: See what?

Me: Didn't you see Mrs. Johnson bending over?

Bubba: No I did not. Now hand me the string of lights.

Me: Fuck the lights—they can wait... Did you see Mrs. Johnson's ass? She is hot, and I am going to duct tape up her husband and make him watch while I tool his wife in their own bedroom.

Bubba: I sincerely doubt that would ever happen.

Me: Bullshit, I am fourteen going on fifteen—she would love my pipe!

Bubba: Trust me, she would not dig your pipe.

Me: Yeah, trust me, she would dig it, and then I would film it and I will make a bunch of dough. It will become a new video series, "Totally Illegal Routing of Hot Wives of Naples Island." Larry Flynt will love it and he will legally adopt me. I will be hanging with John Holmes on porn sets, and I will be routing the finest donuts on this planet and Larry Flynt will hire me to be the youngest executive in Flynt Publications history. (Remember, I am fourteen or fifteen saying this shit.)

Bubba: Fuck, Zalkins! Would you hand me the string of lights! She doesn't care about your pipe, she will never let you rout her, and her husband would beat the shit out of you if you attempted to duct tape him up and bang his wife!

Me: What if I told her it would be the best Christmas present ever?!

Bubba: Get back to work or you are fired!

Me: But we are business partners!

Bubba: Yeah, and soon to be a sole proprietorship.

BUBBA PART 2

God bless my friend Bubba, he's an absolute gem. Now, let's get into the meat and potatoes of one of the best Bubba stories ever. It goes something like this:

We were in Long Beach hanging out at my apartment, we were about 23 years old, and I had this classic pad near a place called Horny Corner in Belmont Shore. To explain Horny Corner, let's just say lots of virgins didn't spend a lot of time there. In fact, if you were a virgin or not into sex, you simply bypassed this landmark near Alamitos Bay. Basically it's a spot where Bayshore Avenue and First Street meet, and where great-looking girls meet beer-swilling dudes hanging out, and try to form an intimate game of naked Twister.

Apartments lined most of the area, and the people living there were way too tan in the winter months. To further define this, most of the people there didn't seem to work, didn't have to work, their girlfriend or boyfriend paid the bills, they were out on Workers' Comp (many for several years), or they were unwisely spending their inheritance.

Most were on a permanent drinking vacation and somehow managed to squeak by and pay rent. This was in the late 80s, so maybe people there are now responsible—it's all changed so much and I really don't give a shit.

So, we were out of our minds butthoused and Bubba declared it was the perfect time to roll to Las Vegas. We were already about an 8-ball deep with chibbies, or whappys, aka blow, and the dialogue went something like this:

Bubba: Hey Z-man (my nickname), I think we need a change of scenery.

Me: Yes, me too…Hey Bubba, you are sweating too much in my pad and it's bumming me out.

Bubba: Let's charge out to Vegas.

Me: Yes, I absolutely agree.

Bubba: Right now, damn it! I will do it! I swear I will drink and drive to Vegas… I don't even care if the cops light us up—I will drive straight to Vegas, no stoppin'!

Me: Yes… I know you will… but right now I cannot feel my face.

Bubba: What's wrong with you?

Me: It's the space coke. I swear I think an anesthesiologist stuck an IV into my lips, cheeks, and beak because I feel like my entire face just had a root canal.

Bubba: Perfect, let's pack our beaks.

Me: Yes, that might just be the cure-all for this condition… Rack up some big rat tails, please!

BUBBA PART 3

O kay, so we loaded up Bubba's Porsche 911 with booze and space coke and an extra shirt in the event we needed to shower and change. Bubba had this killer Porsche bought from some family money given to him. I couldn't even afford a Big Wheel, and if given that type of money to buy a Porsche, I would have bought a skateboard instead and a huge mountain of coke—no need for the nice sled, in my opinion.

We charged on out to Vegas, and Bubba was driving the car like he stole it. We were hitting the Jack Daniel's, drinking cold brews, and packing our ever-lovin' beaks to the hilt with cocaine from fucking outer space. We were completely gripped, and I couldn't talk, which was a good thing—but Bubba, he could talk, and he did for the entire drive.

Bubba: I swear Z-man... liquor makes me great... I will keep driving, I swear... I will drive this car right through the fuckin' hotel lobby and demand warm hookers, booze, and space coke!

Me: That may cause problems with the police.

Bubba: Fuck the cops! Frank will take care of it.

Frank was our buddy who managed the Sahara Hotel, and he could not possibly get us out of going to prison, but Bubba was on a roll, driving 120 miles an hour, fueled by the coke and booze, and I couldn't talk I was so high. "Just leave it alone," I said to myself.

We would have to pull over about every twelve miles to take a leak, because I'm one of those guys that once I have drunk eight to ten beers, my penis turns into "Raging Waters" and I must constantly urinate. Looking back, I should have been sponsored by Depends diapers.

By the eighth time of pulling over, Bubba is frustrated and says, "I swear to God, if we have to pull over one more time for you I am going to shoot you in the face." He's kidding of course, but Bubba had his 9 mm loaded in the car with us. You never know when we may need a gun while blasted out of our skulls on space coke and liquor and driving 120 miles an hour on the 15 Freeway.

We arrived at the rundown Sahara Hotel. This place was cool back in the 60s, but it rocked because Frank would set us up in a room where we could literally have a small circus operate comfortably in it, as well as a few midget gang-bangs. The room was just the right size for Bubba and me. There was plenty of room to wheelbarrow hookers around, and throw empty brews, nine different glass tabletops to rack up rat tails of coke, and lots of beds to choose not to sleep in, because we never fucking slept!

It was about 10 p.m. and Bubba and I were down at the blackjack table, both of us butthoused out of our minds. How do I know this? Well, about nine minutes into playing cards and tipping the dealer even when I lost, the dealer pointed his finger at me and whispered:

Dealer: Excuse me, sir.

Me: Talk to me, captain.

Dealer: Come a little closer please.

Me: No way bro, I swear I am heterosexual.

Dealer: You may want to fix these areas (as he points to my ears).

Me: (whispering) What the fuck? (I grab both of my ears, and tucked into each ear was a rolled up $100 bill that Bubba and I had used to pack our beaks with.)

So, I was thinking, "What's the problem with that? We are in Vegas, this is what people do!"

Bubba and I were destroyed in the casino until about 7 a.m. I couldn't talk, my beak was caked with coke, and my heart was pounding and now located close to my throat. We were seeing guys do the "Casino Walk," you know, those guys who are from some mid-west state like Ohio and they are totally ruined.

They look like they may have sold their daughters for more dough to play 25-cent "Wheel of Fortune" slots—one eye is open, the other is permanently closed due to either total inebriation or because his now ex-wife beat the shit out of him for gambling away their last eight bucks and their home has been lost.

So, it hit us, and out of nowhere Bubba exclaims, "We are going to the Chicken Ranch to rout some hookers!"

I looked excitedly at Bubba, "Yes... yes we are... they all want it at the Chicken Ranch, and I am going to give it to them!"

I was saying this as I knew full well that the space coke had reduced my dick to the size of a thumb tack. But let's forge ahead, damn it! "Line those hookers up... I will rout every one of them and no one will get out alive!"

It was 8 a.m. and Bubba (who is so big he doesn't drive his Porsche, he wears it) and I were just faded. Racing out to the ranch in Pahrump, Nevada is not the shortest drive—it's quite long and brutal, especially when wrecked from countless cocktails and endless lines of cocaine.

This is where it just got better than good, and as loaded as I was I still remember the dialogue to this day. We got to the ranch and we were the only customers there. Bubba and I were stoked, and I had now come down from all the space coke and my dick was qualified to be contracted with De Beers to cut diamonds. I was ready!

They lined up all the women, of whom all but two were smoking hot. I immediately said, "That one there... We are going to spend the rest of our lives together!" (She hates me immediately.) They proceeded to take me into this room where I got to select from a "Menu" of all the varieties of sex packages, like planning a fucking trip to Europe.

I was out of my mind and said, "I just want to fuck you every way possible without extensive injury to either of us, mainly me. I also request you act like you dig it, and I will pretend I am the porn star Peter North working up a nice sweat."

It cost $350 and I discovered I had only $50 on me—I had left my cash in the hotel room. Depression was setting in, and I asked the girl I was with to go find Bubba and he would loan it to me—he won't let me down!

She found him and he gave her the dough, and now I was happier than an adult film star who found out he has no STDs. I carried on with the gorgeous girl who did her best to pretend she was digging it, and I was routing my way into pure bliss when I heard the following from the other room:

Bubba: Bumps? What do you mean, I have bumps?

Hooker: I cannot service you because you have something down there... and it doesn't look right.

Bubba: That's my pipe... and you can and you will service me!!

Hooker: It's not going to happen with those bumps on your dick.

Bubba: Bumps? What about my friend Z-man in the next room? I will bet you he has bumps all over his pipe!

Hooker: Well... he must not have bumps as he is still in there.

Bubba: I will sue everybody! Damn it Z-man, I know you have bumps! I can't believe I have driven your ass all the way out here, to get denied by this ginch and also have to pay for your ass to get your rout on! I am not done with you Z-man, do you hear me!!

I failed to mention that at this time they would look at your pipe and nuts under a bright light with some sort of magnifying glass. That's how they saw the bumps on Bubba's pipe or whatever the hell they were. I guess I didn't have them, I don't know. But I was laughing my ass off and routing this hooker for 45 minutes and she was not happy about it either. So much for the acting job... she's fired!

Well, I finally blew my load—one that would qualify for any money shot in porn, with the exception of Peter North. That guy can literally put a girl's eye out from twenty yards away. I have no idea how he does it, but I applaud that man, and I have a great deal of respect for all the hairdos of girls he has destroyed, not to mention about 76 girls now retired who have to wear eye patches for the rest of their lives due to the bullets of sperm he's unloaded on them.

So, I walked out all sweaty and ruined, and there was Bubba all bummed out and drinking a 7-Up (they didn't serve alcohol). He was talking to the "hell-pig" bartender and I looked like I just finished a triathlon. It went like this:

Me: That was epic... Let's get on back to Vegas, Bubba.

Bubba: No, you asshole... we will leave when I am damn well ready to leave!

Me: What's the problem here?

Bubba: I have bumps, that's the fucking problem—fuck this place and fuck you, Z-man!

Me: I just had a wonderful time here... Let's not spoil the good mood, Bubba.

Bubba: Fuck you, Z-man. We will bail when I am done with this 7-Up... and there is no liquor here—this place lags.

Me: We are out.

Bubba: Okay, Zman.

Me: Okay, Bumpy.

Bubba: Fuck you, Z-man, now we are staying! Two more 7-Ups please!

I hope I painted that picture clear enough. I still find that image one of the funniest of all time...

PART THREE
LOST AT LONG BEACH CITY COLLEGE...

hhh yes, the fun at LBCC. This was supposed to be a new opportunity for me to shape up my act and get some decent grades so I could transfer to one of the University of California schools I loved, either UC Santa Barbara or UCLA. My brother was already at UCSB and on the occasions I went there, it was like a fantasy land of alcohol, drugs, and girls. I couldn't believe people actually went to class there.

But that again is my problem of perception—I think the world is one way, and really it's often the opposite. In my eyes everyone partied, but most people didn't go to the levels that my friends and I would go to. Most people can get really drunk or high and take a break from it, take care of their business at school or at work and not even think about it. For me, drinking and using drugs were my prerequisite for life.

Cold keg beer flowing, pretty girls in abundance, and on the better days a nice fat bindle of cocaine—nothing came close to that. I was in control and could do nothing wrong. I wasn't hurting others, so what's the problem? I was really good at looking outward but never looking inward. I was incapable of seeing that the problem I had in life wasn't with other people, or people I just didn't like or get along with, but the problem with me is actually "me." More of that later, for sure.

Long Beach City College was perfect for me, mainly because a lot of my buddies I grew up with were going there. One of my closest friends and inspirations in my life, Rich Fletcher, was going there for a bit until he transferred to San Francisco State University. Richie is one of those very rare friends that we are lucky in life to have just one of. The beautiful thing about him is that he is solid as a rock, and he is not afraid to tell you what's really going on inside him. He wasn't into all the shit I was into, he would drink with me but that's it, and not alcoholically. Rich would lovingly say, "Shit, Zalkins... you are a mess," and I would l reply, "I know, but I just don't see a big problem with it."

I cannot say enough about my friend Rich though. He has built a wonderful life for himself and his lovely lady on the North Shore of Oahu in Hawaii, living the dream. In many ways I owe my life to Rich, and I will get to that later, as his "tough love" is one of the greatest gifts I have ever received.

LBCC has a bar a couple blocks away called the Thirsty Isle. This place is a real shithole, yet it's beautiful at the same time. Its beauty is not in the way it's decorated, because I think a truck driver and a mechanic designed it after drinking 33 beers each. They serve these massive beers they call schooners that hold about 34 oz. of cold beer, and they were cheap when I was there in 1985.

The beers were around $2.50 and I thought I had won a progressive jackpot in Vegas. I would spend as much time there as possible, and as little time as possible in the classroom. Countless times I would go there for "lunch," which consisted of some frosty schooners, and I would promise myself I would make it to the next class.

That's the thing about my alcoholic behavior. I would often plan to do things, but never get them accomplished. I was a big planner, and a shitty finisher.

I bit off more than I could chew in just about everything I did in life. Everything I did was all the way, 110 fucking percent, but that didn't mean I finished things that I had started. Case in point: Two semesters in a row I would register for 18 units of core classes (pretty much a full load) and then I would dwindle them down to one or two classes.

It would lose its luster, and my drug and alcohol abuse had a way of painting a different picture for me that everything would be just fine. Drinking and using drugs for me was the great persuader, under the influence I can be talked into just about anything and I often do not think of the consequences.

Another ritual I had was drinking on campus. Mind you, almost everyone else was going to their classes sober, but I found it necessary to slam a few of those small Club Cocktails in paper bags, right in the middle of foot traffic like a fucking bum. I remember this well because the Beastie Boys had just come out with their really big album that was revolutionary at the time, and they had a song called "Brass Monkey." Once I found out what Brass Monkeys were and that Club Cocktail made Brass Monkeys, I was all giddy.

"Hey good morning everyone, want a sip of my Brass Monkey?" Fellow students would just look at me and say, "Shouldn't you be at an AA meeting?

I was appalled at their remarks. "What the fuck did you say to me? Did you call me an alcoholic? I am not an alcoholic, drinking makes you great!"

People would say those types of remarks to me, actually meaning well, but I could not see what the problem was.

My parents had had enough of me by this time, and I was staying with a friend of mine named Greg at his parents' home. It didn't last long, and I can't imagine why. One day I was butthoused out of my mind and I passed out on their front lawn with my motor scooter laid out beside me, among several empty cans of beers. Greg's dad, a very conservative fellow, didn't get the humor in this at all, and said to Greg, "I think your friend Todd may have a drinking problem."

It was around that time in 1986 that I realized I drank and used drugs way too much, but I could not find the reason to stop. It all worked for me, and even though I was pissing off everyone around me, destroying friendships, ruining girlfriends, and pushing my lovely mom and stepdad away, I couldn't get it.

My head would just say things like, "I will just get new friends, and my family will always be there and they will get over it." That's what was so odd—my world and my way of thinking was normal, yet wrong and sick in the eyes of others. Looking back now, of course, it's totally absurd. But I had not one clue at all, and my days in Long Beach were numbered.

I was living in a killer three-bedroom house with two guys who went to Long Beach State for a few months, and you will never believe this: they had a soda machine in the kitchen that was full of beers. There were cold Coronas, and for 25 Cents I could have one, which is a major problem for me—I can't have one of anything.

The Corona novelty quickly wore off when they realized I could clean out a case of the fine Mexican beer in one sitting, no problem at all. For about six dollars I could drink a case, and my roommates did not appreciate this much. But the kicker was, one of my roommates was also a cocaine dealer!

What a great living situation for me! I could drink four Coronas for a dollar, and get my cocaine right where I lived (and he would give it to me on credit too—which turned out to be a poor business decision for him). Life was getting better for me!

That didn't last really long... because when you have roommates you have to pay something called rent, and generally to pay rent you have to have something called a job. I was learning as I went along here. So when the third month of my rent came due, I simply did a "midnight move"... southward to San Diego.

I Love La Jolla...

I had an aunt and uncle in La Jolla and I loved them dearly. My uncle Bob was a successful surgeon in La Jolla and was very well respected. They had this sprawling home at the top of Mt. Soledad with a tennis court, indoor pool, koi ponds, pinball machines—the works. They were wonderful people and I had spent many holidays with them, mainly because of their son, my cousin Steven. I idolized Steven. He was probably six years older than me, and I became his shadow when I was in his presence. We got along great, but I know I was a pain in the ass to him and he would often have to tell me to beat it in some way.

So, when I bailed to San Diego, I went to my cousin's house as a refugee from Long Beach. I had only a few bucks to my name, and nothing going for me obviously. Yet Steven, who at this time owned his own home, allowed me to stay with him for a while—of course, until I wore out my welcome. I will never forget his kindness, though, and I have a very warm place in my heart for him as well as for my Aunt Afton and Uncle Bob.

Steven knew how to party, and he did not fuck around! He would start with brews and always go from there to vodka and tonic. That's when I fell in true love with the spirit that looked just like water, and his name was Stolichnaya. Some vodka and cocaine became a recipe for a romance that would last for many years.

But my welcome at my cousin's home was short-lived, and I found myself living in a real shitty apartment in Pacific Beach with an even shittier roommate whom I didn't know.

Pacific Beach was just the right place for a guy like me at the time. Eventually I scored a killer place two blocks from the beach, and I could surf the PB pier within minutes. The little beach town is so cool—they have a long stretch of sidewalk that's right on the beach and it goes from North Pacific Beach all the way down to South Mission Beach.

Some of the loveliest sights your eyes could ever see exist on that stretch of concrete and sand. The best part was you could drink beer and ride your bike all over. Open containers were legal! To me, that was the equivalent of winning the Publisher's Clearing House Sweepstakes.

There were bars everywhere you looked, and a never-ending abundance of girls, and drugs were about as easy to find as the ocean—right in front of you. On a nice day in the summertime you should always have a neck brace handy, because there are so many killer-looking girls that it's easy to develop a stiff neck after certain days of taking in the sights.

It was real common for me to crash my beach cruiser into some innocent person as a result of being drunk and high and checking out the opposite sex. They should have sold "Drunk Guy on Beach Cruiser Insurance" in PB and Mission Beach where some schmuck could have made a fortune.

Getting drunk and loaded, chasing girls, surfing, and repeating this on a daily basis was to me a life without flaws. Inside of me there were a million flaws, but so long as I stayed drunk and high my flaws and shortcomings as a human being were kept at bay.

I loved the place instantly, and even better, I scored a job in a liquor store. One of those run-down convenience stores, I think it was called Qwik Corner right on Garnet Avenue a few blocks from the beach.

That meant free beer for me! I unveiled a brand new policy for employees, self-induced of course. It was called "Drink whatever the fuck I want to drink and not pay for it."

It's hard for me to really explain the freedom I felt in knowing that my beer was now free. All I had to worry about was paying for my drugs, and life was just the way it's supposed to be—high and drunk. "Give me the keys to the beer cooler! You can trust me. I will keep a good eye on the store!"

I'm not sure how much "free beer" I took and drank in my short time being employed there. It was a lot, enough to have some auditor come in and see why the books and inventory didn't add up right.

Before the police could get involved I actually quit working there. I had never been to jail (well, for three hours once) and I knew that there would be no getting out of this. I feared being tracked down by the police for many years after that. I also will be checking with my attorney before publishing this because I want to be sure I cannot be prosecuted. This is twenty years ago—there must be a statute of limitations on "self-imposed free beer!"

I bounced around from job to job, apartment to apartment. I would drink at the beach, snort cocaine when I could find the money, and just live this beach life of going absolutely nowhere. Yet, it seemed that I could remain there doing that for the rest of my life.

I met many people who had lived in Pacific Beach forever, working dead-end bullshit jobs, no real career, no desire or money to own a home. The less responsibility, the better—those are the kind of folks I spent my time with. But there were plenty of responsible people living in Pacific Beach... I just wasn't one of them.

I finally got involved with a steady job with a concrete contractor that paid the bills, and I had a cool roommate from Michigan, named Chris. We got along just great, he was a lot of fun and we loved to drink beer and eat carne asada burritos at the infamous Ramiro's in PB. Chris was a very good friend to me, but after a while he became concerned about my drug abuse, as he had no desire to ever touch the crap that I was stuffing up my nose.

Ultimately he had to move out because he couldn't stand my late night "soccer matches" in our apartment. I use the "soccer match" phrase because when high on coke I would just pace around and make no fucking sense whatsoever. This was another nail in the coffin with someone who was a very good friend to me. My drinking and drug use would get in the way of everything—I just didn't want to do a thing about it.

Alcohol and drugs did their job, they made me feel great, as long as I was willing to roll the dice and ingest the substances. I had many late nights high off the blow when I thought my heart was seizing up, like someone with steel toed boots was kicking me in the chest at 3:00 in the morning and I couldn't sleep.

What's more insane is that no matter how fucked up I got, I always had to brush and floss my teeth. I could be five grams deep into some coke, and countless vodkas and beers on top of it, and at 4:00 in the morning I had to brush and floss before bed. I wasn't even going to bed!

It was impossible to sleep most of the time, but what the hell. If I was going to die at least it wasn't going to be from gum disease!

BURRITO PUNCH

I had met some really crazy characters in Pacific Beach whom I became very fond of and perfectly attached to. They loved to drink a lot of alcohol, and they loved to snort big fat lines of space coke. There were four of them, three brothers and another former classmate from San Diego State living in a pad that was like a one-story version of "Animal House," if you can picture that in your head.

We would watch lots of football, get nothing accomplished, and whiff big rat tails of cocaine every weekend—that is what we did. Rarely would we ever leave the house, because there was no need to. If there's a keg of beer (which was normal for us) and a big baseball size rock of coke on the mirror, why leave?

There was one time I left with the three brothers and one of them had his girlfriend with him, to get more beer. We were too blasted to drive, so we actually conjured up some common sense and walked to the liquor store at about 1:30 in the morning, just before they locked the coolers. If you are high on coke, it is a really bad situation to run out of alcohol. It's damn near tragic.

So, we were leaving the liquor store and were walking back to the "Animal House" to rack up more lines of blow and drink the night away. Across the street were four guys eating carne asada burritos, one of the greatest late night snacks in history. But when you are blasted out of your mind on cocaine, the thought of food sounds about as interesting as the black plague, you really just don't want it.

One of the guys said something wise-ass, and instead of blowing it off, I walked across the street and approached the guy who said the remark. He started to take a bite of his burrito and I just unloaded a left hook that splattered the burrito into his grill and he had guacamole, cheese, and sour cream splattered all over him. A brawl immediately went down, four on four. It didn't help "Team Carne Asada" much that one of the brothers I was with was a former Golden Gloves boxer, and he could brawl like a mother. He took care of two of the guys, no problem.

I was wrestling with the asshole that I had unloaded on, when the girlfriend of my friend let out a huge scream. One of the guys on "Team Carne Asada" had punched her in the face, hard. This was not good, and it did not go over well with us. The "switch" went full on into "fuck you" mode and we beat these guys down in a bad way—I had to be pulled off of the guy I had drilled and I thought I had killed him, for real. There was blood everywhere and he wasn't moving.

We took off back to the Animal House pad and left Team Carne Asada where we found them, except they were beaten pretty badly. The worst part of this was my friend's girlfriend Stacy was just a mess, and this was completely my fault. Had I not blasted wise-ass Carne Asada boy in the grill, none of this would have happened.

I felt like I was now two feet tall, and this poor girl had been punched by some drunk guy, which for me was just completely unacceptable. I was both angry and ashamed all at once. I tried to snort more coke, but I couldn't stand the embarrassment. I went home and crawled into my cave and lay there unable to sleep from the drugs, and the thought of what happened repulsed me and I hated myself even more.

That brawling episode was one of only a few in my adult years— I never really had to fight. I was pretty big and probably scary when loaded, so no one really ever fucked with me. Plus, fighting is so lame and such a waste I never got into it unless absolutely necessary.

If I did, and my "switch" came on, I hit hard and that scared me too. The event in Pacific Beach made me realize that had my friend not pulled me off of the guy, I could very well have beaten the guy to death, and that would have created the kind of problems I wanted nothing to do with.

Deep down, I'm a lover... not a fighter.

YOU MUST LEAVE NOW

After a couple of years in Pacific Beach, I found myself living in a guest house in Del Mar just a few miles north. A friend's girlfriend was having a nice holiday party and I was invited—which in looking back, wasn't the best idea on her part. It was Christmas time and we were all charged up for this evening of holiday cheer.

I arrived at Tracy's house and the place was looking fabulous, all dolled up for the holidays with lights everywhere and all those corny Santa Claus trinkets that the stores charge a fucking fortune for with a 3000% mark-up. Anyway, I had been drinking Crown & Seven at home (my favorite holiday cocktail) and I was feeling the spirit of Christmas for sure.

This was a "buffet" type of dinner, but it was really lavish and Tracy and her girlfriends had gone all out. The food was delicious, and I was easing into my little corner on the couch thinking what a great ass Tracy had, and I was thankful that my buddy was going to be unwrapping her later. "She would make a great present," I thought.

I was about six or seven drinks deep when it hit me. "Hello there, Todd, this is your brain calling you... There's a nice buzz going on in this head of yours, and I am grateful for the Crown

Royal, but it's time to get this party started—let's get some cocaine, right-fucking-now."

I have said that upon drinking only a few beers or cocktails, a light goes on inside my head, and that light says that I need to pack my beak with cocaine from outer space—and five minutes is too long to wait. Everyone at this party was enjoying the bullshit Christmas music we all have to endure every fucking holiday season for days on end, and they were talking up a storm. I was not talking up a storm because all I wanted was a snowstorm, and I wanted it planted right into each of my nostrils.

No longer an option, the cocaine was a "must have." I looked at my friend Steve, and the big talk went like this:

Me: I need to pack my beak.

Steve: Jesus, Z-man, we've only been here a little while, and I don't think that is happening here tonight.

Me: Bullshit it's not. Rudolf the Red Nosed Reindeer could appear with Kris Fucking Kringle right now and say to me, "Don't do any coke tonight, please," and I would tell Kringle and Rudolf to both go fuck themselves.

Steve: Are you kidding me? You really need to get it on?

Me: Does John Holmes have a big pipe?

Steve: What?

Me: Never mind. Yes, I need to get it on and sort things out... In fact, if I don't get my ever lovin' beak packed, I am going to walk up to the buffet and stick my pipe right in the mashed potatoes.

Steve: You wouldn't do that, Z-man, no way, man.

Me: Oh yeah? I wouldn't do that, well fucking guess what? It's on... and I don't care if anyone is going for second servings.

Steve: You are shitting me... Relax, man.

Me: I am going to relax—I am going to relax my pipe in the mashies.

The rest is history. I walked up to the buffet line, dropped my pants and eased my dick and nuts into the mashed potatoes like putting Pop Tarts into a toaster. It was no problem for me at all.

However, Tracy and the entire party had a problem with it, and there wasn't one jaw that wasn't on the ground, plus no one could talk—they just looked at me like I had just crucified a family pet.

Now, a lot of you must be thinking, "He just got that bit from the movie *American Pie*," but no, I didn't. This little stunt took place in 1989 way before most of the actors in American Pie were even in the first fucking grade. It was my version, and it was called "Mashed Potato" pie.

I did my bit of holiday damage and pulled up my pants with my heavily starched nuts and proceeded to say, "Merry Christmas, thank you for dinner, now I am going to pack my beak."

This bummed out those friends of mine for many years to come, and I was never invited back to Tracy's (what a surprise!).

But I did go and pack my beak and have a long and eventually lonely night, which I would get very used to as time wore on.

Footnote: *Please do not try sticking your pipe into mashed potatoes at a party. Regardless of whose party it is. For one, you will probably bum out a lot of people and two, it takes four to seven days to repair the heavily starched genitalia region due to submerging them in mashed potatoes!*

Snow-Blind

Insanity can come in many different forms. I would like to think I'm well qualified on the subject of insanity, so with my Ph.D. in the absurd I will share a nice story with you, one that is really good to read to the kids before bedtime (this is a major exaggeration).

Impromptu road trips were a requirement for me, and they had to involve drugs and alcohol. I didn't do sightseeing trips unless it involved a lot of cocaine and a hotel room where we discussed the sights we had seen or wanted to see. The following is the norm for a "Let's get the hell out of Dodge right now" scenario.

The setting was some local Long Beach pub, preferably a shit-hole—no type of establishment that serves appetizers or has happy hours. We drank in places where people "drink," not socialize. Places that were dark, so no one could see the drugs being passed around.

Friend: I am fucking butthoused, what should we do?

Me: Let's leave town now. Fuck it.

Friend: Yes, let's do that, but where?

Me: Santa Barbara or San Diego.

Friend: Why?

Me: Don't ask any more questions… Start the car! I am going to the ATM. You call the "doctor" to arrange for a pickup of space coke, get a case of cold frosties, and fucking drive like you stole it!

Friend: This is scaring me.

Me: This will be scaring me at around 3 a.m. Now, weren't you supposed to be doing something productive like calling the doctor?

Friend: Oh, yeah.

Me: You are damn right, "oh yeah"—hurry up... let's pack our beaks!

So, my friend Craig and I drove up to Santa Barbara from Long Beach in this thrashed old four-door Toyota Corona of mine. For anyone under 34 reading this, you will not know what that car looked like. So these were classic sleds you could find for under $800 with no hub caps, perfect for surfing, and got decent gas mileage.

I was big, rolling with $56 dollars to my name, a case of cold brews, a nice grip of coke, and my beak-packing friend riding shotgun. We were on a real "winning streak."

We went to this friend of a friend of Craig's (typical), who was this really successful music producer, and at the age of 23 it was a shock to see a guy who rolled the way he did. He had this outrageous house, not that I cared about the house—it was what was in the house that made it the most beautiful house on the planet.

This guy had cocaine that was so pure, it wasn't even white. It was like a light, off-blue color, and when you snorted a small line your entire head went numb, the drip would hit the back of your throat, and you were soon released into a space of heaven so perfect that interpreting it is quite difficult. Picture being out of your mind butthoused and a small trail of powder smaller than your pinky finger lifts you to a special place that only alien space coke can bring you to.

I had snorted a small mountain of cocaine by that time in my life, and this was without question the best blow I had ever had. Everything in my world was immediately perfect as long as that coke flowed through me. For those of you have been there you know what I am talking about, and you don't ever want to come down from that mountaintop.

However, the crash off of coke is something that is hands down one of the most brutal experiences one can go through from partying.

What was perfect an hour ago is now a feeling of dark depression one doesn't want to revisit—except me, of course. There are some experiences that make the crash of a coke high seem like a walk in the park, and they would be coming off of or detoxing from Oxycontin, Fentanyl, and heroin, and we will visit that special hell in a little while, I promise.

When crashing off coke I would get totally depressed, and even worse, insanely horny—and any girl I may have had around has long since left. At around 3:00 a.m., I was ready to fuck the faucets in one of the guest bathrooms given the right lubrication, but I had a better idea! I knew of this quality, fabulous girl back in Long Beach who would administer a total porno-style fuck in exchange for taking her to breakfast.

That's the deal of the century in my opinion, breakfast for killer sex? It just doesn't get any better, plus she had an "onion butt" (that's right, an onion butt—that's an ass so good it makes you want to cry), and I am a sucker for a great ass.

Give me a great body, face, and ass, and I am moving in with her immediately! I do not obsess over a woman's breasts, as the stuff I just mentioned is what does it for me, and please no fake tits either.

I have never been a fan of breasts that could possibly deflate if squeezed hard enough... that's one thing that hasn't changed with me, even in sobriety.

But the problem was, we were all the way in Santa Barbara, 120 miles north of Long Beach, and I was loaded out of my mind. I had a shitty car and it was pouring rain, and even worse was that my windshield wipers didn't work. "Well, screw that... we are leaving now, Craig! I need to get back to Long Beach to 'service' the account."

Craig was not only horrified, but he also knew I was dead serious. We dug out of Santa Barbara high as two kites. We were totally butthoused, and I was hornier than a guy who's been in a war overseas for a long time with no women around. Where were all the women? Not anywhere near me. At 3:00 a.m., most female companions I had ran the other way, which was the best idea—I am sure of it.

I was prepared for this mission back to Long Beach, because I couldn't see through the windshield in the pouring rain but I had on my trusted ski goggles. We hit the highway 101, and I had my head stuck out the window with ski goggles on for more than two and a half hours, all the way to Long Beach—why I wasn't pulled over by the CHP and put in prison to rot for being so stoned, stupid, and careless is beyond me.

But all is well that ends well, I guess. I dropped Craig off at home, and he was so scared he ran upon arrival. I don't think we hung out for years after that night—he is probably still in therapy from the experience. Can you blame him? I was able to make it to the girl's pad, fuck her like I was the porn star that I really am not, take her to breakfast, and then I just wanted to die... normal stuff for me.

Being in my own skin was bad enough, because no matter how much I ever did of anything, it was never enough. The nights would end full of despair and terrifying depression.

Yet I would ramp up as soon as I could, and get right back in the ring. That's the type of insanity my life was all about. Never quite being comfortable, but the drugs and alcohol would give me this buffer that would provide the feeling or illusion that my world was just perfect.

The fact is, behind all the stuff I used to find fun, and there were some fun times, I really just didn't like myself, and I would like myself even less as time wore on.

The Big Turning Point

It was in November of 1989 when I was introduced to prescription pain medications. I was going to junior college at night and working construction during the day. One day I took a bad fall off of my work truck and seriously injured my lower back. I had severely herniated two of my lumbar discs at the L3-L4 and L4-L5 area, but I didn't know it at the time. I couldn't feel my legs immediately after the fall, and I thought I wouldn't be able to walk again.

This sent fears through me that were unexplainable. For a few minutes I just lay there alone on top of the concrete in a nice residential neighborhood trying to feel something in my legs. The feeling came back within a few minutes and I crawled into my work truck and made a beeline to the hospital. I was evaluated and sent home with a little piece of paper—a prescription for bed rest, ice, and something I had never had, Vicodin for the pain.

Never had I taken or even seen a pain pill. My mind-altering chemicals revolved around two things: booze and cocaine. When I had a headache I took an Excedrin with a cold beer—isn't that what everyone does? I was in immense discomfort and I got the prescription filled immediately.

Upon arriving home I cracked a cold brew and took my first Vicodin. I don't really remember much of the experience. I know for certain the edge was taken off and my physical pain seemed to subside a bit. I took a shower and went straight to bed.

The next morning was a whole different story. If a human being could assume the shape of a pretzel, that is how I felt—all twisted up in knots with shooting pain down my legs. I could barely move, and this was really frightening considering I had always been active, athletic, and things like that.

I wasn't your model of perfect health obviously, but I still enjoyed physical activity: surfing, drinking, chopping up cocaine, and sex. All of which are activities designed to keep you in tip top shape so you can be the role model everyone looks up to—not really. Those just happened to be the activities I "excelled" in.

I was scheduled to see a neurosurgeon (a colleague of my uncle's in La Jolla). The MRI results were in, and it was confirmed I had severely herniated the discs I mentioned above. Surgery was immediately scheduled, and it wasn't optional with the way I was feeling.

On February 19, 1990 I underwent a major lumbar laminectomy and partial discectomy at Scripps Hospital. The surgery was long and tedious. Upon coming out of anesthesia I entered a world that was quite puffy and filled with soft white clouds. I couldn't talk very well, but the feeling I had was all warm and fuzzy. I was on a morphine drip. I had never heard of a morphine drip, I had never even been hospitalized, so this was all new to me.

The morphine drip was set to deliver the "goods" into my veins every twelve minutes, I think. Meaning, I had this little plastic thing like a "PEZ candy" dispenser with a button at the end of it. If I wanted more of the morphine, I just pressed the button. Oh boy, did I ever press that fucking button! That little PEZ dispenser became the best friend I had ever had.

One push of the button and I was almost instantly placed in a world that promised warmth and deep sincere comfort with not one bit of pain even close to being felt. I liked that because I don't like pain, physically or emotionally. I know just how to address those issues—I drink and use lots and lots of drugs.

My hospital stay at Scripps was around seven days. There were some really funny incidents that occurred and some not so funny. After a couple of days I was required to take little baby steps with a nurse while placing my hands on a walker. I was instantly reduced to a very frail and weak man. I can remember saying to myself, "A nine year old kid could easily beat the shit out of me right now," and for many, many weeks I would feel this scared and vulnerable.

One day I was doing my baby steps with the walker and the nurse was right next to me protecting me if you will, from falling. I had untied the back of my silly little hospital gown. I have no shame when it comes to seeking a few laughs. Here I was trying to keep a straight face while the nurse stood right by my side, and my butt cheeks were revealed for all to see.

I was 22 years old, completely out of my mind off morphine, loving every second of it, and really wanting the entire surgical wing to examine my bare ass. I would turn and point, "Look nurse, a bedpan!" knowing all the while that my bare ass was a few feet away from some family members visiting their loved one in the hospital.

The nurse would shake her head and say, "Yes, Mr. Zalkins, that is a lovely bed pan. We have a million of them here, and you are welcome to take a few home with you when you leave here…which we all here at Scripps hope is sooner than later."

Ahhh, she was a gem. I loved all the nurses who took care of me, except of course this one nurse. The following information makes me cringe to this day just thinking about it. I can almost feel the pain of what I am about to describe as though it happened yesterday, yet it was nineteen years ago. Okay, after being in surgery for a while the anesthesia sometimes can play with your system, bowels and bladder.

To get right to the point, I had not urinated in quite some time and I was running the risk of a bladder infection or worse. So, you guessed it, it was catheter time! I can remember having to pee so badly but nothing would come out. I was praying so desperately, "Release this pee... let me even pee all over myself for goodness sake! I don't even care where it goes... as I will happily wear it forever... just don't let the catheter man assault my penis!"

Well, after trying to urinate on my own and not being successful, it was time. For those of you who have never experienced it, you don't ever want to—trust me on this. For those of you who have, we should have our own little club or recovery program. We could call it, "My Fucking Wang Got a Plastic Hose Stuffed In It Anonymous!" We could help each other through the true grieving process of catheterization.

It was bad enough that I had to get the damn catheter, and even worse that a male nurse was doing the administration of it. I cannot begin to describe the pain. It was like a plastic rope being crammed into that little mushroom tip of your dick. You know the area where only two things should be coming out: pee and big orgasms! Nothing should be entering—it's an exit-only organ!!

So, Nurse Jekyll crammed this plastic thing in me and the burn can only be described one way: like my penis was a special little extra on the set of the movie *Backdraft*. It was like a blowtorch was going through my urethra, and it seemed to take forever. But it's times like these, at my worst moments, where I can locate some form of humor.

I remember saying to the nurse, "What do you guys do if John Holmes (the legendary porn star with a foot long pipe) was in here? Do you just get six catheters and duct tape them, and cram them in his pipe?"

"Very funny," replied Nurse Jekyll. I answered, "Well, I always try my best."

The catheter got in and I released enough water to fill three "kiddy pools." It was one of those pees that felt so good it was like one of those super-long orgasms that certain women are capable of having. I have always been in complete awe of a woman who has the ability to come for what seems like minutes.

I personally find a big earthquake female orgasm to be one of the greatest things that exist. It's just so fucking sexy to me. So, there I am, moaning "Ahhhhhhhhhhh yessssssss.......here we go.......keep it comin' now.....we are really getting places.....how do you like that Mr. Bladder? Are you a happy bladder now?"

Yes, Mr. Bladder was a much happier vital organ after setting the Guinness Book of World Records for the longest piss recorded in a hundred years.

I then returned to Long Beach to recover from my surgery. It is at that point where I discovered the true value of prescription narcotics, and my world would never be the same.

WELCOME BACK TO LONG BEACH

My mom had helped me secure a killer little apartment on Ocean and Bayshore Avenue (near Horny Corner) prior to my back surgery. It was going to be a long recovery, and I needed to be close to my folks. My mom and stepdad lived just two and a half blocks down the street on Santa Ana Avenue. They had just built their dream home, all custom on two lots.

My mom is an interior designer and has the most incredible talent for making a room come alive. To give an example of how good her work is, most of her clients won't give out her number.

My mom used to make my apartments look really cool with her flair and unique ability. I love the style she possesses, and it's just natural—she had no training or formal schooling for design, she just has great taste and knows how to make a place look like you never want to leave it.

The house they built was rare for Belmont Shore, two lots is really wide. The look was old Spanish-style with big wooden beams in the living room and arched walkways, really thick walls, and great-looking tile. It was a masterpiece.

I was a wreck when I got to their place after being in the hospital. I could barely walk, and going to the bathroom was the ultimate chore. The incision on my back was huge, and the scar looked like Charles Manson had had his way with my low back using a very big knife.

I was in a lot of pain, and to help dull the pain I would take a lot of Vicodin. I wouldn't say I was instantly addicted, in fact, just the opposite. At the time I was taking them as prescribed, every three to four hours along with a muscle relaxer called Flexeril.

The pills made my stomach upset at first, and the Vicodin went to work on my back pain, which was constant. I guess when used the right way pain medications are wonderful, but I will always find a way to do a lot more of something I like, which I have probably demonstrated fairly well up to this point.

If something makes me feel comfortable or gives me a rush, chances are I will be a fan of it. It's just the way I am wired. After a couple of weeks at my mom's home, I would take walks back to my apartment just to try and move around. The sight of me shuffling down Bayshore Avenue with a walker, loaded off Vicodin and Flexeril must have been real fun to see.

I walked at a snail's pace, and everything hurt. Just like back in the hospital I felt really scared and vulnerable. I don't know why, but I was in constant fear of some gang of little kids yelling, "Let's beat the 23-year-old in the walker." I swear a small child could have knocked me down and gone to town on me.

Once I could move back to my apartment, I settled into a routine of watching a lot of movies, reading, and taking the pain pills. I got really good at the so-called "timing" of taking them. Most people would really pay attention to the actual time and say, "It's been four hours… time to take a Vicodin."

My head would just say, "You know, I just took one of those things about a half hour ago and I feel pretty good—how would I feel if I just took one more?" Which I did, and the light was on for me.

When I took that next dose two and a half hours prematurely, I really settled into a nest that consisted of warmth and safety. That's what the stuff did for me. It put this glowing feeling in my cheeks—I could not have been more content because the pain was gone mostly, and I would actually get a little "boost" from the drugs. Not wired like cocaine, just a feeling of "Okay, let's fucking do this. I am ready for this day—what the hell should I do? Damn it, I have a lot of time on my hands, and I want to start a few projects."

That's what's pretty funny about what my head has told me on way too many occasions to count. Once loaded or high, I start to get these fantasies of what I should be doing with my life. Maybe I could get involved with this business or that business, or what about that guy who knows that other guy who could maybe get me involved in this, that, or the other.

Some of the thoughts and ideas may have actually been possible to do. The problem is that I am very, very bad at execution, and it's the follow-through that counts, not so much the idea or the thought. It took my getting into recovery to learn that, but we have some stuff to cover before getting to that part of my story.

A New Direction

y stepfather Darryl was successful in the insurance business. He specialized in business insurance, and handled some pretty big accounts. In earlier years, his brokerage handled the insurance for the Lakers and Kings, and I thought that was really cool because we could go to any game we wanted to at the Fabulous Forum. None of this Staples Center bullshit—the Fabulous Forum on Manchester Avenue in Los Angeles is where some of the greatest sports moments happened in LA's history.

It's where players like Wilt Chamberlain and Kareem Abdul-Jabbar played, and Magic Johnson and Jerry West. As a kid I have so many memories of the Forum, whether I watched it in person or on television, it will always be the definitive indoor location for sports in Los Angeles.

We were at the event in 1978 when the Lakers were playing host to the Houston Rockets. This was the infamous game where Kermit Washington of the Lakers punched Rudy Tomjonovich so hard you would have thought he died. No joke. One punch, and it just laid him out and blood was everywhere. It was really a scary event, and you could hear a pin drop in the Forum.

It was one of those punches that Joe Foreman or Ali would have been jealous of. But it wasn't funny at all. As a kid seeing this, it petrified me. Later on I would know what it was like to be hit by my 6'4" father who boxed in the Marine Corps—stuff like that stays with you.

Anyway, Darryl was instrumental in getting me involved in the insurance business. I had no fucking idea what I wanted to do. I was 23 years old, recovering from a terrible back injury I sustained while working, and I was clueless, with thoughts of, "Where do I go from here?"

Darryl suggested I take some courses at UCLA to get my feet wet with Commercial Business Insurance, and it was the most boring thing I have ever in my life been exposed to.

Watching grass grow would be more stimulating for me than an insurance class. Hell, getting a catheter placed in my dick again would be more stimulating—okay, that's a stretch, but the classes, on an excitement level of 1 to 10, they were less than 1… classes on insurance did not raise my "fun meter" in the least.

What attracted me to Darryl's career was his lifestyle. He had all the toys and a beautiful home, took great care of my mom, drove a 735 BMW and a Range Rover (when Rovers were cool—now everyone in Orange County has one), and he made great money. I was always outgoing, and he thought I was a shoo-in to be a great salesman/insurance broker. He took me under his wing and started to groom me while I was recovering from my back surgery.

I was starting to get around a lot better but still taking the pills, and that's when our pharmacist confronted my mom and me when we were picking up a prescription. I was given 180 Vicodin for the month, which worked out to be about six per day. The pharmacist proceeded to tell us how addictive the stuff was, and that I should start weaning off as soon as possible.

I was like, "Hey, fuck you, asshole… do you see that on the bottle? It says REFILL… Now refill the fucking bottle of pills like you are paid to do, so I can get out of here."

I mean, the nerve of this guy telling me how it is when I have just had a major surgery. I need those pills! In fact I need more than 180 pills—I am starting to like those little white jewels!!

Later on in my disease, those 180 pills would be gone in three or four days, I would always need more, and there would be no stopping me. I would dig to China to get my hands on more of those pills. The addiction was already taking hold of me, and it was only the beginning. I would go on for more than sixteen years of abuse, and I would take the addiction to much higher levels of dependency, insanity, and eventually, terrifying desperation.

My First Corporate Gig

So the classes at UCLA got me exposed to the insurance field, which was so exciting, I knew all the chicks would go nuts! "Oh my god, you are in the insurance business? Let me throw my panties on your desk!"

It was not glamorous work, and the women in the business were always really fucking boring to me, I wouldn't want to bang any of them, and they all looked burned out, which they were, except for a few of course. That business can really suck the life out of people, or maybe that's just my perception of it.

Anyway, I got lucky and found a job in Burbank with an insurance company. Driving to fucking Burbank from Long Beach is like walking from Long Beach to Tijuana. It took a really long time, and it took a huge toll on my back. But I knew how to fix that problem—I took some pain pills. More Vicodin, please!

In the evenings after crawling home on the 5 Freeway I would often stop to pick up a few brews at the liquor store so I could have happy hour in my car. Isn't that what people do?

Hell, if I can't have a party by myself on the way home and take the edge off, what's the point? I deserve some alcohol and drugs! I am a responsible person now, with a boring corporate job with an insurance company! If you were in my shoes you would drink and pop pills too, just to get over the fact that you are driving from Long Beach to Burbank each day!

My head can justify anything. I had an "open prescription" for the pain pills, by the way. It was a Workers' Compensation claim, and my treatment wasn't ending any time soon. Why would I want it to? I was having too much fun popping the pills and falling madly in love with the way they made me feel.

One time I took a file clerk, this really good kid Jason, to my favorite bar for lunch. This place served great hot dogs and cold beer. He had never been drunk before, and I got him completely butthoused out of his mind. I remember getting him back to work, and he was slobbering all over the files he was supposed to be putting away. He got sick and went home. After that, I never saw him drink a beer or any other alcoholic beverage again. That's the difference between a guy like Jason and myself.

Jason got really hammered, had a bad experience, and didn't do it again. Myself, I had bad experiences all the time, and I had to do it again. I absolutely had to drink and use drugs. I did not have much with respect to the power of choice. Once I discovered the magic of what booze and drugs could do for me, I had no desire to say "no." I couldn't say no, and why would I? I didn't really like the way I felt when not under the influence, and things just seemed to move along better when loaded.

I was either "Getting on one, in the middle of one, or getting off one"—that is, referring to getting drunk and high. It was always one of the three.

CLOSER TO HOME....

After I got some claims-examining experience in Burbank, I found a great job in Torrance through a friend of mine. I was really excited to be working a lot closer to home, and I had met this beautiful girl. Stacy was gorgeous, Italian, 5'4", and had a face that could melt you.

I fell in love with her almost immediately when I met her working at her father's restaurant in Long Beach. It just so happened that my stepdad knew Stacy's dad, so it made the introduction easy, but I was a nervous wreck. I was stumbling all over myself just trying to say, "Hi, my n-n-n-n-ame is T-T-T-odd."

When I was in grade school I had a problem with stuttering. I took speech classes to help me with it, but I could still stammer at the drop of a hat. It's really embarrassing for me, and under pressure, anxiety, or fear I still sometimes stutter. I have to take a deep breath and slow down a bit, because my mind wants the words to come out but I can't verbalize what I want to say quickly enough, so the net result is a stutter or stammer.

It was now 1992, my back had recovered fairly well, and I resumed surfing and other activities. I still had my consistent flow of Vicodin, and I managed to even pull back a little. I would just rage on the weekends by coke binging and drinking, and the pills would rescue me after a brutal night. The Vicodin would also be a good equalizer during the work week. My relationship with Stacy was very important to me, so I would try to keep in line the best I could.

The best thing about our relationship at the time was that every other weekend she worked at her dad's restaurant, so I had a "free" weekend if you will. I would have Friday and Saturday with the boys, and when I would see her on Sunday it was pretty much a guarantee that I'd be so ruined all I would be good for was a movie, and that was usually a rental.

That's the selfishness of this disease, that I have now learned but had no clue about then. You see, I always wanted to do something good for Stacy or my mom and stepdad, but more often than not it would be on my own terms. Most guys would have killed for this girl, yet I would just be getting destroyed with my friends, and when the time came to actually spend it with her I was just beat down.

In my pathetic, wrecked state of mind I often would say, "Fuck, this has to stop. I hate myself. I can't stand the guilt and shame of what this does to myself and Stacy." So my Sundays would be riddled with guilt, shame, and pain. But after a few days to recover, by the next Wednesday or Thursday it was time to fire it up and get ready to get on another roll.

The great thing about the pain pills was that no matter how much I drank and snorted, I could be guaranteed at least a little comfort in the midst of all my hell. That probably sounds completely insane, and that's because it is completely fucking insane.

This was the type of behavior that was normal to me, even though I knew I was a mess for the most part, and it all gave me exactly what I needed. That numbing freedom from giving a shit, the erasing of pain—it did everything I could not do for myself.

My addiction will constantly say, "More please, and I will take more of whatever the hell you have got (I just really hope it's the stuff I like) because I want more." I have a disease of "more," and that is a fact—anything to keep me in a different state of mind.

When I was working in Torrance, I really had a blast for the most part. I had a colleague named Kent and he was like the smaller version of me (not in the drug ways, but in the mischievous ways). He had this great laugh, and anyone who has a contagious laugh is someone I want around me at all times.

When Kent would laugh it was one of those things where your insides would get lit up, for real. I would go above and beyond to make him crack up, and when he would, it would light up like Vegas. Getting laughs for me has always been an addiction as well—I love to make others laugh, period.

Kent also liked ice hockey, and he had season tickets to the Kings—it was so sweet. We would finish a work day, go to a Kings game, and we were like two peas in a pod. Laughing, drinking, and enjoying life. He had no idea I was popping pills, but he would definitely know of my struggles with the white devil, cocaine, later on.

One time we had this outside rehab vendor who would take us to lunch. We used Gary's firm to help rehabilitate the injured claimants we handled at our company. It was a great fit because his company did a good job, and even better, Gary loved to drink with Kent and me.

One time during the Christmas season he took twelve or so of us to a big lunch at El Torito Grill. We had a great time, and Gary, Kent, and I would sneak to the bar and do double shots of Patron tequila with a beer back. We weren't supposed to be drinking, but we drank anyway.

Everyone else went back to work and Kent and I stayed for a few more rounds. We must have thrown back ten shots each and several beers in an hour and a half. That much booze in that short a time period would make anyone completely destroyed out of their mind.

Kent and I got back to our cubicles, and after ten minutes or so of us jabbering back and forth, we had a full-scale wrestling match/pseudo-brawl that ended with our supervisor's desk getting trashed, multiple cubicles destroyed, and thirty or so employees looking at us like, "What in the hell is wrong with Mutt and Jeff aka Kent and Todd?"

What was wrong was that we were completely butthoused out of our minds and psychotic.

I just belted out, "Merry Christmas, everyone!" and called a friend to deliver cocaine to my office. Thank God he answered the call, I had the white powder there within an hour, and I was back in the mix again. Time to snort some big fat rat tails and get some work done!

The following week a company-wide memo was sent out to all eight offices in California talking about drinking at lunch with vendors was now grounds for termination. I have no idea what would have prompted such a memo to be sent out! The nerve of those reckless employees!

The pills helped tremendously with those insufferable hang-overs. They were like "agony managers" in a small capsule form. At this time I started to increase my dosage even more. I had to climb the ladder and step it up a few notches.

I simply told my doctor that my back pain was getting worse and not better. It's really tough for a doctor to deny someone pain medications when they have had such a serious procedure as I'd had—this is something I would work to my advantage for years to come.

It was like having an open charge account at some department store. Instead of some beautiful clothing and things of that nature, I had almost unlimited access to the pills. It was Nordstrom for me, but without clothing and crap—I had this special pass to procure all the best drugs with minimal to no effort needed.

During my tenure with this company in Torrance, I was asked during Christmas time to dress up as Santa Claus and spend the afternoon with some underprivileged children. I have no idea how I was voted to be Santa Claus, but they thought I would be good with the kids.

I thought it would be wonderful to do this and I agreed. All the employees chipped in to buy 40 kids or so presents, and it was a really cool thing we were doing. I wasn't much of a "Christmas" guy, mainly because my family didn't make a big deal out of the holidays. I mean, we shared gifts and stuff like that, but there was not a lot of intimate family experience like most of my friends I think had during the holidays.

I was not the Grinch, for God's sake—I am just trying to explain how the holidays were not that big of a deal to me. Having a few nice pills and a Crown Royal & 7-Up got me in the spirit really quick. The combination of hard alcohol and pain pills made me warm up fast, and I would get all aglow and fuzzy. It was that inner furnace that got me lit up, and it kept me coming back like a magic act... the feeling blew me away.

There were so many presents for these kids it took two cars to get them over to the place where we were having our little celebration. My car was stacked to the gills, and I couldn't wait to see these kids and make their day. I put on this huge Santa suit, and it came with the "big stomach" and everything. I was excited about Christmas for the first time in years.

I got to the place where all of these adorable seven- to ten-year-olds were waiting for me like a puppy waiting for their owner to get home. They mobbed me immediately, and it felt great. We got the kids settled down and I sat in this big chair and called their names as they appeared on the nicely wrapped gifts. I had not had any alcohol, but I had for sure taken some pain pills, you know, because of all that lifting of heavy gifts I was doing.

It took a while, and all the kids got two gifts each from what I remember. They were so full of love and joy. Their excitement was contagious, and I felt like I had been a part of something so special. After I said my goodbyes and wished the children a Merry Christmas, I walked back to my car alone.

I got into my car and just started weeping. It had felt so good to see these innocent kids get a brief moment of excitement that maybe they would not have received at home during the holidays. What struck me so strongly was how neat it was that the kids were pleased to have the most simple of things, where my world was always so complicated and full of sickness and getting high. The simple things were no longer amusing me.

These were kids who I am pretty sure did not have the drug problems that I had, and I said out loud in my car, "I hope that none of the beautiful faces I saw ever have to walk the path that I have." I guess it was my soul wanting to take me back to that place when I was seven or eight when the Christmas times were fun, and my Grammy Nel would be there with Eric and me, so full of love.

Grammy Nel had passed away a few years before, and I missed her the most during the holidays. I didn't handle loss very well and I had no coping skills, so I fed myself with drugs and alcohol, which ironed out the many flaws in my system and made my life semi-bearable. The experience I had with those kids is one I hope I never forget, because it moved me in many ways.

I swallowed several pills upon leaving the parking lot—I had to make my good experience with the children feel even better, and the Vicodin would assist me just fine. That's how I would end a great day, or any day for that matter.

OLD BLUE EYES

I am a huge Frank Sinatra fan. The first time I heard "My Way" I was about ten years old and I cried, it was so beautiful. The Chairman has been a hero of mine ever since. My girlfriend called the Mark & Brian radio show in Los Angeles as they were giving away Sinatra tickets when he was playing at the Greek Theater.

I was at my desk, about five or six Vicodin deep, when I got the call, and it went something like this:

Me: Good morning, this is Todd.

Mark & Brian: Well, good morning, Todd... this is Mark and Brian from the Mark & Brian program. How are you doing today? (I immediately knew this wasn't a joke as their voices to me were very recognizable.)

Me: I am doing outstanding, gentlemen—what's happening?

Mark & Brian: Word has it from your girlfriend Stacy that you are a huge Frank Sinatra fan.

Me: You have no idea... yes, I am.

Mark & Brian: Well, that's what she told us. We were wondering if you would like to go see Sinatra at the Greek Theater.

Me: Does Larry Flynt like nudity?

Mark & Brian: I'm sorry, what did you say, Todd?

Me: I said yes... I would love to see the Chairman, anytime and anywhere!!

Mark & Brian: What would you do in order to get these tickets? You are live on the radio with half a million listeners—would you sing one of your favorite Sinatra songs on the air?

Me: Will I sing one? I will take off all of my clothes, run around completely naked here at my office, get terminated from my job, and then sing all the Sinatra you can handle!

Mark & Brian: Well... that's not necessary, Todd, (as they were laughing their asses off). You don't need to go that far... How about singing one of Sinatra's tunes? What's one of your favorites?

Me: The Summer Wind.

Mark & Brian: Well, go for it.

Me: (singing the words in front of a now totally captive work audience while holding the telephone) "The summer wind, came blowin' in from across the sea... it lingered there to touch your hair and walk with me..."

I sang almost the entire song and even included my imitation of the band in the background. Mark and Brian loved it, and I scored the tickets.

Looking back, that to me was such a sweet gesture on Stacy's part, to call the radio program knowing full well I would do anything for the tickets.

Energized by Mother Vicodin and some Flexeril and singing that tune was a real treat. A bunch of my friends called me at work and asked, "Was that you on the radio this morning, Z-man?" I answered, "Yes, it was me, all right. Now look out, Greek Theater, I am coming to see the Chairman!!!"

THE TACO INCIDENT

This little episode I am going to share with you would send my stepdad Darryl and me into an emotional tailspin that would last for many years, in fact I know Darryl is still affected by it to this very day. And now that I think about it, I am as well to some degree.

It was the evening of a UCLA vs. USC basketball game, and this was somewhere in 1991 or '92.

Both teams were very strong this particular season, and USC had this unreal player named Harold Miner, who could just kill you from all over the court and was seemingly impossible to defend. We were going to watch the game on the big screen at Darryl's house, and he was just nuts about his sports on the television.

If a quarter were given for each hour he had logged while watching sports-related activity on that damned big screen, he could have just opened his own sports bar.

There were three of us on this particular evening, myself, Darryl, and his friend Bob. We went to downtown Long Beach, to this hole in the wall Mexican joint called "Los Comadres." This was a popular place for policemen on duty, as well as the local labor force in this thrashed part of town, and actually I had never been there before.

Upon arriving at the small restaurant there were nine or ten customers, including the three of us, so it was real quiet inside and not a whole lot going on. We ordered combination plates involving lots of chicken tacos, and we were having a few beers and talking about the big game that night.

Several Vicodin were "invited" into my mouth to serve as my special appetizer, and I knew it was going to be a quality Mexican food experience, or so I thought. We had just received our plates of food, and both Darryl and Bob were facing towards me.

What happened next is something I will never forget. I remember taking a bite of my food, and looking up to see there were three men walking quickly towards us with potato sacks on their heads with the eyes cut out, and they had very big guns. One had a large shotgun, and the others brandished handguns that looked like "hand cannons."

The gunmen yelled, "Get on the floor you muthafuckas! And take out yo muthafuckin' wallets and put them on the ground!" We immediately got on the floor, and instantly I was shaking fiercely from head to toe. No bullshit, this was the most frightening thing I had ever seen, and it was about to get a whole lot scarier.

One of the gunmen yelled at the small Mexican lady working hard at both the cash register and her waitressing duties, "Give me all yo muthafuckin' money right now, bitch!" He had to repeat this several times, and then suddenly, there was a gunshot that sounded very strange to me.

My impression of gunshot sounds was mostly from the movies, well, that is exactly the difference I am about to explain here. Gunshots that you hear in movies are not nearly the same as "real live" rounds being fired off while a cold steel barrel of a gun is being pushed into your temple. It was really like loud firecrackers.

I immediately thought they were executing every one of us. As one of the gunmen continued to yell obscenities, he fired at the frightened young Mexican woman, and it turned out she couldn't even speak English to begin with.

She couldn't understand the gunman's hair-raising commands. The other two asshole criminals took their large guns and pressed them into our heads as they bent down to grab our wallets. I was so scared out of my mind that I forgot to take my watch off, and they didn't notice, which lends to my assumption that they were a bit scared themselves.

However, I am pretty sure that the level of fear that Darryl, Bob and I were experiencing was just a tad more intense than how the armed gunmen felt, or maybe they felt an entirely different fear altogether.

The first thing that went through my mind was, "This is how I am going to die, and I don't want to fucking die right now," and I thought about my beautiful mother, and how much I wanted to tell her I loved her, and my thoughts shifted to my girlfriend and I wanted to tell her that I loved her as well.

As we lay there, terrified, the front door to the restaurant burst open, and in walked an unsuspecting customer. He realized immediately what was going on, and one of the gunmen yelled, "On the floor muthafucka!" The gunmen were real enamored with that word, and I am now thoroughly convinced they were sponsored heavily by "Team Muthafucka," or they just had no other way of speaking, and I am going with the latter.

The customer turned and bolted out of the restaurant at lightning speed. One of the gunmen chased after him, and I thought for sure he was going to kill the customer dead, right there in the street. The gunman gave up and raced back into the restaurant. I couldn't tell any of the motherfuckin' gunmen apart...ahh hell! Now I am talking like them!

Since I was a kid, Darryl was this pillar of strength, a very tough man and one that you would not want to brawl with. But once a gun is in the picture all bets are off. Instantaneously we were all reduced to weak and helpless human beings and the guys holding the steel were holding the cards, and they could decide to make that evening our last on earth.

I know Darryl wanted to get over on those gang banging assholes, and I did too. Unfortunately, no matter how hard I could drill someone with a fist, I wouldn't be able to stop a bullet.

I could hear Darryl's heavy breathing, like a wild boar being tied up. If his breathing could have been translated into words they would have been something along the lines of, "Fuck you! Put your guns down you sacks of shit and I will end you!" He was right too, but that couldn't be negotiated unfortunately.

We were at their mercy, and I know all we wanted to do was survive this moment in time. I was also wondering if the woman behind the register was now dead, as the gunman had broken off two more shots, and that's what led me to believe we were all heading for the permanent "dirt nap" ourselves.

I guess the robbers got agitated with the fleeing of the customer, because shortly after the man ran out, the guys were screaming at each other to grab all they could and get the fuck out of the place. I remember thinking, "Yes, please bail, that's a great idea."

They did end up leaving, and with them they took wallets and watches, things I could give a shit about. But they also took something of "me" that doesn't involve the material. I had lost something that I can't quite explain. We drove back to my mom and Darryl's house and upon seeing her I just hugged her, and told her I loved her while I shook and cried.

There would be no watching the UCLA vs. USC game that night. That was the last thing on my mind. I was busy trying to locate the part of me that had been removed from my insides.

I went home and took several pills and lay there speechless, but grateful to be alive. For the next several years I would have nightmares that haunted me due to this incident. I would go to a therapist looking for relief, but then I realized I had all the relief I needed in the form of prescription pain killers. I would just "double up" my efforts in this regard, and take even more of the narcotics.

For many years there was an anger that could erupt in me within a millisecond. Anything that made me feel like I had no control or say in a particular matter brought me right back to that feeling of a large barrel of a cold gun running down my head. Never had I felt so utterly helpless, and Darryl did too. My reactions to things out of my control were simply derived from fear that I had never healed from emotionally.

I knew just how to heal emotional wounds. I flush pills, alcohol, and cocaine into my body, and it's the best therapy I could ever dream of, and I don't have to sit on some asshole doctor's couch and look at his 34 diplomas on the wall and tell him how I'm feeling. So long as I have a lot of drugs and they work for me, I am feeling just fine and I can address any situation or shut it off completely. For me it was mainly shutting the world off, it was my own "pause" button.

The geniuses that robbed us that night were on a big roll with similar types of crimes. It turns out that one of their girlfriends took Darryl's Rolex watch to a local pawn shop and the cops traced it back to her address, which they ultimately raided with local law enforcement.

And when they did, they found all three sacks of shit weighing out a kilo of cocaine, and they were fucked. Darryl had to go testify in court later, and tell them the Rolex was indeed his, and he gladly did that. I hope prison is treating them well, but knowing how "well" our judicial system works, they probably only served a few years, who knows.

Moving forward, I made special arrangements in the event I was ever robbed again. I carried a loaded 9 mm handgun with hollow-tip pointed bullets under my car seat, as well as under my bed. I couldn't handle the thought of ever being that weak again, and so vulnerable.

The way I saw it, the next time you wanted to rob me, one of us was going to die. My sick head told me that the odds were now increased to at least 50-50, a hell of a lot better than just me versus the barrel of a gun.

Drugs and more drugs also made me feel as though I had tilted the scales in my favor, and boy was I ever wrong. But there was no way in hell anyone could convince me otherwise....

ONE MORE SURGERY

I blew my knee out playing basketball one day in 1992, and it wasn't a good sign. I tore a couple of ligaments and it quickly swelled to the size of a grapefruit—surgery was not optional this time, either. In as much as I had to have the surgery, it was for me another "insurance policy" for additional prescription pain meds for at least another four to six months, on top of the meds from my other doctor.

This was before the DEA was tracking prescriptions, and well before prescription narcotics were an epidemic in this country, which they are now. I had the surgery, and just like that, the flood gates opened for a new drug for me which was a bit stronger than Vicodin—these little yellow babies. I was in love, I was head over heels in love with a prescription narcotic known as Norco.

I had my back surgeon switch my Vicodin prescription to Norcos, and now I was getting multiple prescriptions from different doctors. Truth be told, it was exciting to me because I could take more, and I wanted more. I had to have more, my head told me, "More pills, I need more pills!!" When I realized I could score more of the drugs and I wasn't getting in trouble for it, that made it okay. It's absurd thinking, I know, but then again I had an absurd mind and it will tell me whatever it wants to when controlled by the pain pills or any other drugs.

I was getting approximately 400 Norcos a month, and that was around twelve to thirteen a day for me. I grew into this real comfortably, and it wasn't a problem. I was working steadily, taking care of my financial responsibilities, and still managed to stay in a relationship with Stacy.

I liked that number, twelve to thirteen. It was just right. Actually, it worked out to about 13.3 pills per day—some days would be more, some less. I always liked to scale back to eight one day, then take seventeen or so the next, you know, because I was in a lot of pain that day! It was like a holiday for me when I could eat more Norcos. I was boarding a plane to "Numb Land" where everything was comfortable and carefree.

This is when things started to go from just walking down a normal street, to turning down some dark alleys and places that would get darker and darker....

The most beautiuful voice I have ever heard...my friend
Bradley Nowell of Sublime/1995

"It All Seems So Silly in the Long Run" —Brad Nowell, Sublime

Upon returning from San Diego and recovering from my back surgery, I had rekindled my relationship with Bud, Eric, and Brad, the gentlemen who formed a band called Sublime, which the world has come to know and love.

What I loved about these guys is the fact that they drank and used the way I did, absent the pills. They would dabble a little here and there, but I was the "pill king" in their eyes. Like a freight train that had no desire to stop, we were a crew of very reckless, out-of-control characters where anything could happen and things could just explode. Rules did not apply, and I liked that a lot.

I loved people who didn't have limitations, and I had that with my friends Bud, Eric, and Brad. There was a huge brotherhood that was like an extended family of the band, and it was a crew of individuals who wanted to set the world on fire, which we did regularly.

Getting loaded full time takes a professional, and we all had PhD's in that department. The party was something that didn't end until we passed out, or chopped the last line.

My love for these guys is undying and always will be. A really fun moment was when the guys asked me to star in their video for their song "Date Rape," which was getting a lot of airplay on KROQ in Los Angeles. Sublime never even really played the song live, but any publicity is good publicity. This eventually was on MTV, and it's raw and fun to watch—very low grade unlike the bullshit million-dollar-budgeted videos these days.

We shot the bar scene at Sam's Seafood in Sunset Beach, and it was a lot of fun. You can see the video by going to YouTube and punching in "Sublime Date Rape Video." I was gassed out of my head, chopping up lines in the bathroom, and the cocktails that Jack Manness was serving in the bar scene were real, and they were fucking strong. The girl in the video who was from Long Beach (I forget her name) was really cute and looked a lot like Gwen Stefani.

I don't even remember much of it all. Booze, pills, and powder ran through me, like any other day—but this was a celebration damn it! I am the date rapist... and how proud I was of this!

The kicker was that Ron Jeremy (the porn star) was the judge in the video as well as the inmate who raped me in jail. The song is a parody and upbeat, and those who have heard it know this. The song does not glorify raping anyone—let's get that straight and it's something I never have found funny, then or now. Okay, we sorted that shit out... let's move on.

There were some very fun times and very sad times with the characters in Sublime. On one occasion we took off down to Mexico, just south of Rosarito. On the trip was Miguel aka Michael (Sublime's recording genius and manager for many years), Eric, Bud, Brad, and I. There was this little enclave of houses right above a nice surf break, and there sat an edifice with two small bedrooms that would bear the infamous name: "The Sublime Pad."

The previous owner of this little shit-hole was Mike Wells (a few years older than me, a total madman, great surfer, and one of my closest friends in sobriety). Anything that we did as a crew involved a lot of alcohol, and it wasn't a good idea for all of us to be together in a foreign country—especially Mexico—with big grips of pills, alcohol, and space coke (which I always provided).

It's funny how a surf session we had in Mexico went, something like this: almost drown paddling out because we were so butthoused, take a wave, either make it or fall off, stumble in to shore, crack open some brews, have a shot of tequila, take a few pills, then pack our beaks with some coke. Isn't that how most fun surf trips are supposed to be?

Okay, this was a short trip, as they all were because we were always so ruined after one day, let alone three. We were on day three, and I had barely slept. Eric and I were packing our beaks like madmen (nothing unusual), then we come to find that Brad had scored a huge bottle of Soma, the muscle relaxers.

I was never really into these, even though I had an unlimited supply of Flexeril, also a muscle relaxer. But these Somas that Brad procured were certifiably made by both Charles Manson and Satan, they were so strong... and so very evil. I thought I had a huge tolerance for anything in pill form, but I was dead wrong.

I took a handful, and passed out within a half hour. Brad took at least twenty of these things and turned into a fucking pit bull. He was out of control, falling on these bushes that have those little "brown stickler" things that you can never get out of your clothes. He was walking like Gumby, all jelly legged and off balance. He would walk up to punch me in the face, and I just moved aside in slow motion and he went face first into the stickler bushes.

Eric and I were having a ball watching Brad go through his "retardation stage" on Soma. He gave up on trying to beat us up and after falling into about nine more stickler bushes, he figured it was time for a nap. His shorts were halfway down his ass with the sticklers all over his red butt cheeks, and Eric and I couldn't stop laughing.

It was a real "Kodak moment," and thank God I happened to have a Kodak throwaway camera, so I took a bunch of shots of Brad climbing into the van with sticklers on his ass, and shots of him in the middle of his Soma nap.

These photos proved to be so good that one of the shots actually made the inside cover of Sublime's multi-platinum hit album that made them famous throughout the world. If you look inside the CD, it's the shot of Brad climbing in the van with his red ass cheeks blazing—if you look closely enough you can see Eric laughing while holding the bottle of pills.

On our way back across the border things got pretty interesting. The border agent asked each of us what our nationality was, and all of us (except Brad) said we were American. Brad was in a pill-induced state of sleep on my lap when the border agent said, "What about him?"

I shook him to wake him up and the agent asked his nationality, but Brad may as well have been speaking Chinese because all we heard when he tried to speak was, "Bluuuuuuaaaaaahhhhh." The agent just shook his head and said, "It's obvious that one of you had more fun than the rest of you." We took that as a compliment, and the green light was lit for us to bail home across the border.

We got back to Long Beach and pulled up the van behind Brad's house. It was late at night, and we could hear Brad's soon-to-be-wife, Troy, was pissed. It took three of us to carry Brad to the front door of the house—we opened the door, dropped Brad like the big ball of human bubble gum that he was, and split.

We ran back to the van and could hear Troy screaming at Brad, and at us too. We split for home to try and figure out what our names were and how serious our brain damage was from this three-day fiasco.

One of the worst days of my life was up in San Francisco the day after Sublime played what was to be their last show in Petaluma, just north of San Francisco. Petaluma was an affair of epic proportions.

My friend Pat Conlon and I had rented a Lincoln Town Car to drive up and meet Eric, Bud, Brad, and of course Michael, their producer and soundboard genius.

After the show, blasted off booze and pills (no coke—I was saving that for the next night's show in San Francisco), I tried to drive all of us back to San Francisco in my rental car, but I kept driving into the wall of the theater. Jon Phillips (the band manager and my good friend) took over, saying ,"Z-man, you are way too fucking butthoused! Get out of the car now."

So Jon drove, and Pat and I stayed at Blaine Kaplan's house (Sublime's booking manager) just down the street from where the band was staying. I was in the back seat of the Lincoln and as hammered as I was, I can never forget Brad resting his head on my shoulder after playing his ass off at the sold-out venue. He missed his wife and baby boy Jakob, and made it verbally clear that he wanted to be with them.

The next morning was one that is tattooed into my brain like the bad dream that it was. Pat Conlon and I were driving back from breakfast and trying to put the pieces back to the puzzle from the night before. Our bodies and minds were a disaster, and we were so ruined from the night before (a sign of a real good time, right?).

As I was parking the car by Blaine's house I saw Greg Abramson, who directed the "Date Rape" video. As I backed in with the passenger window down, Greg leaned in the car and said, "You guys won't believe this—Brad is dead."

"Oh God, no," I said, "No fucking way, bro! ... No fucking way."

We made our way up to Blaine's flat and there were people all over the place in total shock with looks of utter disbelief and sadness. I didn't know most of the people in Blaine's house, but I knew then it was real. Both Pat and I immediately lost our fucking minds.

We all loved Brad very much. One week before his passing we were in Vegas celebrating his getting married. He had a baby boy, Jakob, who was around six months old at the time. "This can't be happening," I thought, but it was.

I was later told by Blaine that Brad had tried to contact me at 4:00 in the morning, but I couldn't be awakened. I was too fucked up, and too passed out. This struck me like a bullet right between the eyes. I was not good with loss, and I was incapable of coping with grief. I was an expert at feeling nothing at all—this was a situation I wanted to feel none of.

Everyone we knew was just completely wrecked as a result of his death. It could have happened any time, I guess, what with rolling the dice with black tar heroin. It just didn't seem possible to me that Brad could be gone. Brad had been clean from heroin for a short time, but the story goes that some guy at the Cal State Chico show gave the band pills, cocaine, heroin, and other "goodies" the night before I met up with them in Petaluma.

Brad's death broke a lot of hearts. He had a beautiful baby boy and a lovely wife, and had only been married for a week at the time of his passing. I had become close to Jim Nowell (Brad's dad) and I am close to him to this day. I have seen pain on his face at times that only a parent can wear. I hurt for Jim and of course Troy and little Jakob.

This tragedy haunted me for many years. Knowing that he had tried to get a hold of me before he overdosed was like broken glass stuck in my nerve endings. It hurt all over and I would beat myself up over this for a long time, something I had no control over whatsoever. I was completely incapable of dealing with his loss, so I did what I did best—I tried to cope by reaching for more of what it takes me to kill the pain I feel from the world… and that is a lot of pain killers.

In looking back on all the years of my drug use and the patterns, twists, and turns I traveled, I can say without a doubt that my drug use accelerated to the point of no return when we lost Brad. I couldn't process it—I was so broken over it, and I felt so bad for Eric and Bud who, with Brad, were developing so much as musicians. In only a short time the world would have known them and they would have been household names.

In the time that followed, I would make real sure that nothing could hurt me at all anymore. I would numb myself to a new level. So, I went about traveling that road, and that road would eventually render me totally insane.

Jamming in Northern California. From left to right: Ross Fletcher, Eric Wilson-bass player from Sublime, Me, Miguel-founder of Skunk Records and recording engineer genius.

Part Four
"A Vehicle for My Party"

After Brad died I dove deeper into my addiction of prescription narcotics. I was knee-deep in Norcos, and they just wrapped me up in so much warmth and glory I couldn't get enough of them. I didn't know you could chew them for a rapid release of the drug, so upon learning that, I was having my own "buffet" of Norcos and eating them as though they were PEZ candies.

I loved PEZ candy as a kid—who didn't? They came in these tiny little packages and had great flavors, and they even looked like little prescription narcotics now that I think about it. You could often buy the packs along with the little dispenser that you loaded the PEZ into, with little cartoon characters as the plastic handle you pull up to release the magical candy.

I found it funny to pack little Norcos into a PEZ dispenser; they didn't fit right, but I would break up the pills so I could have a little laugh when popping the narcotic. The PEZ/Norco dispenser game didn't last long though, because I only found the humor in it for a couple of months. What used to be fun with respect to using these pills was becoming less fun, and more of a chore.

Earlier I mentioned a band from Long Beach called the Falling Idols—I love them to this very day even though they don't play except at reunion shows for Sublime's label, "Skunk Records." Some friends and I formed a band called "Corn Doggy Dog and the Half Pound" and started to play covers from the Falling Idols. It was the perfect excuse for me to use lots of drugs, drink lots of alcohol, and live a life of playing shows and having long four-day weekends.

As a kid I had idolized the Falling Idols, and now I had the opportunity to sing their songs on stage with some of the original members of the band who are very close friends of mine even now. Our friendships go back more than thirty years, and my relationship with each band member is special and weird in its own unique way.

Our Falling Idols songs were the best and they were so much fun to play live, but we had some original songs too—some even written by me. John Cougar had a few songs I found pretty cool in the early MTV days, "Hurt So Good" and "Jack and Diane" (you young readers will have to "YouTube" them). These are really great songs in their own right (I have a point here I promise), and the videos were gritty and cheaply done, the way they ought to be.

I am not much of a singer, but more of a comedic front man so I have been told, so I rewrote those Cougar songs to reflect the titles, "Pull Some Wood" and "Jackin' My Ham." Both songs I wrote about jerking off, getting my pipe smoked, and getting major stiffies, all of which to me are very important activities. For those of you who don't agree, you are only lying to yourself, but I am okay with that, seriously.

We would play locally in Long Beach, and eventually we would have the privilege of opening up for our friends who were in better-known local bands. I'm not sure if they gave us the gigs because they felt sorry for us, or because we could pull off a song or two decently. It's neither here nor there—at the end of the day, playing in this band was a complete excuse to allow me to march on with my addiction and get away with it, sort of.

All of my friends in the band knew I was insane, but the woman I was with (to whom I would ultimately be married for two years) never knew the extent of my sickness. The long weekends of playing shows and coming home a shattered mess was as normal as breathing in and out.

We had a great relationship with the guys from Black Fly's, the anti-establishment sunglass maker in Orange County, and we would play some of their parties. One time at the Galaxy Theater they had this really killer Christmas bash where we played with my friends, "The Long Beach Dub All Stars" (a great band with remnants of the Sublime and other legends from Long Beach). My band was opening up, and we wore tuxedoes, all decked out and looking sweaty and not very handsome.

I had my girlfriend and her sister make this three-foot plaster penis that we glued fresh green grass on, and I fondly called it "the John Holmes Chia Pet." I took this big rod out on stage and announced I was coming out with a new line of novelty products, and the John Holmes Chia Pet would be available at all Target and Wal-Mart stores after the New Year.

It was a big hit—I still find that funny to this day, and I know others do too.

One night up in San Jose we opened up for our friends Slightly Stoopid. Most people in bands like to hang out after playing and case the joint for free booze and girls, where I had a penchant for maybe throwing down a drink or three, and packing some coke in my beak, then it was straight to my hotel room.

I had this obsession about being clean, so I had to shower immediately, and then I would crawl into my darkness of chopping lines and eating pills and then watching the sun rise.

The next day we were in this hotel restaurant having breakfast, myself, Scummy (bass), Kenny (guitar), and my longtime friend and original drummer from Falling Idols, a guy nicknamed Mudd.

I was so taxed from the night before, and my head was caving in, so I threw down eight or nine Norcos to ease my suffering. There was this kid about ten years old having breakfast with his dad, this fucking kid would not stop staring at me and making this face I will never forget. So I grabbed a steak knife that was on the table, pointed it at the child, and said, "Listen to me, you little rat bastard… If you keep fucking looking at me I am going to kill you and your daddy."

This didn't seem to go over really well, but I think the father was shitting his pants because the cops were never called. I loved all the great mob movies, especially *Goodfellas*. I could easily turn into

Joe Pesci, Robert De Niro, or Ray Liotta and break off something like, "I swear on my fucking mother's eyes, if you don't stop looking at me I will leave you where I find you, you little cocksucker you."

That type of language wasn't generally used towards kids, and I know now how wrong it was, but I was not good at dealing with things when I was on a big roll of drugs and booze. I would reserve my really poor behaviors for the special moments with adults whom I couldn't stand, and there would be plenty of those people, especially when the nightmare of Oxycontin was introduced into my daily regimen. Once on that shit, all bets were off.

Being in this band allowed me the flexibility to get really destroyed publicly, tell lots of x-rated jokes on stage, and berate the guys in the band, all because deep down inside I couldn't stand myself, and getting loaded into oblivion shut everything off for me and gave me brief moments of peace. We used to joke about how the band was a "vehicle for my party"—truly, that's all it was, a big excuse for me and any others willing to risk their lives for an evening of "pushing the envelope" one more time.

Sometimes I had to have UPS or FedEx be the vehicle for my party. For instance, one time my friend Miles (the singer for Slightly Stoopid) and I were flown over to Germany for a week to record with this German band called SKUNK. Now, I am not sure whose bright idea it was to offer me a free trip to Europe with all expenses paid along with an unlimited bar tab at the hotel (they would later regret that).

I wasn't about to be without cocaine on this all-expense-paid fiasco, and not wanting to carry it myself and risk prison in Germany, I just sent it "overnight" to my hotel room. Both Miles and I got completely butthoused on Virgin Atlantic on our way over, and upon checking into our hotel a beautiful front desk girl said, "Oh, Mr. Zalkins, you have a package that arrived for you."

"Oh, that's just wonderful! Thank you for that, Ms. Wienerschnitzel, I really need those important documents," I excitedly replied.

The bar in our hotel had the best beer I have ever had, and we could drink all we wanted—and we did. Then we would just race up to our room, rack up a few lines of space coke, and say, "Fuck, isn't Germany perfect?"

I may have won a few of the battles in that crazy head of mine, but my addiction and the progression of it would ultimately win the war and really take over me—and this was all right around the corner.

Hanging in the secure arms of my
mom, one month old in 1967.

That's me on mom's lap, my brother Eric on dad's lap. I think I was already pushing my brother's buttons at this time, 1968.

I can actually see the love on my dad's face as he holds me as a baby. I wouldn't see this expression a whole lot as I grew older.

*I was only a year or so old when this was taken.
My dad passed out from drinking too much, note the
cigarette still burning in his right hand, 1968.*

*Check out this shot of my mom and dad as newlyweds. It
looks like my dad already wanted to bail out of there!*

*Prom night, 1985. Guess which one is me? (I'm the guy
with glasses and a foot long cigar...I never smoked it,
but I definitely snorted a huge pile of space coke)*

*Bradley Nowell and me, on his wedding night,
1996. I would be with him the following week in
San Francisco where he passed away from an
accidental overdose. It still haunts me to this day.*

Me and Bradley Nowell's son, Jakob.
I love this picture.

Taken in 1995, after a very long night of partying at
the Sublime pad in Baja California, Mexico. If I close
my eyes for a second I can still feel that prolific hangover.

*Me and one of my closest friends in the world, one who
never gave up on me. Gregory "G-Force" Ferruzzo, on a
surf trip somewhere in mainland Mexico mid-1990's.*

*My buddy Pat Conlon from Rockaway Beach, NY. A
talented artist and a hell of a good friend.*

Taken in January of 2006 with former world champion surfer Mark Richards from Australia. I was fat, sweaty, and addicted. I would carry on for another twelve months like this until I completely fell apart.

My Grammy Nel, my mom's mom, and one of the sweetest and generous human beings I have ever known.

My best friend in the whole world, my mom.
To her left is Chanelly, Bardot, and Broulee'.
Gotta love those French Sheepdogs!

THE JOY OF SURGERY

Most people have surgeries to repair something that is wrong with them, with the anticipated result that they will be better off physically as a result of having the procedure done. For me, I had a few surgeries that were necessary, plus a couple of surgeries that were performed but were more "elective."

I used to like that word elective, "I elected to have surgery to fix my knee." That was the biggest bunch of bullshit! I had two very serious surgeries on my left leg only because I knew it would be the Disneyland "E" Ticket to a plethora of good pills.

This was my fail-safe guarantee that I would have a consistent flow of pain medications without having to worry about hunting around for doctors. Most pill addicts will drive to China to find a doctor who will prescribe the good shit, like Oxycontin, Fentanyl, and Morphine. Nothing will stop the addict determined to get their pills—nothing. No roadblocks, SWAT Team, or other Federal Police force can get in the way of a pill junkie scoring what they need.

Multiple doctors are really common for pill addicts, and they were for me because one doctor could not prescribe enough of what I needed. I am in a lot of pain for God's sake, and I need lots of doctors—as well as a dealer to keep me in "the game."

Very seldom does a pill addict get away with only one doctor, and if that's the case one of a few things is going on:

1. The doctor is overprescribing and will soon be losing his or her license to practice medicine.
2. The "addict" just isn't eating enough pills yet!
3. The addict is on a "supplement" program, meaning they are getting more pills either by stealing from friends, family, pharmacies, or all three.

Don't take my word for it, I am merely commenting on what it was like for me. I needed two doctors and a dealer, plus I would steal pills from family members or friends—and it still wasn't enough.

Here's a timeline for my surgeries:

2/19/90- Back Surgery (required).

4/91- Left knee surgery from basketball injury (required).

10/92- Left knee surgery from bending at work (doubt it was required).

3/94- Left leg tibial osteotomy (not required). This surgery was major, and was just the first part of a two-surgery process. I am bowlegged, so the orthopedic surgeon thought it was best to straighten out my left leg by severing the tibia below the knee and putting a steel plate in on the side of the knee to straighten it. This surgery was way more brutal than I anticipated; it required a week in the hospital up in Santa Barbara, and during the procedure an artery was accidentally severed—oops! The doctors had to call in a vascular surgeon to repair this "accident," and I am affected to this day from it.

12/94- Left knee ACL replacement. This was the second part of the two-surgery process. By the time this surgery took place, my left leg was suffering from total atrophy—looking at me you would have thought the surgical leg was starving, it was so skinny, and it looked very much like the poor souls who endured so much hell in the German concentration camps.

At this point, I was in a great deal of pain from both parts of the unnecessary two-part surgery—and this was really all a grand scheme I had in my head to provide myself with endless "scrippies" (my nickname for prescriptions). I had no problem at the time with surgeons severing my tibia and inserting steel, as well as being on crutches and a huge brace for months, all for my "safe passage" to obtain more pain pills.

I endured all of that crap above for the sole sake of a pill guarantee, and I could never admit it to anyone else because never would I want to expose my weaknesses to others that I was a junkie, a "true blue" pill junkie who also loved alcohol and cocaine.

But the pills would become my "everything"—they would replace booze and coke for the most part, becoming my "savior," and ultimately tear me apart.

I Want To Go Bigger

From 1995 through 1998 I struggled with the physical ailments caused by unneeded surgeries. None of these things are the fault of anyone but myself, and I took these high risks for the safety of scoring future drugs. I carried (and continue to carry) the burden of all of these unnecessary procedures upon my back. I don't know of too many people (other than really sick pill addicts) who are willing to have knives and saws cut into their bodies and who will risk permanent disability and long recoveries for the sake of obtaining prescription narcotics.

I was not only willing, I was determined to stay in a state of a "train wreck" physically so any doctor could just look at me and without saying much, get out a pen and while starting to write on a prescription pad say my favorite words, "So, what's going to help take this pain away, Mr. Zalkins?"

"Ahhhhh, that's right, Doc, now you are speaking a language I understand... You just keep writing, and put lots of fucking refills on that little piece of paper, and while you are at it feel free to put down a very large quantity because I am in a lot of pain here," my mind would say.

It was a sweet moment when I would see my doctor get down to business and start scribbling the special medical language down on that special piece of paper known to me as a "scrippie."

Remember *Charlie and The Chocolate Factory?* Remember how exciting it was when poor little Charlie found the golden ticket in a Wonka Bar? That's exactly how I felt the moment I received my fresh prescription.

"Just keep writing down those large quantities, and lots of refills, doc," I would say to myself. You never know how much pain I may get in, so write down a few extras in case I am in a tight spot. All this crazy shit would race through my head because I knew within an hour I would be cashing in my prescription for some little white, yellow, or turquoise gems that would make me all warm inside, and would provide me with all the euphoria the drugs unleashed.

I was now living in Silverstrand Beach (Ventura County) and working in Santa Barbara as a commercial insurance broker, trying to find a way to earn half of what my stepdad Darryl was earning. It was around this time (1999) that the doctor I was seeing was starting to say things like, "You really are taking a lot of the Norcos. We should look into weaning you off of these."

"What did you say? Why would we want to do that? It's these pills that help make my level of pain manageable," I said in a panicked state of urgency.

"What I am suggesting, Todd, is that we move you on to something stronger. We can always have the Norco for breakthrough pain, but my fear is that you are taking too much acetaminophen or Tylenol and that your liver and kidneys could be damaged."

Oh yes, now I get it—something stronger, sure, and breakthrough pain. "What is he saying? I don't know, but I think I like it. But let's be really careful and look after those vital organs, because I have a real killer life I am leading and I don't want any Tylenol messing up the good times I am having," I thought to myself.

I just nodded with ecstatic anticipation. He continued, "Let's try some small doses of Oxycontin, which is very effective for pain... It's time release, and you can have 120 Norcos a month for breakthrough pain."

For a split second I freaked out because I had heard about the Oxycontin epidemic on the East Coast where people were doing the craziest things like robbing elderly people who had the drug, and there were even older people who were dealing the drugs they were supposed to be taking for things like cancer pain, and stuff like that.

I had always thought, "This shit must be really good if grandmas and grandpas are turning into dealers."

In all my years of using I never encountered 82-year-old Grandma Madge dealing 8-balls of space coke out of her Buick on her way to play bingo with her girlfriends. This Oxycontin had to be packing a really major punch if it made people do the shit I was reading about, and it was getting much worse with pharmacies getting robbed at gunpoint and things of that nature. People were simply becoming out of control with Oxycontin.

I could never imagine how I would cope with having to score all of my pills from just dealers or having to steal them. This may sound sick, but I thought, I'm not that type of guy—I have surgeries in my medical history and all my pills are prescribed by licensed physicians.

My diseased head will flat out tell me exactly what it wants to hear to stay on the path of self destruction. There is no other way for me. It's simply a one-way street that cannot be negotiated any other way.

"I am a special addict," I said to myself, and I won't start taking a drug that is turning grandmas into dealers and high school kids into criminals. So, what was my immediate response? "Yes doctor, I agree, it's time to take it up a notch and take care of all this pain."

This was the official launch of my addiction into the "major leagues" if you will. Please do not take this as some rite of passage or bragging right, because it's not. But from the moment I started to ingest Oxycontin my need for drugs would change, my personality would be altered even more than it was, and the path I was on would lead me through the gates of hell, to a place even worse.

I walked away that day with a prescription for 240 Oxycontin (20 mg) (in a few years I would be taking 10 times this amount). I had 240 of these little pink gems and 120 of the yellow jackets, or Norco's. They were yellow and a jacket because they kept me warm. Then I called them "little yellow orphans" because they needed a home, and that home was in my body. I liked to have fun nicknames for my drugs—it kept things interesting and plus you need to speak in code when talking with other junkies. It is a top priority to have your own "special drug language," or at least it was for me.

It's important for me to point out that the more pills I took, the more pain I seemed to have, and then I would—of course—have to take more pills. There is something that happens psychologically that tells me I am in more pain, yet here I am more medicated than ever before.

So I never really knew how much pain I was in because I wasn't off the pills, coke, or alcohol long enough to ever know what my level of pain really was. This was a very scary scenario for me—I knew I had some legitimate pain, but was it the type of pain that could be treated with Advil or something over-the-counter?

I obsessed over it, but it didn't actually matter—the pills I was taking clouded any rational thinking. I was hooked, and there was no way that Advil or anything else non-narcotic could cure my ills. I needed narcotics... very strong narcotics.

Not only did I have some physical pain, I also had many other demons that were emotionally related that required me to medicate myself. The power of these pills is hard to explain to those who have never had them. For those who have had the experience of taking hardcore prescription pain pills, there is not a lot of explanation necessary, but I cannot assume all who are reading are pill addicts, or pill addicts in recovery. Just keep reading, and I am sure you will get the gist of it.

GAME ON

It was in late 1999 or early 2000 when I received the scrippie for the Oxys and "breakthrough yellow orphans." I hope by now I have demonstrated an escalation of the demand for more drugs, and how my needs would rise. I was progressively getting worse, never better—there were new levels I had to get to, and I had just been prescribed the method of that transportation, Oxycontin.

Oxycontin is a very strong opiate medication that is supposed to be taken orally, and it's time released into your system. The "Oxy" is short for the drug Oxycodone, and "Contin" for continual, they should say, "Once you try Oxy you will continue to use it!" A few months later I would discover the joy of chewing Oxys, then a couple years later snorting them like no tomorrow.

My first experience of taking this drug was profound. There are a lot of things I have forgotten as a result of my pill addiction, and some timelines in my story are basically "blank spots," meaning I can't get real specific because I can't fucking remember anything. More of that later—back to the first Oxy experience. I don't take one of anything, so I took two of these little pink beauties and washed them down with a Diet Coke. The pills are very small, smaller than Tic Tacs.

I was driving on the 101 Freeway admiring the beauty of the ocean en route to Santa Barbara. Then it came....bammmmmm!! This warm rush filled my veins and poured through my system. I had to pull over my car immediately because I hadn't felt something this intense before. My jaw became soft, my temples were ringing with joy, and I was this soft, plastic, gummy person that became a fixture of the seat in my car. I lowered the seat back, and my eyes twitched.

A teardrop came out of the right side of my eye. Any bit of physical pain I had was gone... this was much more powerful than the Vicodin or Norcos. I was instantly delivered to this pinnacle of goodness that can only be described as, "This is exactly how God and Jesus Christ want me to feel." This is pure religion—nothing should feel this good, but it is feeling this good and please don't ever take this feeling away from me.

Aside from any physical pain that was now totally eradicated, the drug did something more. Emotionally I was dropped off at the doorstep of some residence where everything in life was okay at that point in time. No troubles, no struggle with life stuff—my world was instantly placed in a state of utter perfection.

I love sex, and the effect of the Oxys was just as fantastic as the beautiful moment before orgasm when the entire world stops for a second and the only thing that matters is getting off. I have always thought that one of the most beautiful things in life is when a woman reaches that point of climax and her orgasm sends her entire body into an uncontrollable frenzy.

To this day, a woman getting off is a much better experience for me than my getting off, that's the truth. And in that moment, I realized I now had the drug that makes me feel like a chick does when she comes—the floodgates of warmth opened up into every cell in my body as a result of this magical pill.

I was giddy like a schoolboy's first crush, with that feeling of floating on air, and it was not going away... at least, not at first.

I Want to Feel Like This Forever

I had no idea that the ticket to paradise in the form of a small pill would bring me to my knees and produce more pain and sickness than one could ever imagine.

Given the opportunity to take something that will eradicate my fears, make me feel like God and Jesus want me to feel, and on top of it make me believe I am experiencing something close to a woman's orgasm??

Hell, I don't ever want to get off this ride. As a quick side note, my referencing God and Jesus with how Oxycontin made me feel is not a wise ass remark—I simply had this spiritual type of magic carpet ride that I felt only God and Jesus could provide because it was so heavy.

That's really how I felt at the time, and I was crazed for more.

Now I was in love for the first time. I had thought I knew what feeling good was, but Oxycontin was really giving me the extra hug and long kiss on the inside of me. It didn't take long, though, for me to have some of the side effects. Aside from the heavy nod I would experience, I also started to itch like fucking crazy.

The first thing in my mind was, "Oh no... not some bullshit side effects! I want to get along with you, Mr. Oxy—we are going to have a beautiful relationship, just please take away this fucking feeling like all of my skin has been dipped into poison ivy and we will be getting along just fine."

The nod, which I mentioned above, is this moment where your neck loosens up like it has been broken, your eyes start to flutter, and you drift off into your little dream world provided by the best travel agency I've ever known, Opiate World Travel.

Nodding off could be really dangerous, and many times I would swerve on streets and highways just missing moving cars as well as cars that were parked.

I have never won the lottery, but the fact that I never killed anyone in a car, or a pedestrian, or just drove my car through a crowded storefront should make me feel like I won the lottery, because I never should have gotten away with the constant danger I subjected my fellow man to.

I think God just had me pay for it in other ways, and we will get to that point of the story for sure.

On Oxy, I would scratch my arms incessantly to the point where they would bleed. In the first three or four months I had scabs all over my forearms and hands. If a client asked me what had happened, I would just tell them the truth. I would say, "I was hiking, and I fell into some poisonous bush and had to be rescued. I am lucky to be alive!!"

That's how pathetic I could be. What am I going to do? Tell the real truth? That would come off real well, "Yes, those scabs you see are a direct result of my falling in love with a heavy prescription pain narcotic called Oxycontin. Would you like to get hooked with me and start your own scab collection?"

Telling lies in my addiction got to a point where I actually believed some of my own bullshit. That to me is just another example of where this sickness leads me. In fact, telling lies was more interesting to me and it became more like a little game. I had to lie because almost every single activity I was engaged in was involving some untruth, if I considered it a "partial lie," believe me there was a shitload of deception in the mix.

I became very good at "archiving" my lies too. This was a technique that was highly effective because there were many moments where I had to reach back into my archives of lies and deception so I could continue to tell you the truth. Or, the truth as I see it. I don't give a shit about what your truth is—when I am in my addiction there is only one fucking thing that matters, and that is for me to stay high, or "stay well."

Maintenance

Staying well is a junkie's term, and to define it is easy: It means to keep on the drugs at all costs to avoid getting sick, because if I don't have a regular stream of Oxycontin, Norcos, and Valiums racing through my system I will get so fucking ill that I will be no better than a corpse with a pulse.

I could not take a day off once I was addicted to the pills. Addiction doesn't take any days off, and it doesn't give a shit if you aren't in the mood to get more drugs. Addiction doesn't care if you have to lie to the doctor or to your spouse or loved one, or if you have run out of the pills too soon and it's too early for a refill. Are you kidding me?

If you have run out of the magic little pills you had better find a way to fix this problem, because within hours there will be invisible bugs crawling all over your skin—one of the worst feelings you could ever encounter.

I experienced running out a few times, not many, and all I know is that the world could be collapsing around me, loved ones could be dying in front of me, and given the choice I will take the pills over anything else. The addiction is that powerful. Show me a pill junkie who tells you otherwise given the same scenario and I will tell you his or her name—that would be Pinocchio—because a pill junkie can rarely tell the truth when in the thralls of their addiction.

Here's a good example:

I was out in Las Vegas visiting with my mom and I had forgotten to bring my supply. San Clemente, California, is a long fucking way from Las Vegas, and if you are a junkie starting to feel sick San Clemente might as well be another fucking planet in another fucking galaxy, just trust me on this one.

Before I ever packed for a trip, before any passports or travel documents or even money was assembled, the most important thing for me to remember to pack was my vast assortment of pills. I would package them neatly, and they had to be accessible at the drop of a hat—if I was in some bullshit line at the airport that I couldn't tolerate for more than three minutes, I had better have a few Oxys or Norcos within reach.

I kept the pills everywhere, and always on my person. Never would I check my luggage and risk the chance that my pills would not arrive at my destination, I could give a shit about my clothing being there, but if my beloved pills weren't there I had a problem that was equivalent to World War Three—just ugly.

I always kept some in my pocket and the bulk of them in my backpack, which never—and I mean never—left my hands. Try to take my backpack and I can pretty much guarantee there will be a homicide in progress. Have you ever seen a desperate mother looking for her child? It's like that. Take away my pills and I have lost everything—they are the most important thing in my life.

Where was I? Oh yes, in Las Vegas, visiting my beautiful mother but out of my pills. My head started spinning out of control, my breathing accelerated, and my forehead, back, and armpits were sweating with no end in sight. My temper was out of control, and I was screaming at the top of my lungs…"I cannot believe I left my fucking medicine!"

This is the point in my story where I get to completely come clean with you and say that I have a major problem with prescription pain medications, but maybe you have gathered that by now.

It had gone far beyond being in physical pain—I could no longer tell you what was real or not, and all I possessed was this light that flashed in my head that said, "More pills, more pills, I need more pills."

The worst part is, I was an Oxycontin addict and I was out of Oxys. There was no way I could get the drug called into a pharmacy in Nevada—impossible. Oxycontin is a highly monitored drug by the DEA and you must have an original "triplicate" prescription to have it filled.

This enormous sense of anxiousness took over me, and it came down to this: Either I get a hold of someone back in Southern California and beg them to drive out to Nevada with more drugs, or I am going home and I have only been at my mom's house for two hours.

How in the hell do I explain that to my mom? "Ummmmm, sorry, Mom, I have to go back home because I am a pill junkie and I left all my shit there," yeah right.

I got so lucky. My assistant at my office had access to a shitload of pills of her own (you have to hire junkies if you are a junkie), and I also had a huge prescription of Norcos waiting for me at a local San Clemente pharmacy. I begged and pleaded for my assistant to drive out to meet me, and she did.

By the time she arrived with the pills I was a wreck. I could barely stand upright, my muscles ached, and I was shaking like a guy naked in a snowstorm despite the beautiful afternoon in the Nevada desert. I immediately chewed up seven or eight Norcos, and I was happily melting in my car seat about twenty minutes later.

My Swinging Moods

My moods were always contingent upon one simple thing: my pill count.

If I had just scored a huge grip of pills, I was in the best mood I could possibly be in. This doesn't mean I would be running around doing cartwheels or pinching the cheeks of little kids telling them how cute they were. But if I had just seen both of my regular doctors and my dealer, I was vaulted up to the ceiling with high-grade prescription narcotics and my life couldn't be better.

Now, to reverse that scenario, if I was getting low and the weekend was coming up, or I burned through my pills too fast, it was the most agitated state of mind I could possibly be in. I would be short with my clients, bank tellers, friends, neighbors, mail carrier—you name it, they were on my "fuck you" list if I didn't have an ample supply of pills. Somehow, this made perfect sense to me and my guard always had to be up.

I always knew if I was getting low, and I didn't have too many moments where I was totally screwed, but all it took was one moment of running out and it was a very dark place to be in. The moment your body requires more of the opiates, it's very good at letting you know. Your body will punish you, and you will be thrown into the worst muscle spasms, sweats, and nausea, it's something you don't ever want to endure.

We have all had the flu and I think it's one of the worst things we can live with for a week or two as human beings, but when your body is craving the pills and the medicine they deliver, it's just like the flu—but ten times worse, and I mean it.

My mind would race and spin out of control, and my legs would be the first parts of me to get really weak. Plus, there was a sense of urgency that was mind-boggling—my next handful of pills was the only thing in life that makes or breaks me, and it was just a horrible feeling that turned me into something not of this world.

The worst time that I experienced was once when I had run out of pills and I was truly stuck. I can't remember the exact year, as I do have a lot of blank spots in my memory from my pill and drug usage. I do know I was not on the Oxys yet, but I was in the full blown stages of Norco addiction. It hit me on a Saturday mid-morning, and I would suffer all the way until Monday morning at around 11 a.m. All I could do was lie down in a ball and sweat and crave, sweat and crave.

I had no options at this particular time. This is one of those experiences where I would say, "Hell would be a vacation compared to the place I am in... Hell is like a picnic on Hawaii compared to this. I am somewhere in Satan's house, and all of the worst people in history are at his pad: Stalin, Hitler, Pol Pot, etc., and they are having a keg party, and I am tied down to a huge butcher block and all of these fuckers get to torment me for two solid days."

That is the best way I can describe my ordeal of running out of my pills and having to endure the withdrawal for three days. But as bad as this experience was, the experience of my ultimately getting clean and sober would make this look and feel like a walk in the park.

Fishing in La Paz 2000.
The drugs were still working for me at this time.

FEDERAL OFFENSE

Now the Oxys had me on a pretty good path for a while, and I stopped the itching of my skin. I was already using two doctors: one who prescribed Norco, Oxys, and Valium, and another "backup" doctor who wrote me a scrippie for 240 Norcos a month, my insurance policy to avoid getting dope sick.

About two years later, though, I had to be plotting and scheming for more pills. I was being prescribed close to 400 Norcos a month, and I was now getting 240 of the 40 mg Oxycontin.

Plus, I would buy Norcos from friends willing to score a scrippie from their doctor, they were always bullshit small amounts of 40 or so, but those 40 or so could keep me well for a day in the event I had run out of pills—heaven forbid. I also had a guy I could buy 100 or so from every two weeks.

So, I had about sixteen to twenty Norcos a day plus the eight Oxycontin a day for my steady habit. This would put most people in a coma for sure, if not kill them. My tolerance level was increasing substantially and I was just trying to stay ahead of running out.

For the first four to six months I was taking the Oxycontin I would get pretty high, numb and warm. After that, I was chasing the feeling I once experienced when I pulled off the 101 Freeway on my way to Santa Barbara. I would be trying to recapture that feeling for some years to come, but never finding it again.

I stole a prescription pad from one of my doctors one time, before the triplicate prescription pads were really official-looking and the Feds were monitoring doctors and patients. I tested fate one day and wrote a prescription for Norcos. I had had endless streams of pain pill prescriptions filled in the past, and here I was committing a federal offense by forging a prescription—and I failed to indicate on the prescription "how many pills per day" to be taken.

Right in the middle of filling the prescription, the pharmacy technician says, "I will just be a second. I need to call the doctor to verify the dosage."

I should have had some Depends on because I just about crapped my pants. I pleaded with the pharmacy tech, and she knew me really well, and I always complimented her on how pretty she was. (It pays big time to have the pharmacy tech or assistant on your side. These are the people who can make or break you, and ruin your day. They have the power to clear your prescription early so you can get your drugs, and they can also just give you a break, which I got many times.)

So I was begging her, "Come on Susie, you know me, I take it six to eight times a day, look up all of my past refills."

Any hard ass would have verified the dosage amount, found out it was bullshit, and called 911 to have me arrested. The punishment for this crime is immense, and I will be checking with an attorney before this is published to ensure I cannot be prosecuted, even though this was a long time ago.

Upon getting that scrippie filled I got into my BMW 740iL and wept like a seven year old boy, screaming, "This is fucking nuts! I am fucking losing it here." But then I calmed down, ate seven or eight Norcos, melted into my car seat, and had forgotten all about this horrific incident about an hour later.

FEDERAL OFFENSE 2

One time I was in a rare bind—I was completely out of Oxys and Norcos and I couldn't get any for a few days. For me, a few days without my pills seemed like an eternity. I had to ingest my medicine every few hours just to keep from shaking and breaking out in cold sweats and getting ill very quick. My dealer was unreachable, and there were no friends or family I knew of who had undergone a recent surgery which would enable me to bribe, or if necessary steal what I needed to keep "straight."

For anyone who has been there, it is your darkest hour. I remember this quite vividly because this only happened once. It was Friday afternoon, so that shut the door on any doctor's visits, and the weekend was here, meaning Urgent Care would be my only bet and they wouldn't write any good drugs due to the increased awareness for prescription pill addicts storming into their waiting rooms for more pills—and Vicodin was now like baby aspirin to me.

I had to act quickly and be very resourceful. I had this one doctor I was seeing who wrote me very small prescriptions for Norcos, maybe 60 to 80 at a time. I had already burned up my refills with the scrippie he had written me for sure. I had no choice in my eyes—I was going to have to "call it in." This is something I had never done, only thought of, but never actually executed.

I was going to call the pharmacy where the prescription had been filled, and act as though I was a doctor's office helper just calling it in for a patient. I hadn't had a dose of Oxy or Norco in a few hours, and my level of anxiety was rising big time.

This was a horrible thing to be doing, and I didn't feel good about doing it. As a junkie though, I am willing to go to any length to get what I need, lying, cheating, stealing, manipulating, you name it. Those are all prerequisite character traits of a junkie.

Show me one pill junkie who says they aren't dishonest, and I can guarantee you he or she is nothing but a lying, criminal, screwed up junkie. I know that I even started to believe some of my own deceptions and lies.

I had to pull the trigger and score more "yellow orphans" aka Norcos. There was no way of calling in a refill of Oxys, you just couldn't do it. So I called the pharmacy and it went down like this:

Me: Hello, Ms. Pharmacy Tech... this is Dan T. Mann with Dr. Johnson's office. (Of course, I used an 80s porn star name, what an idiot I was!) Umm, yes, I was calling in for a refill for a Todd A. Zalkins.

Pharmacy: Sure, what's the prescription for?

Me: Norco

Pharmacy: Quantity?

Me: 120, one pill every four to six hours per day.

Pharmacy: Any refills?

Me: Yes, two please.

Pharmacy: Okay, we will get it ready.

Now, there is no sound on this earth more beautiful to my ears than, "Okay, we will get it ready." I let out a huge sigh of relief. I was in my car, and I was looking out of each window as though the SWAT team was going to descend upon me. I felt like Ray Liotta in *Goodfellas* at the end where he is blasted out of his mind off of coke, there are helicopters above, and he is paranoid beyond description.

Thirty minutes or so later, I took a few deep breaths and walked into the pharmacy. This is where my feet instantly turned into cement blocks, they became very heavy. I knew that what I was doing was not only wrong, but carried a very serious penalty if I were caught.

However, the choice to not go in was silly—I had to go in. Otherwise, I would enter the gates of hell called "opiate withdrawal" which involves cold sweats head to toe, the feeling of thousands of bugs and spiders crawling all over my skin, muscle cramps, the worst diarrhea you can imagine, and constant shaking. I was not prepared for that—I would risk going to jail to stay "well," as if that made any sense at all.

I got to the counter, already sweating profusely through my dress shirt, and the pharmacy knew I was not doing well. I tried to play it off, but you could tell by looking at me that I was a strung-out maniac who needed more pills—nothing more and nothing less.

Surprisingly, the pharmacy girl just grabbed the sack on the shelf (which is another beautiful thing), and rang it up. I paid for it in cash and got the hell out of there, tearing the bag open as I left the counter, my hands anxiously working the top of that fucking plastic pill bottle. I poured six or seven into my hand, chewed them up into a disgusting yellow paste, and grabbed a Diet Coke from the cooler and pounded half of it.

I was relieved—I had 120 Norcos for two and a half days, just enough to get me through until Monday. This gave me time to find my dealer to get more Oxys or Fentanyl as well as finding one of my many sympathetic and charming front office girls to get me in to a physician. I easily had twelve to fifteen to choose from, all up and down the coast.

The doctor's assistant, nurse, or office manager could be the best or worst friend a pill addict has ever had. I would always be very kind to them, which they deserve anyway, but I had to go overboard and secure their friendship, or at least have them as my ally.

I would buy beautiful bouquets of flowers for my favorites, and by doing so I guaranteed myself a "pass" in the event I got into a sticky situation. This was no different to me than taking care of a good client of mine. You always want to "service the account," and my way of servicing the account was sending some nice flowers to the doctors' assistants from time to time.

In hindsight, yes it's sick as hell and completely insane. However, at the time, it made all the sense in the world and then some, and there was no way in hell you could convince me otherwise.

"THE WAITING IS THE HARDEST PART" —TOM PETTY

Being a full-tilt prescription junkie meant that I had to spend a lot of time driving to doctors' offices, sitting in their boring ass waiting rooms, and looking at these magazines in which every other page is dedicated to an advertisement for treating either depression or male enhancement. Damn it, I am not depressed and my dick works just fine—I am in a great deal of pain here, where is the doctor!

I always have thought that as necessary as doctors are, they are the rudest fucking businesspeople on the planet. This is due to one thing and one thing only: appointment times.

When I have an appointment with my doctor for 10:15 in the morning that does not mean I get to relax in his special little waiting room until 11:25 just to be transferred to another cold, bullshit room to change into a gown and then be seen by 11:50.

Anyone else in this world that ran their business like a doctor wouldn't be in business. Why? Because no one is waiting an extra hour to see their accountant, insurance agent, auto mechanic, kid's schoolteacher, or principal, nor would I expect them to. I am just not that fucking important, yet for some reason we all put up with the arrogance and self-imposed "flexibility" of the good old doctor.

One time I had a 9:30 appointment to see my "pain management" doctor in San Diego, and I showed up ten minutes late. The front desk Nazi said I had to make another appointment. Some folks might accept this, but most wouldn't even if they aren't waiting for the "holy scrippie" for the drug of their choice.

To tell me I will have to reschedule my appointment because I am ten minutes late is just totally nuclear. This is the type of incident that could have police involvement, and I mean that.

"Little Miss Nazi front desk bitch" had better have a loaded 9 mm stainless-steel berretta with hollow-tip bullets because I am not going anywhere. If I have to follow the doctor home, I will fucking do it. If I have to interrupt his tennis match or bullshit golf game, no problem. If I have to interrupt his kid's lame ass play at his lame ass criminal private school, I will do it, and if necessary I will threaten him physically.

Some of those things I mentioned above I have done—I will allow you to pick which ones.

Here's what I told the lady in San Diego who told me to "reschedule." "Uh, Nurse Jackie... I have seen Dr. Williams for years, and he knows my history and the necessity for my pain medications. I am also on a high blood pressure medication which, if it is not refilled, I could be driving my car and have a heart attack... on top of this I have waited for Dr. Williams in the past for a total of about four days due to his triple-booking appointments and other criminal activity. Lastly, if I don't get in to see the doctor I swear on my life I will take off all my clothes and act as if there is absolutely nothing fucking wrong with me, and if that 87-year-old bag has a stroke from seeing my pipe half hard, it's all your fault."

This happened, and she responded with, "That is not necessary, Mr. Zalkins, and you don't need to talk to me that way. You can go in now, but don't let this happen again." She was mortified, and I didn't give a shit because I needed a prescription and I needed a nice refill quantity on it as well—two or three times would be nice.

The other "fun part" of being addicted was all of the bullshit I would have to hear when waiting for the prescription to be filled at the pharmacies. Normally I was sweating profusely, highly agitated, and in the worst of moods. My eyes would be all puffy and glazed, and the word patience didn't exist in my vocabulary.

The worst was when there would be only one pharmacy assistant or "tech" as they call them. It would be just my luck to be standing in that wonderful brightly lit pharmacy and have to listen to some "tech" explain the reason why some asshole's prescription can't be filled.

Often these were older people, and I really had a sense of compassion for the retired guy who fought in World War Two or the elderly woman picking up cancer medications for her husband.

But all bets were off when some random, healthy asshole was questioning the pharmacy and their policies, saying how he now has to go home and wait for it to be filled, and blah blah blah.

The first thing I would say was, "Hey Ernie, or whatever your name is, we have these things called cell phones? You can actually call the pharmacy and they can give you a yes or a no if your prescription is ready. It's real simple—I do it all the time."

I did this more than once, and came very close to getting into a full scale brawl, and I wanted every bit of it. I loved to tell someone else why they were being the asshole and how they were deficient, yet if my scrippie wasn't ready and I didn't call to check because I just thought it would be ready—look out, things were going to get out of hand very quickly. If Ernie chose to say the same thing to me that I mentioned above, he would be sucking meals through straws for months.

This is just another example of how selfishly determined I would be to get my drugs, even though I never intended to bum someone out if something went wrong, I generally did because my brain was simply starting to fry from all of the years on pills. I couldn't see it—everyone else could see it, but not me.

SAN CLEMENTE

In the fall of 2001 I was done with my marriage and I couldn't stick around anymore—it felt like something I should never have gone through with. My way of getting out of the marriage was sheer torture for my poor wife, as she was just the innocent victim. She did nothing wrong and there were a lot of things I did love about her, but I couldn't see the things that were good—all I could do was exploit the bad, which was the only thing my diseased and sick head would tell me.

My wife and I had bought a beautiful home in Ventura, close to the surf spots I loved but rarely visited anymore. She stayed in the home in Ventura and I moved to San Clemente in south Orange County. I have some great friends down there, plus I wanted to be as far away as possible from where I was, because I always think my life will improve if I just pick up and leave. So I got lucky and negotiated a nice deal with the insurance brokerage I worked for in Santa Barbara, enabling me to start an insurance brokerage of my own.

Although highly addicted to pills at this point, I was also still functioning in the workplace. My decision to leave my marriage took a serious toll on me emotionally because I felt extremely guilty for hurting my wife as we were only married for two years.

I would pop more pills to push these feelings down, and when I would binge drink and snort coke, I would go deeper and farther than ever before.

I don't do guilt well, especially knowing that I was responsible for wrecking the marriage, but my head told me, "I need to be on my own" so I jumped headfirst into growing my business in San Clemente. I had a beautiful office on Del Mar Avenue right up the street from the pier. Work and pills consumed me, if I focused all my energy in that area of my life, I wouldn't think so much about the guilt and shame of my leaving my wife in Ventura.

Today my ex-wife has remarried, and from what I hear she's happy and has a beautiful baby boy. She deserves to be happy after all the crap I put her through. They say "Hindsight is 20/20," well that means really good vision and I could not see anything clearly during those times, not with my addicted eyes.

I quickly got established with a doctor in the San Clemente area and I still had two others, one in Ventura and another in Santa Barbara. I had other doctors in other areas, but those were "cash and carry" doctors so I could fly under the radar and I only used them when really in need. Why would I want to use a cash and carry doctor when I had killer health insurance that paid for everything?

If I had taken the pills I was using in 2005 and 2006 (the height of my pill taking), became a pill dealer, and sold them on the street, I would have been able to make $25,000 to $30,000 a month. That's right, a month.

Pills are big fucking business, and I know, because I would sell some "overstock" of my 80 mg Oxycontin for $55 to $80 per pill!!

My insurance co-pay was only $10 for 240 of those turquoise 80-milligram gems—on the low end, that prescription alone would be worth $13,200. That's just one scrippie: take the other three to six I was getting a month and I had a "Scrippie Goldmine."

I was now being "legally prescribed" 400 Oxys per month from two doctors, not including another 300 to 400 Norcos, not including my dealers and other doctors I would call just to make me feel "pill rich." There were actually some moments where I was stacked to the gills with prescription pain meds, and it wasn't enough—I needed to feel "pill rich."

This meant I would go to one of my unsuspecting doctors who were very kind and who had no idea I was so deep into my addiction, get another scrippie or two, and have so many bottles of the shit that it made me feel like some pathetic "Pill King."

Now you know why so many pharmacies and hospitals are being robbed for all of the best pain medications, it's big business. Dealing wasn't a long-term thing for me, though; I sold to one or two friends of mine for a short period of time.

If you're going to score some pills from me, that's all fine and good, but if you think I'm going to deliver them or meet you? Good fucking luck—it just isn't going to happen, and you had better plan on doing a few errands for me as well, like picking up my dry cleaning and getting more yogurt and granola at the store. If you don't come to my pad bearing the fine gifts of strawberry yogurt and a box of granola, you are fucked. Come back when you have my yogurt!

I wasn't the guy making pain medication deliveries. I was too comfortable with my war chest of pain meds and my huge bowl of yogurt and granola, sitting in my big leather lazy boy chair watching Forensic Files or C.S.I.—that was a big party for me!

Somehow I managed to buy a nice home in San Clemente (not buy it outright, but put the dough down and make payments). I was away on a business trip, and while I was gone my mom just went to town getting the place all dialed in. When I returned I couldn't believe what I saw, those "Extreme Makeover" shows have got nothing on my mom. She got this place looking so comfortable and classy in just about a week—it was killer. It made being at home a real joy, and I felt that joy for a little while when I moved there in 2003.

But the excitement I had for my new home was gone in weeks, and it was time to return to the active grind of addiction. Very seldom would I be able to stop and smell the roses—in fact, there were no roses for me. My motto was, "take time and stop to snort the Oxys."

A few months after I was settled into my house I got this wild idea to get off of the pills. The doctor's visits and chasing the drugs were getting tiresome, so I figured a stay in the hospital would get me fixed up. There was no rationale whatsoever to this decision, it was just another phenomenon to me.

I cannot stay on one subject or task at any given moment, I am completely irrational with my thinking, and I can barely retain anything that's been said to me. Out of nowhere some outrageous idea or insane thought would come into my head and I would have to act immediately on that sick instinct.

Since I have been clean and sober I have heard from countless friends and acquaintances that my pattern of speech and the way I communicated during my years of using was just baffling. I have heard the following at least 100 times since I got clean, "We couldn't understand anything you said, your eyes were always glazed, and you were bouncing off the walls so much we couldn't stand to even talk to you."

The scary thing is that when I was sick I thought nothing was wrong with my speech and appearance. I knew that I had a very serious addiction to the pills and I could not get off of them, but I thought I was just fine. My perception was that I was a fine communicator, but the fact is I was completely fucking insane but I simply didn't realize it at the time.

So, out of nowhere I wanted to get clean. I just wanted to try to be proud of something for a change, as opposed to being so sick of myself. But I had absolutely no idea what a commitment it would take to get well from this addiction, and I still had a lot more pain to endure.

REHAB PART 1

I checked into South Coast Hospital in the fall of 2003 to detox off of the prescription pain medications. That's all I wanted to do: get me off of these pills, please. My thought was I would check in, let them drug me up, and I would punch through the other side of this silly addiction and then my life would be perfect.

I was dead wrong—I had a brutal detox from the get-go. I had been taking so many pills for so long, I was just miserable. For whatever reason, though, they did manage to get me to sleep during the night which was a blessing. Getting up to go to the bathroom was a hell on earth, that's for sure.

All of the opiates back your system up to the point of making your system highly toxic. You're not "regular" at all, and it's very common for us pill junkies to take massive amounts of laxatives. Once you start to truly detox you have these "blow outs" almost every ten minutes, you are crapping your brains out and it is very unpleasant, you sweat, and your stomach feels like Mike Tyson used you for a sparring partner.

There's really nothing quite like that special misery when detoxing off of opiates. If there is a hell on earth, I would put detoxing from prescription pain medications as one of them.

Being in detox was pointless. The staff wanted to push me towards rehab and have me go to these fucking ridiculous "Twelve-Step meetings," get a sponsor, and work these things called Twelve Steps. "Are you kidding me? I'm not going to AA—what I have here is a mild problem with prescription narcotics. I only snort coke and drink alcohol during the holidays."

I wanted nothing to do with anything a doctor or counselor was telling me. Just do your job and medically detox me off this shit, so I can get back to work and be all that I can be! The rehab doctor at the time told me, "You have a very serious problem with prescription drugs. You can't beat this thing on your own."

That's it, I said to myself, just watch me! I will kick this fucking shit and then I will come back and kick the shit out of you, "Dr. Lying Criminal Know-It-All... You don't know how tough I am—I have been around, you know? I can fix me, no problem." That's exactly how I felt at the time, defiant to the core and not wanting to hear anything you had to say, especially if it could help me. I don't need your help, and I don't want it either. I'm cool, I've got this handled....yeah right.

The first three days of the detox were heavy, but I was a bit stronger by days four and five. I was ready to go home. "I am off this shit... I told you fuckers I could do this! Get me out of here and take this plastic wrist band I.D. or whatever you call it and stick it up your ass! I have things to do, I am a busy guy."

They discharged me right away because the worst of the detox symptoms really were gone. Even though they recommended I stay for the 28-day program and get involved in some type of Twelve-Step group of recovery, I shunned that immediately, and while I was driving away I told them to stick the Twelve Steps right up their ass—I needed a beer!

FLY AND THE FAMILY STONE

That's exactly what I did, too. My brain was on overdrive and I wanted and needed a drink, big time. I was cranking Sublime's classic album *40 oz. to Freedom* in my Ford F150 and I was going straight to Fly Industries, the home of Black Fly's Sunglasses. These guys would never turn me away and were always down for a sick party, and I was the guy to bring it to them on this special day with a reason to celebrate: I just got out of rehab!

I could write an entire book on my experiences with the guys from Fly Industries. I love all of them, and they know how to get it on in the best of ways. The do not fuck around! I like people who get right to the point, "Just chop me up a fat rat tail of coke please, give me several shots of this and that and let's get things moving along here."

I strolled into Fly Industries on a Friday I believe, fresh out of rehab. I was admitted to the back area where some of the crew was hiding from me behind their desks. I was on a mission, and they all knew what that meant. I was going to drink, and soon after I would demand cocaine, preferably the good stuff from outer space.

First, I made a beeline to the rest room, tore off my rehab bracelet, and stapled it to the "wall of fame-or-shame." Black Fly's had the most unreal shit taped and stapled up all throughout their crazy warehouse, and I loved visiting there. I would always be amped up to the gills when I went to Fly's because I knew we were going to get into some quality trouble and my hair may as well have been on fire, "Let's do this! Let's fucking do this!" I would say.

We went straight to Malarkey's on the Newport Peninsula, and got right to it. Shots and beers, shots and beers, and more shots and beers. I am off the pills now and it's time to celebrate this achievement, drinks all the way around for me and my friends.

Probably not more than an hour into our drinking, I started to unleash one of my favorite lines for my drinking partners, "Pack my beak, damn it! Somebody here is going to pack my ever lovin' beak right now," this was my immediate demand for cocaine.

It doesn't take very much time from my first drink of alcohol to trigger that desire for cocaine. It's a guarantee that if I drink, I will be craving blow—and if I have to fly to Peru to get it, so be it.

It was a rare occasion I didn't have coke on me. Here I am, fresh out of rehab after shaking for several days from an opiate detox, and I am craving more booze but I need cocaine, immediately.

I am pleading with the guys I am drinking with to pack my beak, and they have none on them. I said, "Fine, here's the phone— start dialing." I don't like to waste time. Within a half hour I was trying to flip over the pool tables because I needed to have my beak packed, causing a total scene. I was asked to leave that fine drinking establishment, and the guys I was with were over me, and who can blame them?

"Well I am over it. I am going to Long Beach to try and pack my beak," I told them. So, I drove to Long Beach, seriously intoxicated and right out of rehab. Think about it... I was just in the hospital to kick some drugs, and hours later I am butthoused out of my fucking mind and on a mission to procure coke. I don't think I could spell the words, sane, rational or denial.

This was one of the very rare nights in my life where I would not score coke. I mean, rare as rare gets. Of the thousands of times I wanted cocaine, I may have failed to connect maybe ten times. That's a serious batting average, because I took my using very seriously. Failure to connect with my dealer or your dealer is not an option, and it's just completely unacceptable! I will score my drugs at all costs.

Without the aid of cocaine I could never drink all that much. The blow always gave me the ability to drink more and stay up longer. I was close to blacking out and somehow I made it to my mom's house in Belmont Heights. I passed out, and the very next morning I was really dope sick for pills, with the usual shaking, sweats, and muscle aches.

All bets were off—I was one day out of the hospital, hung over like sin, and I needed some pills, now! My mom was unaware of the depth of my problem at this stage, and I told her I really needed to get to the hospital "because my back hurt." I had a large scar on my lower back from my 1990 surgery, so there was no denying that I could very well have back pain at any given time. Not that I never had any pain, I just used it as an excuse to get what I wanted, when I wanted it.

We went to the emergency room at Long Beach Memorial Hospital where I was admitted and given a nice big shot of Dilaudid, and immediately I was given that warm blanket of opiate heaven where both God and Jesus Christ were holding me tight, and everything was okay again.

When it would hit me strong like that, a little voice would go off in my head saying, "It's okay, Todd... I'm here. I am going to take good care of you—you are safe now." Just like a mother to her ailing child, the opiate pain medication gave me all that I needed: warmth, comfort, joy, safety, and love.

I was given a prescription for a small amount of Norco, around 20 to be exact—of which all were gone by that afternoon. I now had a dealer in Costa Mesa, and this guy was rock solid and was always holding large amounts of little yellow orphans and Oxys. It was the weekend, so there was no way I was going to see any of the doctors on my prescription roster.

The guy I bought pills from in Costa Mesa was heavy, meaning he did not fuck around. He generally had a loaded firearm with him and he had massive quantities of Norcos; the Oxys were too expensive and I would just wait to get those from my doctor. I could buy plastic jars of 100 Norcos; I would usually buy 300 to 400, and I think they were two bucks a pill. My giving this guy $600 to $1000 was standard—I never bought the minimum, always the max he would give me. I don't like to run out, ever, so I will pay whatever it is I need to pay to get what I need.

This was a serious guy though, one you would never rob, ever. I never had to do that—I was lucky that I had some health insurance, a few bucks in the bank, and some friends who were willing to help me out from time to time. Any fool who found it a good idea to rob this dude would find himself dead as disco, and health insurance just wouldn't do you a bit of good if you chose to steal his grip of pills.

BACK TO WORK

So my bright idea about rehab didn't work, and a lot of them don't. I managed to stay off of the narcotics for less than 24 hours upon being released from the hospital. The idea sounded good to me, but sounding good and really wanting this to work were two completely different things.

A quick fix to everything is how I like it, and the quicker the better. Waiting for anything doesn't work for me. Whoever said "patience is a virtue" was never addicted to Oxycontin, nor did he ever have to wait in line to have his fucking prescription filled going through opiate withdrawal.

Somehow I managed to work really hard and make decent money, enough to pay my bills—and more importantly, keep my cache of pills at a nice level. Just because I had good health insurance didn't mean I didn't spend a shitload of money on scoring my pills from dealers, probably to the tune of $3,000 to $5,000 per month in cash, all depending on what was available.

My appearance and my using were progressively worsening. I was gaining a lot of weight from lack of doing anything physical, my face was bloated, and I would sweat constantly. Some clients of mine would say, "Gosh, Todd, you sure are sweating badly today. Are you okay?" I would reply, "Oh sure, I'm fine. I just worked out hard this morning and I probably got ready a bit too quick without cooling down."

Bullshit like that was common for me to say. I certainly couldn't reply, "I'm sorry, but I am totally toxic from taking absurd amounts of Oxycontin, Norcos, and Fentanyl. I am the sickest son of a bitch that I know, and by the way, do you have any pills on you?"

Other clients just flat out told me, "Todd, we are making a change. We won't be doing business with you anymore." The fact is I was a very scary looking guy. I am almost 6'4", and at my heaviest I weighed 265, and that along with my insane-looking glazed eyes and non-stop perspiring—who in the hell would want to do business with me?

After I was told this in person by a client, I proceeded to crawl deeper and deeper into darker places. I made up my mind I would no longer go to see clients in person unless absolutely necessary, and if I did have to go see someone it would be first thing in the morning around 10 a.m. so I would be semi-coherent. And isn't that funny, "First thing in the morning, around 10 a.m.?" I don't think that is first thing in the morning to most people, but to me it was.

By that time in the morning I would only be six Oxys deep, a few Norcos, and three Valiums or so, you know, to go with my morning coffee. Isn't that what people do??? By the afternoon, forget it. I had one eye looking one way and the other eye partially closed, and not making one bit of sense. I should have had a collection of eye patches on me.

I could also go from "zero" to "fuck you" in a millisecond. For instance, one day after the really disappointing loss of a nice account of mine, I was stuck in traffic just south of Irvine on the 405 Freeway. I was in my lane and looking straight ahead (which was rare), when some asshole cuts right in front of me and as he's doing so he flips me off.

When he flipped me off, my "fuck you" switch went immediately on. I threw my BMW in park, jumped out of the car, and proceeded to scream "Oh yeah? Fuck me? Fuck me? Is that how it is you little cocksucker?" I proceeded to bash in his car with my fist and started to kick in his window and windshield. He couldn't move because he was pinned in traffic, not to mention petrified with fear along with what looked to be his wife in the car screaming like she was being raped, and I didn't give a shit, I was seeing red.

There were no questions asked and no discussions necessary. I proceeded to dismantle this fucker's car, and if he had gotten out I probably would have committed homicide—that's how insane I could get in a heartbeat. I didn't have many of these encounters, and I can only imagine how horrified others were on the freeway watching this and trying to get home.

There I am, this big, sweaty madman kicking in some guy's nice Mercedes. But I had a good reason, right? He cut me off and proceeded to say "fuck you," well, that was unacceptable and it was important for me to show him how an insane pill addict reacts when flipped off.

What's really amazing is that I wasn't arrested, nor was I ever contacted by police. It was still light outside and anyone could see my nice silver 740il, and the sick, fat, sweaty guy driving it.

The poor guy is probably still having nightmares and his wife is still in therapy as a result of my actions. If I ever could find them I would certainly like to apologize for my behavior, but I doubt they want to see me anytime soon.

I saw a photo of myself recently taken during that time period and I couldn't even tell who I was looking at. It was me all right, wearing clothes spotted with sweat, with a fat, bloated face and eyes you could see right through. I'm so grateful I don't look that way today, but I am much more grateful to not feel that way today. But I still had a hard road to travel to get from there to here.

ANOTHER QUICK FIX

My pill addiction was constantly worsening, so in 2004 I decided to go to the Waismann Clinic in Orange County, which has a "revolutionary treatment for opiate addiction." Their marketing material states that they can have you return to a productive life in a matter of days after going through their treatment process.

They claim to have the best "success rate" in the industry, which might be true, but they don't tell you how many of their patients actually have stayed clean and sober—at least they didn't tell me, anyway. But I didn't care because once again I wanted that "quick fix" to my problem, so for $10,000 I was "all in."

I was really excited about this step that I was taking, and the place had so many good things to say about their procedure. It's a nice facility and the people there were very kind and comforting. This detox is a medical procedure under anesthesia that induces and speeds up the withdrawal while the patient sleeps.

Waismann goes on to say that "other treatment centers or rehabs have less than 10% of a success rate after the first year due to the physically addictive properties of Norco & Oxycontin." No shit, I understand that. The recovery rate is way less than ten percent for us pill junkies, I have often heard that 1% to 2% of Oxycontin addicts actually get one year or more of sobriety or clean time—it is that tough to get off of this crap once it has you in its grasp.

So, I went through the treatment, and all I can say was that the experience was very, very heavy. While under the anesthesia I had some of the most psychotic dreams ever, and upon coming out of the anesthesia I tried to immediately tackle the nurse and grab her tits. She was hot, and I thought she wanted it.

I was completely delusional and all hooked up to these monitors and IVs, and I was trying to grab the nurse's tits. I had no idea what I was doing. I later apologized, and she told me she had seen worse happen. I didn't want to know what that meant—probably some idiot just like me with a raging hard-on chasing the staff around yelling, "Kiss me, I am now drug free! How about a quick blow job, honey!"

What I remember of this experience was how weak I was for several days. It was really tough just to walk a few steps, and I would be out of breath as though I had just run a marathon when I had just walked ten feet. For the most part I would say that the clinic did what it was supposed to do from a medical standpoint. In a week or so I was very glad to be off of the pills. But the fire within started to burn, and soon I was drinking like a fish and packing my ever-loving beak with massive amounts of cocaine.

The moment I felt strong enough I went surfing with some buddies at the San Clemente pier, and I passed out in the water. My friends carried me to the lifeguard station where I was told to lie down as they gave me oxygen for several minutes. They told me to go home and get rest, and that I had no business being in the cold ocean water after the procedure. I was too weak to paddle, but I had thought it was a good idea.

I was very grateful for their assistance, but I had some things to go sort out. I was released from the lifeguard tower, which I took as a full blown "green light" to hightail it straight to the bar.

"How about some shots of Jaegermeister please... With some beers to back them up," and within 25 minutes I was calling my dealer for some high-grade cocaine. It was on, and my friends and I drank and packed our beaks all night. I was ruined the next day, but I managed to not go and seek out the pills to cure the hangover.

PART FIVE
A BANDAID FOR A SERIOUS WOUND

I actually managed to stay off of the pills that time for about four months. This was the longest I had gone without prescription drugs in my body since 1990. I was drinking more towards the weekends and snorting space coke eight to ten times a month—like playing golf, only on the weekends.

My pill problem was licked, or so I thought. I really had no desire for them, but my return to pill popping came about in the most random of ways. A girl I was dating had a nice quantity of Vicodin, and I knew she had them but I didn't even think of asking her for some of her little white pills. I was off that shit and wanted nothing to do with them.

I was enjoying sex now more than ever, so I wanted to keep that as one of my hobbies. Once you are off the opiates your libido starts to fire up like a freight train on methamphetamine. I could not get enough sex—it was the most beautiful thing in the world, and I didn't want to give that up.

I was working at my insurance brokerage office one day, and out of nowhere I had this horrible headache. I am not one of those people who get lots of headaches, when I do get one, it's from snorting big grips of coke and drinking several cocktails and beers, and that's just a hangover. But the following is something I will never, ever forget:

I hadn't been craving pills, I hadn't been chasing doctors, I hadn't been stealing pills from friends, I hadn't been calling my pill dealer… I just had a raging headache, and what popped into my head was, "I could call Carrie and get one of her Vicodin—she would give me one or two."

So I did. I called her up, and it was one of those things like asking if she had any Diet Coke in the fridge. It was that easy, and she said specifically, "Are you sure you can take one of these? You have been doing so well." In my head I went straight to "Hey, I am a Waissmann method graduate—I am cured!" Yeah, right.

I figured it was only a headache, and I thought that a nice pain pill would fix it. I hadn't taken any opiate pain medication for a few months. There was no way I would go back to how hard I was going—it's totally impossible. I would never go to those depths I had gone to before. I just won't allow that to happen. I went to Carrie's house and had some great sex, and then she pointed to the bag of pills, which held probably sixty Vicodin. Any good pill addict can estimate within one or two pills how many are in a jar by shaking it or in a baggie just by eye-balling it.

No bullshit, I only took two and said, "Thank you for the porno style sex, and I will talk to you later." I took one of the pills upon my return to my office and washed it down with a Diet Coke. I didn't take them both at the same time, and that made me feel like I was okay and my old habit of taking several had died out.

Within ten minutes I got that beautiful warm feeling, and floating on puffy clouds, and it was all good. My headache was gone, and I wasn't screaming, "Damn it I need more fucking pills—where are they?!" I felt as though I had conquered a major problem and I was living proof that I could still take a Vicodin when I needed it.

In fact, I held the other Vicodin until the next day, when at the end of the long work day I popped the pill. On my way home from work I got the "warm fuzzies" again, but now a light went on in my head. Maybe I should have some Norcos as a backup—but no Oxycontin, those are too hardcore—just some Norcos. I will just keep them in the medicine cabinet for when I get one of those "headaches" that I normally never get. It couldn't hurt though, right?

The very next day I was in the office of one of my doctors complaining of new and further back pain. The beautiful thing was that I had been off for almost five months, and every doctor I had seen previously welcomed me back with open arms and I could get prescriptions wherever I wanted.

The pilot light for my addiction was back to the "ON" position, and those two Vicodin I got from Carrie would plant the seed for what was to be the most maniacal drug binge in my lifetime. The cat was out of the bag, and the cat wasn't screwing around. I was back, and on a mission.

SLEEP APNEA, WHO ME?

In 2003 I went to a continuing education conference for my broker's license down in San Diego. I went down there with a buddy of mine in the insurance business, named Tom. We shared a room at the Hilton, this is something I never did, share a room with another guy. But I think they were all booked up and the conference was right there in the hotel for two days. As much as I love my buddy Tom, I wish he had been a 5'7" blonde with blue eyes and of the female persuasion, but that's not what happened.

What did happen was that Tom got no sleep whatsoever. He's one of these guys who don't drink, don't do any drugs, and he is just a good husband and father to his two beautiful daughters. He's also a God-fearing man and is involved in his church in a big way.

Here's Tom, the straight-laced insurance broker rooming with insane Todd Zalkins, the out-of-control, sweaty, drug-addicted, part-time insurance broker because he likes to "play old punk rock on the weekends" guy.

As a joke, I brought along this ridiculously huge pullout porn poster of these super hot chicks getting nailed with dicks the size of canoes. I taped it up in our hotel room and I said, "Goodnight, Tom, sweet dreams, and say hello to those lovely girls."

Tom was completely mortified and could barely look at the poster of wonderful porn filth, "That's real pretty, Todd... real pretty... thanks for bringing that," he said in an exaggerated tone. I think I said, "I will bet you they don't have anything like that in church!!" There was no reply from Tom—he was done with me for the night.

Tom didn't sleep, he said I snored worse than anything he had ever heard in his life, and to this day he jokingly says he's still tired from that experience seven years ago. He was really concerned because he said I would be snoring in a profound way, and moments later there would be dead silence, and then maybe I would cough or start snoring again.

Either way, he said I should get it checked out and that there was definitely a problem with the way I breathed when I was asleep.

The next night Tom didn't sleep either because he was in fear I would die in the hotel room from not breathing. He was really adamant about my getting this checked out, and he was also adamant about the fact that he would never, so long as he lived, ever share a hotel room with me again. He means that to this very day.

I eventually got checked out at a sleep institute in San Clemente. It was pretty cool, they hook you up to a million monitors, and you're in this really comfortable environment, and you go to sleep—you go there like at 9 or 10 at night, then you leave in the morning after they have monitored you all night.

The questionnaire that I filled out before this evaluation had two special, specific questions that were very important, but I didn't find it important in the least to answer them truthfully:

*Are you currently taking any prescription medications?

Answer: No, Never.

*Do you drink alcohol or use drugs? If so, how often?

Answer: Rarely. Maybe a drink or two a week.

I am the lying asshole criminal of the decade for not being even remotely honest with the sleep clinic. But why would I want to be honest with them? I can't even be honest with myself, and I don't want some sleep doctor calling all my doctors telling them the pills are affecting my sleep. I might be dying in my sleep, but I am not going to have my precious sleep interfered with because I am cut off from my access to triplicate prescriptions.

This was serious, though. The sleep doctor contacted me immediately and said the following: "You have a very severe form of sleep apnea, one of the worst cases I have ever seen for a man of your age. You stopped breathing 40-50 times in the middle of the night and for a man your age (35 at the time) this is not very common. You need to call this number today and get set up for a CPAP breathing apparatus."

CPAP stands for Continuous Positive Airway Pressure, and this machine is used for critically ill patients in the hospital with respiratory failure, and for newborn infants. I was probably the first one mentioned, a "critically ill patient" who was knee-deep in the addiction to prescription narcotics.

I was prescribed one of those machines, and now I was really on a winning streak—well, that would be a slight exaggeration. The only reason I stopped breathing in the middle of the night was because I was under the influence of so many Oxycontin, Norcos, and Valiums—this had nothing to do with "Sleep Apnea." Had I answered the questions truthfully (like that would ever happen) it would have given heart attacks to the ones evaluating me.

*Are you currently taking any prescription medications?

Answer: Yes, depending on the day, anywhere from twelve to sixteen 80-milligram Oxycontin, ten Norcos, a Fentanyl, and three or four Valiums. That's per day by the way, and it's important to point out that the Norcos are strictly for "breakthrough" pain.

*Do you drink alcohol or use drugs? If so, how often?

Answer: Hell, yes. I don't drink every day, but I binge drink if I do, and that will entail eight to fourteen beers, another ten vodka tonics (triples), and four to six grams of high-grade, quality cocaine. That would be a normal night of partying.

I would love to see the photo of the doctor's face if he saw the answers written how they really should have appeared. I don't think the CPAP machine would have been prescribed—I am assuming it would have been more like a prescription to get my ass into rehab, immediately.

So, in effect I was overdosing nightly and if I didn't start wearing this oddball-looking mask attached to a machine that pumps air into me, I could die in my sleep.

This struck me really hard because the sleep doctor was not messing around. He indicated it could not wait another day and that it was possible that if I didn't wear this breathing apparatus, I could die in my sleep on any given night.

So I caved in, fully knowing that it wasn't sleep apnea—it was the disease of opiate addiction, and now I would have to wear a breathing mask just so I could see the next day.

Not once during this time did I think about reaching out for help. Deep inside I had an opinion of about a "3" on a scale of "100" with respect to how much I liked myself. The pain of getting off the pills is too much for me to handle, so why try?

I cannot tell you how many times I thought about not turning the CPAP machine on at bedtime, and just praying that I drifted off into a permanent sleep. The desire to die was now frequently on my mind.

Oxy Highway & "Death Sticks"

I had a cash-and-carry doctor in Santa Ana, a pain specialist doctor in La Jolla, and three other doctors to get regular scrippies from, as well as a friend in Long Beach who sold me 800 mg. Fentanyl lollipop "death sticks" as well as Oxys if I needed them. I never turned them down—if my buddy had the Fentanyl death sticks I never refused to buy them, ever.

The Fentanyl sticks are these little suckers that actually taste great and you are supposed to let them slowly dissolve in between your cheek and your gum line. I call them "death sticks" because Fentanyl suckers are shaped like a suppository, they are bone white, and taste like candy. They are also made for people in the most severe pain—cancer patients, people in hospice, and otherwise those on their deathbeds.

This is powerful medicine, and I would estimate that one of these sticks packs the power of five or six 80-milligram Oxys, all in one wonderful-tasting sucker. For me, I waste no fucking time— slow release is bullshit. I want fast release, and fast relief now. I am in a lot of physical and emotional pain, so I chew through the death stick within 30 seconds. (They should rest on your gum line for a half hour, minimum.)

I had all of the angles covered for my drugs, with multiple doctors and dealers, and I was prescribed close to 500 80 mg. Oxycontin a month, with a low street value of $27,500. This doesn't include all of the Norcos I scored by scrippie and the Fentanyl death sticks I was buying from my friend. I was taking thirteen to sixteen 80 mg Oxys a day—these are the big ones—along with eight to twelve Norcos, and a couple of 800 mg Fentanyl death sticks.

This is easily the equivalent of 100+ Vicodin a day. That is how deep I was going, and I was just blasted out of my mind, but that's how I wanted it to be and there wasn't any turning back or putting the brakes on.

This was 2004, and I was spending more and more of my time at home and becoming addicted to anything on cable that had murder-solving in it: Forensic Files, Cold Case Files, you name it. If it had a deep, scary, narrator's voice attached to the program, I was recording that shit on TiVo. I was so in love with Forensic Files that my girlfriend at the time got me an 8x10 autographed photo of Bill Kurtis, the host of the show. I still have it framed—I love that guy.

My entire world revolved around the following: Keeping enough drugs in my house at all times, keeping enough yogurt and granola with raisins in the kitchen, and keeping several boxes of "Dulcolax" laxatives in the house, of which I would take six to eight a day to ensure I would take a dump twice, maybe three times a week. Now, that's healthy.

The opiate pain meds slow everything down—your metabolism, your system in general, and all vital organs, including causing shortness of breath—and for me it was a death wish because my using actually required me to be on a CPAP machine to keep me alive.

With all of that stuff mentioned above, I was having a really great time with my life. Not really. I was rarely seen smiling, and I wasn't finding things in life fun—in fact, no one really saw much of me anymore. I was buried in my cave.

A shot of me and my buddy Rick Hazard. Things would get a lot worse than they appear here in this shot in just a few short years.

HAZARD AHEAD

At this time my friend Hazard and I started to snort the Oxys; I had had no idea I could do that. I am a slow learner, what can I say? Hazard, being a good friend and junkie, showed me how to do this. I knew you could chew the little turquoise gems to unleash the quick effect of the pills, I had been chewing Oxys and Norcos for a while now. But snorting? No way.

What you do is you soak the Oxys in a little glass of water for a couple of minutes, so the coating rubs off without any of the drug being wasted, and you are left with a pearly white pill custom-made in Satan's own laboratory. To this day I am convinced Oxys are the devil, because getting off of that shit is just a beast. It's so damn hard, but people do it, I did it, and I want to see and hear of more people doing it—that's why I am writing my little horror story.

Hazard and I would take six to ten Oxys and wash them all at once, then take a big binder clip (the kind you use to keep thick stacks of paper together) and mash the pills up into a sweet little white powder. Then we lined up long "rat tails" of Oxy powder.

Upon whiffing one of these bad boys, it is over, you are immediately put into a state of what we would call "perma-fucked" because you are good for nothing—you are lucky to make it to the fridge for the yogurt and granola, and then stumble into your television area to curse at "Dog the Bounty Hunter."

Speaking of Dog, what is up with that guy? He smokes like twelve packs of cancer sticks a day, wears 34 roach clips in his hair and leather bands around his arms like a porn star from the 80s, and his hair looks like a bad version of Bret Michaels from Poison.

He bumps around in his hell ride with his wife who has titties the size of a fucking boat dock, and the kicker is that the rest of his crew dresses the same way, with big cans of Raid to spray the fugitives with and big flashlights used to beat the shit out of the guy who's gassed on meth and rapping shit about his wife's big titties....Sorry for that rant, but I find it funny for one, and secondly, Dog rules... Don't fuck with the Dog!!

Okay, back to the fine art of whiffing big forearm-sized rat tails of Oxys. Upon graduating to this fine method of living, there really is nowhere else you can go—I could never shoot it up because I have had a lifelong fear of needles, which is why I have no tattoos and why I am alive today. Had I not had a prolific fear of needles I would have shot up long ago and died—there is no doubt in my mind.

So, we would whiff two or three of the Oxys each, all at once and melt into my living room furniture where I would punish my buddy Hazard by showing him repeats of "Dog the Bounty Hunter."

We were a real pair of pals, I tell you. Both of our lives completely revolved around keeping Oxys in our system. That's where this shit takes you. I have never met someone that just "uses Oxys on the weekends."

For the young kids and really anyone else out there thinking of trying Oxy casually, run the other way. I know some people who tried Oxy once and never did it again, but I also know far too many people who tried it once, got hooked, and are either now dead, strung out, or wish they were dead. I can relate to every bit of it.

Oxycontin is a masterful persuader, and once it gets its "hooks" in you it's very difficult to back away from. You want more, and soon enough there are no options—once the game is on, the drug seems to win time and time again.

One of my all time lows was when I had a huge pile of Oxys, enough to kill a full wing of residents at Betty Ford, yet I found it necessary to obtain a giant softball of black tar heroin, just to play with and smoke.

This heroin ball was as big as my fist, and I am sure that if I had that thing in prison I would be on the Forbes list of one of the richest guys in America. Hazard and I were just blasted out of our skulls on Oxys, and we would "chase the dragon" (smoke heroin) for dessert.

What's really ludicrous is the fact that it wasn't even doing anything for us, really—maybe for a few moments, but we were just too numb. The Oxys already put us in a state of total melted bliss, but to create some more fun a little black tar heroin just did the trick.

If my neighbors only knew what was going on inside that house of mine, there would have been a Federal Arrest Warrant for me.

Hazard, My Personal Assistant

I often had a very cruel sense of humor during this time. Hazard often depended on me to score some Oxys for him. I had all the access to the drug, enough for several addicts, not just me, by way of having multiple doctors and a dealer as my ace in the hole when necessary. Junkies are very good at knowing when their junkie friends are going to cop more pills—there's like this weird sixth sense we all get when something is brewing.

Hazard was so on top of this it was ridiculous. He knew what day I was seeing a particular doctor as well as the time of my visit, and what city this doctor was in. He was a real conscientious junkie friend—like a concerned mother he would frequently say, "Now Todd, remember you have that appointment down at Scripps hospital next Wednesday. Now don't miss that, as we all don't want to be dope sick."

The funny thing is that no pill junkie I know has ever missed a doctor's appointment for their refill. It just doesn't happen. I could cancel important business meetings, dinners with friends or loved ones—you name it I would cancel it—but never would I cancel an appointment to get a new triplicate prescription from my doctor. If I were without wheels, I would walk twenty miles if necessary to get my scrippie, this point should now be well made I believe.

The cure for me and all my problems in life was that winning lotto ticket known as a "Triplicate Prescription." Only the best of the best with respect to pills are prescribed on triplicate, and by now all doctors writing triplicates were scrutinized intensely by the federal government, maybe the DEA—I forget which entity, but it's serious and they don't mess around.

Pain management doctors make it very clear before treating you as a new patient that you must "not be under the care of another physician receiving similar narcotics." Are you kidding me? I needed to have two regular doctors, doctors on the side in every region of southern California, a dealer, and also friends and relatives to steal pills from when I could.

So, if my appointment was at 10:00 a.m. to get a new scrippie, I kid you not, Hazard had already taxed my voice mail by 10:25 making sure it was all good. If I did not return his call by 10:40, he was on me again via cell phone. Here's where the cruelty lies: I knew Hazard was "jonesing" like a mother, and he needed more pills to stay well, so when I would pick up his call I would say, "I'm sorry Hazard, but I can't hear you. I must be in a bad cell area... and you are breaking up... I don't know if my cell will ever work again."

Hazard would be losing his fucking mind by mid-afternoon. I would lead him on to the point where, looking back, it was so uncool of me. If the shoe was on the other foot I would have been homicidal over the ordeal.

To add insult to injury, there were countless times when after screwing with Hazard for seven hours or so, when it was finally time for him to cruise by to pick up some pills, I would ask—well, demand—that he pick up my dry cleaning as well as some yogurt and granola at the supermarket.

By this time, Hazard was almost going into seizures from not having any Oxys, and he would be forced to pick up yogurt and cereal and dry cleaning. The nail in the coffin for Hazard was when I intentionally locked my front gate.

There's poor Hazard, sick as a dog, holding my dry cleaning and yogurt, screaming for me to unlock the gate. I am probably thirteen Oxys deep as of 5:00 p.m., all numb and drooling like nothing was wrong. What a complete prick I was!

Heroin, Oxys, Fentanyl death sticks, Norcos, Valiums, and lots of coke inside my pad—I was just reeking of good living. I look back on this nightmare and I cannot believe that was me, but it was, and I still had some more suffering left in me. We will get to that for sure.

Rehab Part 2

It was late in 2005, and once again the constant chase and struggle of maintaining myself on all these prescription narcotics drove me to rehab. I obsessed over the notion of being off the shit, and I dreamt of how nice life could actually be if I were to get clean.

This was only in my dreams, because actually getting clean and sober takes a real, honest gut check and an enormous amount of desperation, and I wasn't ready. Subconsciously I wanted to be off everything, but I had to dig even deeper to locate my bottom. In the meantime, I checked in once more to South Coast Medical Center in Laguna Beach for another detox.

I recall one of the counselors talking with me, and the talk went like this:

Counselor: (looking at some medical chart) It sure looks like you take a lot of these opiate pills... Oxycontin, Norco, Fentanyl, Valium.

Me: No way—you're kidding. You must have the wrong chart, I am in here because I want to stop smoking pot. I can't get enough pot.

Counselor: Are you serious? I apologize, I must have the wrong information. I will be right back.

Me: Sounds good to me... and I hope you find who that chart belongs to... Sounds like he or she has a very bad drug habit.

Counselor: (returning a few moments later) Well, Mr. Zalkins, it appears you are a real wise guy today, aren't you? I did have the correct chart after all.

Me: Are you sure? Because I could show you photos of my bong collection on my cell phone—I have some of the biggest bongs you have ever seen.

Counselor: Are you through, Mr. Zalkins?

Me: Yes, I guess so... I apologize.

Similar to my rehab experience two years prior, I suffered for several days in detox, wanted nothing to do with a Twelve-Step program of recovery, detested all the counselors, and just wanted to feel better quickly. I managed to get through a whopping four days, and then I split. I went straight to my dealer's house in Costa Mesa and "re-gripped" with a shitload of pills.

It takes whatever it takes to want to actually do the work to get clean and sober, and there is a lot of work involved, at least for a guy like me. For me to rehash all the bullshit that happened in rehab that time is a waste of paper and a waste of your time. The experience was almost identical to my previous failed attempt at South Coast Hospital.

The bottom line is that I was in total fear and I wasn't ready, only a part of me wanted it. That's the problem, being the all-or-nothing person that I am, partway didn't count—it's one or the other, and I still had some more sickness to work on.

LET THE BAD TIMES ROLL

I found myself going into 2006 addicted once more. In fact, I had not entered a new year not addicted since I was a kid. This would be about 24 years of solid drinking, snorting, and popping. What's one more year? I don't know of any other way to live, plus I still have access to all of this disgusting medication that's supposedly legal.

One thing is for sure, I don't use the damn pills in a legal fashion, and I am scoring, popping, and snorting enough of these things to kill lots of people, yet I am still alive and I have not one clue as to how or why.

Using a CPAP machine to keep myself from dying each night was another reminder directly in front of me as to how sick I really was. Each day I woke up, took off this mask that kept me alive one more night, and shuffled (not walked) into my bathroom to take a leak. The stone tile was very cold on my feet, just like my heart. I didn't move quickly anymore unless it was to race to the pharmacy before they closed.

Life was a real struggle—I often stared into my bloated face in the mirror and saw my sad eyes and said, "Look at what you have become. You don't want this life—there is no beauty here, and you are totally fucked."

That scenario gives you a taste of what my mornings were like for years. The killer warm feeling the pills used to give me had stopped.

They don't do what they used to do, I am scared to death of trying to get off, and my insides now run cold and dark. I have tried so many times, I have done rapid detoxes for $10,000, I have done medical detoxes at home, I have been to rehab twice, and no matter what I try there seems to be no light at the end of the tunnel—because I am too goddamned scared, and I cannot admit that to anyone.

The physical craving for the pills is tremendous when detoxing, and each time I tried I felt more naked and raw than the previous attempt at getting off. It was my brain and body telling me that I was getting sicker and sicker, and that the end of my road among the living was not far off.

The idea of dying was so appealing, yet each time I went to bed at night I managed to turn on the CPAP machine one more time, to see one more day of my sick face in the mirror and to feel those cold stone tiles on my feet.

Countless times I said aloud to the CPAP machine, "All I have to do is not turn you on and not wear your sad little mask, and maybe I will just drift off into a permanent sleep. Waking up and chasing that shit is now such a chore—why do I put you on and desire another day of life? I don't live life. I am not a participant of life, not even a spectator, my eyes are closed and I can't see the truth. All that exists for me is my addiction, and nothing else is a joy because I don't find joy in anything."

The reason I could never go through with leaving my breathing mask off and risking death in the middle of my sleeping was because I had a miniature speck of hope that someday, maybe, I could turn things around. Someday, maybe I could ask for help and finally surrender. But not now—I have more drugs to take and I am surviving. In a really sick way, I am surviving.

GETTING DONE

2006 was a very difficult year for me. My world got smaller and smaller, my business was failing (or I was failing my business), and my level of isolation was at an all time high. Rarely would I go into my office, and if I did, it was to pick up commission checks that had arrived. I would race to the bank and race home to my cave where I could hide and not be seen by anyone.

Fear was all encompassing, and I felt safest at home with the door locked, the phone turned off (which didn't matter anyway because no one was calling me anymore), big jars of assorted pills, lots of yogurt and granola, and TiVo. That was my life, I was vacant of anything good.

My standard attire consisted of pajamas with either race cars, footballs, or funny looking dogs on them. I would drive down the hill from my home in San Clemente wearing these comical looking jammies, slippers on my feet, and a baggy sweatshirt to go to the market and stock up on more strawberry and raspberry yogurt, and of course granola with raisins.

I have no idea why I liked that crap so much. The customers and store employees must have found me to be such a joy to look at. Sweat running down my face, zero patience in the world for some asshole in front of me, and a shopping cart filled with—well, you know what was in the fucking cart... lots of yogurt and granola.

My demeanor was that of a homeless person, but I had a home. Most homeless people generally do not want to look you in the eye; they are defeated human beings and I wasn't any different. I could not look you in the eye, and I couldn't make one bit of sense because my speech was getting worse with my progressed addiction.

Having a place to live wasn't going to last much longer anyway—I hadn't truly worked a full week in more than two years and I was very non-productive in every facet of my life. I too was a defeated human being.

For the most part I have very little recollection of the first six months of 2006, yet for whatever reason I can remember most of the end of 2006. I remember almost every bit, yet I was more loaded, sicker, and more insane than I had ever been in my life. Go figure.

FURTHER DOWN

In early September of 2006 I was reaching further down emotionally and physically, and I was really at the end of my rope. You are probably thinking that I should have been at the end of my rope some time ago, but my path is what it is, and it's painful for me to reopen this chapter of my life.

But writing this book is about finding hope where there is none, and if this helps one person punch on through to a better life, it was worth my taking a trip back to the worst time in my entire life.

It's September 23, 2009 as I write this and I have a heavy heart, not so much because of what I am getting ready to write, but because my stepdad Darryl passed away a few days ago from the advanced stages of diabetes. He was a good father figure to me as a child, and I put him through a lot of hell in my teens and into my adulthood.

We had some incredible times together, and our most special moments were going to the UCLA football games together and wearing our hearts on our sleeves, win or lose. His illness reminds me all too well of the disease of addiction—slowly but surely it takes and it takes. With diabetes things start to shut down, they amputate some toes, they amputate a leg, the kidneys shut down, they put you on dialysis, the eyes lose focus, and the body cannot take any more, and that's what happened to Darryl.

He fought his disease the best he could, and in the end the disease took over.

Addiction is very similar, to me. It slowly robs the human being of his or her personality, their love, their ability to function properly—addiction takes hold of everything, including the spirit of the one who is suffering, and the soul goes with that too. Nothing to me is sadder than an amputated spirit and soul. Eventually there comes a turning point, and that is whether to face this sick addiction or succumb to it. Very few of us face it successfully, but we can do it, together.

Something told me to give it another shot to get off all the pills, yet again. I was getting much more desperate than in my previous attempts. Now, I would sweat constantly due to being so toxic, if I had been placed into a cold meat locker I would still have sweated profusely.

I was like a "sweat faucet" that ran at all times. Upon exiting the shower in the morning I would start perspiring, and by the time I was dressed my clothing looked like I had been in the rain without an umbrella, but there was no rain outside.

My body had been resenting the drugs for a long time, and something was changing. The Oxycontin and other pills were no longer doing for me what they did in the beginning. The little turquoise 80-milligram pill that gave me the warmth of a nice blanket was turning on me—it was no longer giving, it was taking.

My level of fear and agitation was on a constant rise, and no matter how many of the pills I took they didn't perform the miracles that they had done in the past. The blanket of warmth and comfort the pills provided was now much thinner, and even the Fentanyl death sticks didn't work.

HOME IMPROVEMENT

I wanted to buy another huge ball of black tar heroin, but I had this tremendous fear of needles, so that wouldn't work. I decided I would do another "medical detox" at the home of my girlfriend at the time in Newport Coast. I figured I would get through an upcoming fishing trip to La Paz I had scheduled with my good friend Steve, and come home and kick the habit—alone, of course.

The thing with me is that I do not want to seek outside help, I want to fix everything on my own, and this time I meant business, or so I thought. The other medical detoxes I had tried twice before, the two other medically supervised detoxes at home, and the $10,000 rapid detox/blood transfusion at the Waismann Institute were mere memories now.

I was determined to get clean—not sober, but clean. I had no intention whatsoever to stop drinking alcohol, and I may as well include cocaine because if I was drinking there would be blow involved. I wasn't drinking with the regularity I did years before—I was a pill addict, a straight up hardcore junkie. That was my problem, I thought, and I was hell-bent and focused on removing the pills from my life. Then everything would fall into place just fine and alcohol and whatever else I did was fair game.

Any pill addict can identify with the emotional turmoil of running out of the pills. Let's get this straight: Junkies and drug addicts are hands down the most ruthlessly determined people that exist in this world. There is no distance I will not drive to score, there is no limit to the lies I will tell, and if I have to break laws to get what I need to stay well so be it—that just comes with the territory when you are a crazed pill junkie like me.

If all the junkies in this world got clean and put all the energy they used to get drugs into some type of legitimate business, it would make Microsoft look like a fucking two-man gas station outfit. The time it takes to stay loaded and the energy involved literally had become my full time job, and my part-time job was getting more yogurt and granola.

Any other junkie who disagrees with that statement is one of the following: either they are not a junkie, or like most junkies they are so full of shit they can't admit the truth. I never wanted to hear the truth from others, but I knew I was a completely insane crazed junkie.

My closest friend Rich who lives in Hawaii would say, "Come on bro, you need to man up, strap on the boots, and kick this shit you are on... You can't lie to me, bro—you are so fucking sick it's ridiculous and it breaks my heart to even see you this way."

When I look back, my friend Rich's verbal bashing and unconditional love demonstrated that I wasn't fooling anybody. I needed to get well, but I was this walking contradiction living in a world of disgusting addiction, and I was in too much fear of the sickness that you experience when trying to get off—that was my biggest barrier, fear.

I was running out of pills in La Paz as planned. My last pill popping, chewing, and snorting would take place on the flight back home to Orange County. I would go to the medical detox doctor the following day who would create for me a hell on earth; a pill addict going through a detoxification from Oxycontin and Valium is one of the most extreme forms of sickness one can experience when it comes to getting off drugs.

Nothing gets good quick—trust me, nothing. You don't just cash in your chips and stroll into a detox program and expect to feel good in a few days. Anyone who has ever detoxed quickly and felt good in a week or two was never a pill addict to begin with. The ones who feel good quick are the ones who have toyed around with Vicodin for a little while or "tested the waters" with pills for a few months.

I was on this stuff for well over a decade, the opiates were deep into my tissue and even into the bones. An extreme anxiety came over me as I took my last few pills, and they did nothing for me at all—it was only delaying the impending doom of trying to detoxify.

Human Beehive

I took my last Oxy at around 10:00 p.m. on a weekday, and I was to see the doctor in the morning around 9:00 a.m. The discomfort started about four hours after my last dose, so at around 2:00 in the morning I was a mess. My skin started to crawl and the nervousness and shaking started to take hold of my entire being. My head was like a pinball machine, bouncing around like crazy, and my brain had flashing lights demanding, "What in the hell is happening here?"

It's a sight you would not ever forget to see a guy like me, sick as a dog, stumbling into a doctor's office. My face was pale, I could not write. I was drooling and slobbering, and shaking uncontrollably. No way could I drive a car. My girlfriend had to drive me, and I curled up in the front seat hugging myself and racing my hands up and down my arms like it was going to make a difference.

At around 10:00 a.m. I was given a Subutex (Buprenorphine), an opiate blocker that helps with the massive cravings and makes you feel good almost instantly. This is given to opiate addicts for their first five to seven days of detox, this magical tablet dissolves rapidly under your tongue and you get a very comforting feeling as a result of its powers. I had only had this once before during a home medical detox I had tried a few years earlier, which was not successful, as you can probably guess.

The little tablet dissolved instantly under my tongue, and within a couple of minutes my hands stopped shaking, my skin stopped crawling, and I had dodged another bullet—or so I thought. I would not be getting any more Subutex, this one was only to stop me from crawling off the walls and settle me down for a few minutes.

If I could unzip my skin and grab a "new suit of skin" to put on my body, I would do it. I would do anything to make this pain and nausea go away. It is ongoing and there is no end in sight. Every second feels like a minute—and an hour? Forget it. You just want the sickness erased from your system. My skin felt like little bees were stinging me everywhere, and it was non-stop.

I was given the drug Suboxone to take under the tongue every four hours or so. It helps the symptoms from the withdrawal, but not entirely. In fact, I think the Suboxone is the only thing that stood in the way of my committing suicide—a very attractive option when you are getting off of Oxycontin, Norco, Fentanyl, and Valium.

I was given something to sleep, I believe it was Trazodone, and that seemed to help me sleep for a few hours—but I had rats gnawing on my neck and back, and invisible spiders sped around on my skin like I was a human buffet. I swear I could feel these creatures but I couldn't see them, and this torture lasted for several days. I was very weak and could barely walk to the bathroom, liquids were the only thing remotely interesting to me, and soup broth was about as much as I could get down.

The biggest task I had was walking downstairs to turn on the television. Everything I watched I couldn't relate to, and people seemed so different to me while I detoxed. I trembled and shook and cried to myself, "Is this even worth it? I can't get to the other side of this, can I?"

Please Take Me from This Place

A t about day eight or nine I could actually walk without running out of breath. As junkies we get very weak in the muscle department, simply because once you are a full-time junkie you don't do a damn thing. My physical activities consisted of eating big bowls of frozen yogurt and granola, slobbering, nodding out in my big leather easy chair, and watching anything on cable that involved the solving of murder.

Once I regained a sense of balance at about ten days, I was still absolutely miserable. All of a sudden, like a train going through my head it hit me: I want a fucking drink! Right fucking now! I want to feel different and I think alcohol will do the trick for me! I don't want pills, but alcohol is okay, right?

Fuck it. I need a change of scenery—Long Beach, here I come.

I showered and nervously put clothes on (I had been wearing pajamas for months, because I like to be real comfortable while drooling and watching TiVo). I was off to Long Beach, my hometown, where I could find some friends who like to drink like I do, and I knew what would be coming the moment the buzz set in— my craving for cocaine, and a lot of it. I got into my convertible Porsche Carrera and raced up the road about twenty miles.

I had about as much business owning a Porsche as the DMV had even letting me operate a motor vehicle. I had bought the car in Newport Beach when I was gassed out of my mind off Oxys and booze. I thought to myself, I work really hard, and a Porsche is exactly what will make me feel better. I think I enjoyed that car for about eleven minutes after driving it off the lot, because I don't enjoy anything when I am addicted to pills. I had forgotten what joy was altogether.

In Long Beach I went to the infamous Joe Jost's on Anaheim Street and met some friends. I am sure I looked like I had just been dragged out of the grave and propped up. I took a sip of alcohol and it tasted shitty to me, but I wanted a lot more and then it didn't taste shitty anymore. The beer was flowing through me and then, bam!

That green light in my brain went on, the one that says, "It's time to get a grip of blow and snort our brains out." It was all coming together nicely. I was drinking, and soon I was going to be snorting some good old-fashioned cocaine from outer space. I had a great blow connection, straight mob stuff, and the dealer liked me a lot. On the holidays he would even give me a bunch extra as a "gift"—what a great guy!

After several schooners of cold beer, I called up my coke dealer and picked up about fourteen grams of Mafia blow. It's funny when a drug dealer says, "It's good to see you, mang." My dealer's attempt at saying "man" always had a "g" at the end so it sounded like Pacino in *Scarface*. "It's good to see you, mang"—I just loved hearing him say that to me.

That Lovin' Feeling

There was always a really great feeling when I knew that I was going to be scoring drugs, almost like a "high" before I even got high. The moment I knew it was "on," you would think I had just gotten away with robbing a bank—my attitude would be upbeat and life was wonderful. The flip side, however, was a whole different scenario. I didn't have too many experiences of not being able to score coke or my pills, I was a good "planner" for my drug use and I didn't fuck around in this regard.

Back at Joe Jost's I was ready to hear, "Night Train" by Guns N' Roses. That song played at full-tilt volume would put me into an indescribable frenzy. When Axl Rose screams, "Loaded like a freight train, flyin' like an aeroplane… feelin' like a space brain one more time tonight!!!" I simply lose my mind. Rack up some big rat tails of coke, mix me up a huge vodka tonic, and let's celebrate—I am off pills!

Some of the friends I was partying with said something like, "Yeah, it's good you are off all those pills. That shit is dangerous, not good for you."

Yeah, and lining up ten-inch lines of cocaine and throwing down tumblers of vodka is the healthy alternative. Sick as it may sound, as long as I was off all the pills, my using coke and booze justified itself. This doesn't mean I felt good about myself, though. I completely and utterly despised myself.

But feeling different is where I need to be, and I need to chase that feeling down dark alleys, to different area codes—hell, I will chase it to a different time zone if there will be enough drugs there for me.

I found myself in a spare bedroom at my friend's house. It was 4:30 in the morning, the birds were chirping, my head felt like a bus ran over it, my nose was a mess, my eyes were glazed over, I hadn't slept, my heart was skipping beats from all the coke, I was wearing the CPAP breathing machine I was terrified to not wear, and I said to myself, This is what it's come down to.

I am not in my own bed, I am in Long Beach, cold and alone, addicted, sick, and twisted. God, if there's a gun in this house put the barrel to my temple and squeeze the trigger now—it would be a privilege for me to die right about now.

This incident occurred in September, around the third week, and it would spark the biggest mission of drinking and snorting I have ever experienced in my life. The fuse was lit, and it wasn't long now until my world would explode and come to a screeching halt.

Choppin' Lines for a Party of One

Out of the next ninety days of my life I would proceed to drink and snort coke for about 78 of them. I barely slept and lost about 30 pounds, but I thought, "Just as long as I don't take any more of those fucking Oxys." And it would still get worse before checking into rehab in February of 2007.

I was on a tear—my head just demanded a steady flow of cocaine and alcohol. Never before was I an everyday user of cocaine. My friends and I would go on a binge, cool it for a few days, and then drink some more and that green light for cocaine would be triggered.

For sixteen years I was on a steady diet of pain pills, booze, and cocaine, with the pills being the dominant controller of my life. My heart was starting to hurt physically, but I would still race to the coke pile to ingest more of it.

I wanted to be off the pills more than anything in the whole world, and I was, but I could not shut my head off. It would not calm down, and there was this insatiable appetite for more and more coke and booze. I thought it was just a phase, as I was still detoxing from the Oxycontin and Valium.

My days were spent like this: no sleep, if I was lucky, maybe an hour or so from 4:00 a.m. to 5:00 a.m. No coffee was necessary to wake up, as I would rack up a few lines of coke and start the day, and this was accompanied by a few Bloody Marys or beers by mid-morning.

By 11:00 a.m. I would start to feel straightened out, but this would only last for a few minutes. At 11:20 or so, the craving for more blow and alcohol would set in. I was chasing something I could never reach or capture, ever again.

I was in my office pretending to work two days a week with the blinds drawn, and one light on to allow me to see the pile of white powder. Paranoia was my hobby now, and I would jump out of my skin just hearing the fucking mail slide through the little "mail slot" on my front office door.

I was barricaded, and a few times I took a cab home from my office because I couldn't walk—thank God I did. I am not going to mislead you though, I wasn't at my office very often, and if I was I couldn't talk to any clients on the phone (I was losing them all anyway). I just managed to put on some decent clothes and raid my office fridge for beers while I lined up more coke and wondered if or when I was having a heart attack.

After being off of the pain pills for twelve days or so, I felt it necessary to obtain some more Oxycontin and Fentanyl sticks to help ease the pain of the vicious coke and booze hangovers.

The pain I would feel coincided with the depression that the cocaine/booze hangovers gave me, made me want to dissolve into a grave, yet it was so easy to pick it up again and charge on through for another mission of pain and suffering.

I am really good at putting myself through severe emotional and physical pain as a result of using. I just don't want to address any life problem without drugs as my coping mechanism. Why would I? I know of no other way, and plus, I am a professional at using—and at feeling miserable.

This cycle went on and on for close to 80 days. My afternoons and nights were spent in Long Beach in the spare room of a friend, shaking and paranoid as I dove deeper and deeper into a cocaine-induced psychosis.

It was a raging "fuck the world" mission of Oxycontin, morphine pills (which I just scored), cocaine, Fentanyl, and liquor, and not once did I feel great. The best it ever got during this time was a feeling that I didn't need more, and that lasted only a few moments and then I needed more. Any fellow addict can identify with this empty, dark feeling—if not you aren't a sick addict, most likely, and I hope you never have to experience what I did.

Life isn't fair and I knew that, if life were fair I would have been dead or in jail. The "good times" of drinking and using drugs had faded into the abyss long ago. The laughter among friends and the funny pranks were now replaced with extreme antisocial behavior and a minimal circle of friends.

The telephone was only used to arrange a drug purchase from my dealer to score drugs and to call someone to meet me to use them—no longer was I returning calls from clients, and real friends and family members had stopped calling long before.

Me and one of the best friends I've ever known,
Rich Fletcher. Taken while visiting him in Hawaii
around 1998.

My Wake up Call

I was slowly dying and deep inside I knew that, wishing it would end much quicker. Somewhere I had crossed this invisible line from somewhat caring about living, to being hell-bent on giving up on it entirely. Breathing wasn't interesting to me anymore. When I crawled back to my home in San Clemente it would be cold inside from not being lived in. It would be very cave-like as I sat in a chair with lines of coke, a glass of vodka next to me, and the room dimly lit.

Looking back on this time of my life I realize I had not laughed for months, maybe even years. Nothing was remotely funny, and I think I had lost my sense of humor due to this sickness. Once you really start to lose the things that matter is when you contemplate the meaning of your existence.

I had no sense of purpose at that time, the days were now longer and longer, and my heart was skipping beats. This was a sign that internally things were shutting down—the body can only be so forgiving and tolerate so much abuse.

It was in late November that I received a call from my dear friend Rich in Hawaii. The news was horrible... his ex-girlfriend from years past with whom he was still friends had overdosed from a combination of alcohol and pain medication. I had known Cammie since I was in seventh grade. We were the same age, and she was one of the most beautiful girls I had ever seen.

On top of that she was very sweet and had just a classic way about her. This was the type of woman who caused car accidents due to her physical beauty, yet I always knew she had beauty on the inside too.

It was serious, and she was in a coma. Eventually there was a liver transplant procedure performed and from what I understand she was on life support. She would end up passing away more than two years later after being hooked up to machines that kept her alive. That is the price tag that can come with this horrific disease, and it easily could have been or should have been me long before.

For the first time in my life I realized that if I didn't get help I would soon die. It took the falling of a former school classmate to make me realize this. Wake-up calls come in different ways for people; for me it was hearing about this beautiful woman, Cammie, who was so full of life and had a son, and had never lived the life I had lived or traveled the sick paths I chose to travel. It was one of those things where you say, "That should be me, and not her."

I forever owe my wake-up call to what that amazing, beautiful woman went through. God bless you always, Cammie. Since her passing I have forged a very close friendship with the father of their child, Jimmy. Of all places, we met at a recovery meeting where Jimmy shared about how Cammie had passed away a few days before.

I attended Cammie's wake in Long Beach where many heart-broken people gathered in her honor. It was a small "high school reunion" of sorts, but I know that everyone there, and myself included wished we were there for other reasons.

Today I have a friendship with Jimmy that leans more towards that of a brother, straight up he's family to me. He has more than twenty years of sobriety, and is a great single father to their son, Shante.

One of the most beautiful things is that we often surf together, the three of us, and it's a real joy to see both father and son ride waves together. Occasionally we all ride the same wave together and scream, "Carpool!!!" in unison.

LIFE OF THE PARTY

Before my good friend Rich called to tell me about Cammie, it had been many months since I had talked with him. The last time I had seen him it was a disaster. He had come to Long Beach from Hawaii to celebrate his lovely mother June's 80th birthday, which was going to be a surprise party. Anyone who knows Rich's mother loves her, she is a wonderful human being, and I love her very much.

I was invited to June's 80th birthday celebration and I didn't even attend, although I had planned to be there. What ended up happening was I drove up to Long Beach with a nice bouquet of flowers for June, but I was early for the party. So I took a nap on their concrete porch induced by several Oxycontin, and from what I have been told it wasn't a pretty sight. I was slobbering and incoherent as Rich and his friend Dylan showed up early for the party.

I just handed the flowers to Rich and said, "Tell June Happy Birthday for me... I am not feeling well, my back hurts." What a bunch of bullshit that was—I was just an embarrassing, sick pill junkie who could not be present for a dear friend's birthday party. But that's what I did in my addiction—I failed with my commitments.

Failing to come through is something I was specialized in, and if I didn't feel up to doing anything (which I never did) I would just create some bullshit excuse about my back not feeling well or not even let you know I wasn't coming.

Why the hell would I? I will only do something if it's convenient for me or if I am well enough to attend. If I don't have one or both of those going for me, all bets are off and I am not doing a damn thing. The only thing attractive to me in my pathetic addiction to prescription pills is a comfortable chair, lots of yogurt and granola, and TiVo loaded with a lot of forensic murder-solving shows I can watch for hours while I drool on myself.

This sounds pathetic I am sure, and that's because it is pathetic. But I knew of no other way to act when I was deeply involved in my addiction. I seek the cozy warmth and comfort that all those pills provide—it's my oxygen, my food. It's everything to me.

You can put me anywhere on this planet, and as long as I have a big grip of my Oxys and Norcos and a comfortable chair or couch, my life is perfect. Hell, you can put me in the middle of the streets in Calcutta on New Year's Day during a soccer riot, and I would just smile with the comfort and joy that opiate pills provide me with. Or so I believed.

So there's an example of what I would do to my best friend in the world, on a day when I should have been present to celebrate his mother's surprise party, but I chose concrete steps and drool in the corner of my mouth.

Rich's phone call planted the seed that my number was coming up, but I still wasn't all the way done. It would take another two and half months of total cocaine and alcohol abuse, along with getting back on the train of Oxycontin, Fentanyl, and morphine pills one last time.

I didn't stand a chance against this disease. I had played my best hand and I lost. No matter what I did, no matter how I mixed up the ways I drank and used, I would never get back to that place of ecstasy where it had once taken me. Everything had officially stopped working, yet I carried on, the wounded soldier of addiction on his last tour of duty.

Cut Off

It would be an injustice to those reading this if I didn't tell you that at this time I had been "fired" as a patient by my doctor at Scripps, and that was a loss of 240 Oxycontin—the big ones, 80 milligrams. My prescription count for Oxys was down from 400 to 160 per month. Having this happen to a junkie like me is no different than a patient with a life-threatening illness like cancer being told, "I'm sorry, Mr. Zalkins, but I just can't treat your illness anymore. I can no longer give you the cure."

I had been given a warning by my doctor at Scripps after they were notified that I was also seeing the "cash and carry" criminal doctor in Santa Ana. I had gotten away with one warning, and I flew under the radar for a while and avoided detection, but all triplicate prescriptions get logged into some computer system where they can track all your refills.

That cracks me up today. If there was a printout of all the pharmacies and doctors that I saw for "treatment" and to pick up drugs, it would look like the "Thomas Guide for Junkies."

Dozens of major chain pharmacies from San Diego to Santa Barbara plus mom and pop independent pharmacies (they were my favorite) had been visited by yours truly.

One of the things that used to really crack me up was when the pharmacy tech-assistant would say, "Did you know these drugs are very addictive, Mr. Zalkins? Have you had Oxycontin and Norco before? We would like the pharmacist to review the instructions with you."

I would have a look of astonishment, and pseudo-concern, "No kidding, they are addictive? I had no idea... Yeah, that's a good idea—let's gets the pharmacist over here for a review of how I should take these... I don't want to develop a problem with these pills just because of this little bit of back pain I am having."

What a crock of bullshit. What I really wanted to say was, "Thank you for that kind offer, Stephanie, but you are talking to the world's authority on pills. I have lied and cheated to get these little gems for more than a decade. Now, do us all a favor and tell the pharmacist you just sold pills to the Professor of Pill Takers, and help save the environment while you are at it—there is no need to staple the fucking little receipt, with the little fucking instructions, onto a little fucking bag. It's a waste of paper...

"Plus, the moment I turn around from your little white counter I am going to tear open the bag, steal a Diet Coke from off the shelf, chew two Oxys, with a few Norcos as a backup chaser, and melt into your parking lot... Are we clear here, Ms. Pharmacy Tech? Oh and Stephanie, one more thing? I should also have you be aware that I love pills so much my brain tells me to stop breathing 40 to 50 times each night, and the only reason I am alive is due to the assistance of my trusted CPAP machine."

Never did I say something as ridiculous as this to a pharmacy employee. These people were the most important people in the world to me—even more important than my family and loved ones.

In my disease if the ship is going down, I would dread the decision if I could only "take one person with me"—the person keeping me loaded and from getting sick versus a loved one, it's a very tough call.

This is the thinking of a very deranged person. But when you are as deep as I was with the prescription addiction, it will dictate every move and decision. Nothing is clear in my head, and I am totally irrational. So long as I have my supply of pills I can get through my day, if not then get the hell out of my way because nothing will stop me from getting them. Let's all just get along here—give me the pills I want and need, and this world will be perfect, for now.

I was now officially cut off from the doctor who wrote my scrippie for 240 Oxy's a month, and even the "cash and carry" doctor in Santa Ana was notified to cut me off in late November of 2006. Moving forward, I had to depend on one doctor, one dealer, and a friend in Long Beach.

That's okay though, this is just a temporary inconvenience, or so I thought. I can seek and find other local doctors to supply me with what I need to stay comfortably screwed.

Junkies are very resourceful, and I am on the Board of Directors for "Junkie Resource, Ltd." But I wasn't going very far anyway—the drugs were no longer able to drive the "making Todd feel good train," so I just supplemented with Vitamin Cocaine.

ME VS. MOTLEY CRÜE'S BODYGUARDS

It was around this time (late October or early November, 2006) that a guy I know in San Clemente had two all-access passes for the Aerosmith and Motley Crüe show down at Coors Amphitheater in San Diego. Bumout was a local artist in San Clemente and we had some mutual friends in common. He had somehow sold one of his paintings to Tommy Lee, the drummer of Motley Crüe, and he liked his artwork—hence our connection for the passes.

Bumout and I had it all lined up for us to go see the show, and I of course paid for everything which is what I usually did anyway. We took a limo down there, stocking it with enough booze to kill an infantry and enough cocaine to make our own snowboard run. I was a mess going into this debacle, having not slept right in weeks and still charging on this prolific pill-chewing, space-coke-snorting, booze bender.

I was still excited though. I loved Motley Crüe's first album, "Too Fast for Love." Back in the day, my friends and I would play "Live Wire" over and over and break everything in sight, and I still love that song. People would have killed for these passes, and I had been excited to go for weeks.

Aerosmith were some of my all time heroes and they can still rock like a mother. I think it was 1978 when "Live Bootleg" came out—I was eleven years old, and when I heard it I loved it instantly. It was a double album that opened up to these incredible photos of the band that to me was the epitome of rock and roll. When I heard "Sick as a Dog" and "Draw the Line" on that record, I lost my mind.

Before the limo picked us up, Bumout and I were throwing down beers and shots of Jaeger. I started to pack my beak with coke and I couldn't wait to hear, "Kickstart My Heart" by Motley Crüe. That song was written by bass player Nikki Sixx from his basically being brought back to life after overdosing off heroin, after being pronounced dead! The fucker was brought back to the living, and he wrote that epic, charging rock song as a result of the near-death experience.

The crazy thing is that I would listen to "Kickstart My Heart" at full blast, a song about almost dying from drugs and an experience I believe Nikki Sixx got sober after, yet I was racking up massive lines of coke and doing shots of booze like it was water, and just thinking, "What a great fucking song this is—please line me up more rails of cocaine!" That made perfect sense to me at the time.

So we got down to San Diego after crawling in traffic and having to piss nineteen times on the way down, and of course snorting more coke every time we stopped. But I had planned way ahead, I had big vials of coke all ready, no chopping necessary, so we snorted in the limo, in bathrooms—it made no difference. I brought about half an ounce with me, about fourteen grams, which is plenty for a few people going to a rock show. Isn't that how people get ready to go see their heroes of rock?

We were late to the show, and what was the song I heard as I raced up to will call for our passes? Motley was busting off "Kickstart My Heart" and I was so anxious to get in to the show. I had ten grams of space coke in my pocket, you know, for when I was going to "bro down" with Tommy Lee after the Crüe killed it on stage.

I was sweating and holding up my plastic "All Access" pass to the security who were everywhere. I managed to get to the side of the stage where no one else seemed to be—the people with all access were on the opposite side, so I thought I hit pay dirt. Just me and these security guards, and I was about ten feet away from Nikki Sixx.

There were these two little fuckers on stage wearing Skull masks and they were obviously tied in with the band. One of them rolled up to me and said I couldn't be standing where I was, he was aggressive but not being a total dick.

I replied, "I have this all access pass."

He said, "I don't give a shit."

I said, "Suck me off, you queer, I am not going anywhere."

Within seconds a Samoan security guard the size of an apartment building appeared. This guy was big—the type of "big" that no matter how loaded you are, you know that this person could kill you just by breathing on you. That's how gnarly this guy was, and he was not fucking around at all. It would have taken an elephant gun just to get this guy to slow down from beating me.

He grabbed me by the neck, and I immediately apologized, and he just told me to, "Shut the fuck up."

I was completely butthoused-drunk and high off coke as I was walking with this "Samoan Mountain," and there was something in me that said, "I am going to die, and this guy is going to fucking kill me," so I said nothing.

I had enough blow on me to land me in prison for sure and there were cops everywhere. I was escorted out of the VIP area but I still had my pass, so I went to the very front row of the show. Being the intelligent chap I am I took it upon myself to get the attention of the guys on stage with the skull masks. Once I got their attention I was flipping them off, telling them to eat a dick, and suggesting that they should perform fellatio on one another in front of the 20,000 guests.

This was again poor judgment and behavior on my part. I was soon joined by a San Diego Police Officer and a security guard. The cop ended up being the nicest he could possibly be, and he simply said, "You are going to have to settle down and stop pissing off Motley Crüe's personnel."

I had huge rocks of coke in my pocket, several grams in glass vials, and I immediately responded, "Yes, sir. I will settle down immediately." And I did, until Aerosmith was on and played "Draw the Line" (a song dedicated to the snorting of cocaine) and "Sick as a Dog." I had found some other guy I didn't even know and we were arm in arm crashing into people losing our fucking minds to the music.

We were those two guys out of 20,000 where half the crowd was saying, "Look at those two stupid-drunk assholes." That's exactly what we were, insane and a complete embarrassment, plus scaring most persons within a hundred yards of us. Don't ask me how I managed to avoid arrest, as I most certainly deserved it.

But the grand finale was when we were hanging out by Tommy Lee's trailer after they had played. (Bumout had done some artwork for Tommy Lee as I had mentioned earlier, so they "knew each other" in a Hollywood, bullshit kind of way.)

The kicker was when we were finally let in to say "Hello" and meet Tommy Lee, and I was introduced by Bumout and Tommy Lee replied, "Is that the insane motherfucker that wrecked my assistants tonight?"

"Uh, yes, that was me but I am no longer that nuisance," I replied.

Tommy Lee just laughed at me and said, "Jesus Christ, keep an eye on your boy here, Bumout—our guys almost had him killed."

I was breathing this sigh of relief, just saying to myself, "No shit, no fucking shit." I immediately bailed out of the trailer feeling like a really not-so-wonderful type of guy, and I assaulted the Jaegermeister Machine outside Tommy Lee's trailer. You know you are a rock star of substance when liquor companies like Jaeger put "all you can drink" dispensers of their not-so-inexpensive booze wherever you play shows.

I have not had any liquor companies sponsor me, although maybe Club Cocktails could have sponsored me as the "Dirt Bag Who Drinks on Campus Guy" and I could have received free Brass Monkeys. However, I could definitely be the official spokesman for Oxycontin, and my television commercials would sound something like this:

"Hello, my name is Todd Zalkins. You can call me OxyTodd. I love Oxycontin! I love the way it makes me feel, it removes all my physical and emotional pain, and I also am really addicted to this shit—I will forge prescriptions and lie to all doctors just so I can get it.

"Oxycontin is the best thing that's ever happened to me and for some reason I just can't stop taking it I love it so much, Oxycontin has destroyed my life and it will destroy yours, so fucking run from this crap as quickly as possible!"

The criminals who make Oxycontin probably wouldn't approve of my improvised plug, but I could definitely be their spokesman.

The limo ride home from the Motley Crüe & Aerosmith show had the same ending as several hundred other nights. I couldn't get high anymore no matter how much I used, it wasn't fun anymore, I couldn't have a good time doing anything, and I was losing my mind.

So, I was dropped off at my house in San Clemente at around 1:30 a.m. where I chalked up some lines of cocaine as I sat in the lazy boy chair and looked around at my home. I was all alone... it was cold, three bedrooms and two and a half bathrooms of coldness.

The walls were reeking of addiction and unhappiness. I just sat there stoned out of my head in my leather recliner thinking, this should have been a really fun night. But it wasn't fun, and I don't think I had experienced a fun night in about five or six years.

Me and the best step-father a kid could ever wish for,
Darryl Wright. This shot was taken in the mid-90's,
well before I had graduated to Oxycontin.

A Junkie for a Fan (UCLA vs. USC)

Since I was a young boy I went to the UCLA football games with my stepdad, Darryl. He was psychotic for UCLA football, even though he played at Long Beach State he was raised as a Bruin by his dad who had graduated from UCLA.

I had dreams of going to UCLA all of my childhood, but there is a certain requirement to get into that fine learning institution— "good grades." I ceased getting good grades in junior high school, or middle school, or whatever the hell they call it nowadays. Drugs and alcohol is what I studied, and I studied really hard.

Some of my best moments as an adult were when Darryl and I got closer after having been distant due to my behaviors from drugs and drinking. When I became dedicated in the commercial insurance field he saw me turning around, and I was just starting my addiction to the prescription pain medicines.

He and I would go to some really neat places when UCLA was playing away, like to Seattle to see them play the Washington Huskies, and many other beautiful environments.

We would always cap off the day with an unreal dinner—Darryl loved great food and we would seek out the best of it, often driving way out of the way just to try some special dish at a little restaurant he had read about. I enjoyed the drives in the rental cars after the games, as I would pop a few Vicodin and either celebrate the UCLA win with Darryl or we would be in agony over the loss. But great food always made a bad loss okay, especially when four or five Vicodin were my appetizer and dessert.

The UCLA–USC games were the biggest each year, and we would be really charged up; on game day we turned into borderline lunatics, and I am convinced it is the greatest rivalry in all of college sports. Even though a lot of USC fans say that playing Notre Dame is their game of the year, just check out a Trojan fan after they have lost to the Bruins—it's like someone died, and the same applies to us as Bruin fans. If UCLA loses, which they have done a lot lately to USC, it's just a killer.

In 2006 the Bruins were really outmatched against a very heavy-duty USC team, ranked #2 in the nation I believe, while the Bruins were unranked which wasn't a surprise. The Trojans had it all—speed, size, and talent. The game was in November as always, and the Bruins were major underdogs. The funny thing about this rivalry is that anything can happen, and I have been witness to the most unreal comebacks as well as utter heartbreaks from losing in the last seconds.

On the eve of the big game I was a nightmare, but I was going to the Rose Bowl the next day with my friend Bumout. The big game is very special to me and I have never partied hard the night before (on the night after the game is a whole different story). But this time, Bumout and I found some other guys to party with and I found myself taking three hits of Ecstasy (not my drug of choice), snorting several grams of coke, drinking like it was going out of style, and chewing Oxys. That's how I spent the evening of the big game—something I had never, ever done.

I got about an hour of sleep and woke up to three or four huge Bloody Marys, triples for sure, plus I racked up several lines of blow while Bumout was still asleep. I felt like an Amtrak had hit me, but after throwing down some Oxys and Norcos, I felt all right.

My feeling decent lasted about thirteen minutes, and then I started breaking into these horrific sweats and my hangover was brutal.

But it was game day and we were going! Bumout and I got on the freeway, and I had several vials of coke ready to keep me going. Never had I brought drugs into the Rose Bowl, especially on a day like UCLA vs. USC. We arrived in Pasadena and a friend of mine met us at a market so he could buy some blow from me. I snorted blow every chance I got, at the supermarket and in my car. My agitation was out of mind as we were fighting to get into the parking lot, the game was sold out and things just moved a lot slower than usual.

The lot was full, so we parked in the residential neighborhood of Pasadena where we had two coolers full of vodka and beer. I was now drinking the vodka straight and several beers, as well as ducking into my driver's seat to pack my beak with space coke, and I thought I was doing okay.

I was far from okay—all of the years I had had so much passion for such a huge rivalry, and a day that was bigger than Christmas for Darryl and me (Darryl was in the hospital at this time suffering from the advanced stages of diabetes). My heart was skipping beats and sweat raced down my face, and I could not change the way I felt—I kept going hard with the alcohol and drugs.

I saw kids and adults hustling into the game, and here I was the biggest scumbag on the planet. I hadn't slept at all, and I was piling cocaine into my nose, one nostril was starting to bleed, and I could not get enough alcohol into my system. Nothing felt right, and yet I kept marching on in my sickness, pretending I was having a good time. I hadn't had a good time in years. We took the long walk into the game and I reached into my pocket and chewed a few Oxys to "straighten out," like that was really going to work.

Inside the Rose Bowl both Bumout and I saw UCLA upset USC 13-9. This was one of those days where if both teams played this game a hundred times, USC would have beaten the shit out of UCLA 99 of them. The Bruins played inspired defense, and their young, inexperienced quarterback played smart and made some huge plays.

Never in the past had I left my seat at the Rose Bowl for this game unless to rush to the rest room to take a leak. I spent probably half of this game inside of the bathroom stuffing my beak with blow as I hid out in one of those filthy stalls with toilet paper and piss everywhere. For me, it was the place I needed to be. I was buried in my "urinal cocoon" to be safe and away from people while I trashed my system with more drugs.

After the game, all UCLA fans were just ecstatic and the USC contingent looked like they couldn't find their lost puppies. I was with Bumout walking to my car, and I threw down some Oxys and I could not walk correctly. It must have been a real pretty sight, I am sure. We got to my car and it wouldn't start—the battery had died from leaving everything open and cranking music for three hours while we drank and snorted.

At that moment, I realized how truly empty I was as a human being. I didn't have much time left to live, I just knew that, and that's a very scary place to be. My car not starting was just like my life—my batteries were dying out, and I felt like the loneliest person on the planet.

Merry Fucking Christmas

My hangovers from the coke and booze were too much to handle, so I started taking more and more of the Oxycontin along with eight to twelve Norcos a day. I would snort the Oxys and chew the Norcos to bleed whatever I could out of the small pills, hoping for the effect I missed so much. I was also "lucky" enough to score some more 800 mg. Fentanyl death sticks as well.

So I was back on the train, what was to be my last run. I continued to use coke and drink and use the death sticks and Oxys to save my ass in the morning. My clothing no longer fit me, I would constantly sweat, and I rarely left the house. I was scared of the fucking mailman, and even scared of my neighbors—I would duck as soon as I saw them; just knowing that I looked like hell and that I couldn't carry on a sane conversation had me in a constant state of fear.

Talking with others was out of the question as I would just stutter and drool, with both of my eyes shifting in different directions.

Early in December, I could no longer sleep at all. I went with my girlfriend at the time to see her extended family in Vancouver. Everyone I saw seemed to be happy and joyful. It was the holidays and people were lit up, the city was beautiful, and I was just dying inside. I was sleep-deprived, addicted to opiate pain medications, cocaine, and alcohol. I was starting to become delusional—often when I looked at something, I would have to shake my head really fast, shut my eyes and open them, to validate that whatever I saw was real, and that is a scary spot to be in.

We always stayed in a beautiful hotel when we went to Vancouver, and it's such a magnificent place. The food there is amazing and the people were always very kind every time we visited. But on this trip in 2006 during the holidays, everything in me had gone cold and black. I would overhear people talking, saying things like:

"We are going to Mom and Dad's. The whole family will be there, all eleven of us, and then we are going skiing at Whistler," or, "Grandma makes the most incredible pies at Christmas, you should all come over."

I would hear people conversing like this and listen to all of the love going around, and yet I couldn't identify with any of it. I could remember being happy, at least some of the time, but I could no longer manifest a marginal smile or belly laugh.

To me that is just heartbreaking, when you can't reach down into yourself and change what's going on. For me, that was a sign that everything I had done up to that point with drugs and alcohol had truly turned against me, and I could take no more.

BURY ME

Each morning on the 19th story of the hotel as my girlfriend was getting ready, I would be on the balcony drinking a beer, having not slept and wanting to jump to my death. I thought how easy that would be, but something in my head said, "Shit, that sure would hurt for a millisecond."

That's the type of fear I was operating in. I cannot even come up with a good suicide plot because I'm convinced the pavement will hurt me for a whopping millionth of a second or the bullet going into my brain sure will sting. How fucking nuts is that? I guess it's that insanity that kept me alive, because I had no real desire to live, which was getting more and more apparent by the minute.

On Christmas Eve I had not slept in nineteen days. I had stopped the cocaine use for the time being, but as tired as I was I would just lie in bed fully aware of how much I wanted to sleep. My head just wouldn't shut off, as though the circuits in my brain had exploded and there was no chance that it would function properly.

This scared the shit out of me. I would look over at the woman in my bed sleeping comfortably, happy in a deep sleep, and all I could do was wish and hope for a better day. Maybe I will sleep the next day? But the "next day" never came, and I couldn't understand why I couldn't rest. I was no longer stuffing coke into my nose, which was the thing that usually kept me awake—now it was just Oxys and Fentanyl sticks, and nothing would settle me down.

It's safe to say that at this point I was totally insane. There had been some pressure by my girlfriend for us to get engaged and I could understand that. She had put up with a lot of my terrible behavior, and much more that I would never subject her to because she wasn't into drugs at all. The pill addiction was no secret, and she knew how badly I wanted to get off them. As we were on a walk through Stanley Park, a place I had enjoyed many times before I was so sick, I got on one knee and I proposed.

In my mind I had a good idea that I was insane and had no life coping skills remaining. I know for certain I had no business asking for her hand in marriage—I was dying anyway, and I knew that. My selfish, addicted head didn't want to be left alone, so I thought maybe she could help fix me. She had done as much as she could, but I have since learned that no one in this world can get someone well unless the one who is suffering and addicted has the desire or willingness to change.

At Christmas Eve dinner I excused myself from the table and returned to my hotel room, alone and crying uncontrollably. I could no longer get a nice warm effect from the pills, yet I was petrified to even get clean. I had to do something, and so I lay there with puddles of tears talking to God.

"God, please help me… I know this is not how you want me to live, but I know of no other way… God, please help me." It was a happy time for all the people around me, during Christmas in beautiful Vancouver, BC, but I was the most lost soul there. All I could do was lie in my hotel bed, look over at my nightstand with tears streaming down my face, and put the CPAP breathing machine on to keep me alive for another day.

It was at that moment I realized I was going to get help and be serious about it for the first time in my life. But I would go on popping every pill I could get my hands on—and drinking and snorting blow as well—until February 16, 2007.

I'M ALL DONE.

Upon returning home from the worst Christmas in my life, I led a caveman existence in my cold home in San Clemente. From the outside you would think a stable, middle class guy resided there; if you went inside you would see a home without any life in it, so cold that you could see your breath when you exhaled. My fireplace was no longer being used, I was no longer going to the side of the house to get firewood, and I had loved doing that once upon a time.

I had a heater that worked throughout the whole house, but I wouldn't use it. I liked to be bundled up in pajamas and sweatshirts and thick socks, scared to death of where my life was now. The front gate was kept locked to prevent any neighbors knocking on my door. I was scared of all human beings, any noise to me was foreign, and every fiber of my being was connected to a circuit connected to my worst fears. I was the "Supreme Isolator."

I had hardly slept in 23 days, so I figured why not add to the misery of not sleeping and buy a huge amount of coke and snort until the wheels came off. The best part of my day was after about nine or ten lines of blow in the morning plus some Oxys, when I would put the top down on the Porsche and race around my neighborhood cranking, "Sympathy for the Devil" by the Stones. I would play that song 25 times in a row as the cocaine dripped into my throat and the pills glazed my eyes, celebrating how fucking awesome the Rolling Stones were.

I was chopping lines for a "party of one." With large piles of coke, I would nervously chop and form lines in my home office, kitchen, and living room—that way I didn't have to remember where the coke was when I wanted to snort more. There were now morphine pills I scored called Kadian, plus Oxycontin and Valium in the event I would attempt to sleep, but it seemed pointless.

I could no longer eat, and the worst part of my day was prying myself up from my leather chair, putting my slippers on, and sliding to the bathroom to pee. This was a major chore, and when I would get back to the safety of my leather chair I would put the straw in my nose and snort the space coke that no longer affected me. My throat was permanently numb, and my mouth had this disgusting taste from all the alcohol and lack of proper food intake.

My system was rebelling against all the drugs, and it would no longer let the "happy" light come on as a result of ingesting the pills, coke, and booze for so many years. My body was putting up its final stand against all the narcotic torture, and it resented me more and more. My body hated my mind, and my mind hated my body.

I Can See You

The scariest thing happened during this time. In late January of 2007, I was having another fun night of "lockdown," just myself, jars of pills, and plates of powdered cocaine. I had thrown down several Valium at around 11:00 p.m. to try and get some sleep, with the CPAP breathing machine on, of course—something I had grown to despise.

Outside of my bedroom on the hillside I saw a man's face looking directly at me—he was hiding in this bush, and he wouldn't stop staring at me through my windows. I stared back, fixated on his face. I couldn't tell exactly what he looked like, just a white guy staring at me, and he wouldn't stop.

I got into this staring contest with him, and I thought I was looking directly into the face of a psycho killer who was going to break into my house and kill me. I said, "Get the fuck out of here, you asshole, I am going to call the police. And if you want to break into my pad right now, do it—I will stab your eyes out and fuck your skull." I had no idea what I was saying.

After my taunting and negotiating with the psycho killer had failed to reel him into my home, I made a 911 call to the San Clemente police station:

911: 911, how can we assist you?

Me: There's a psychotic man staring at me through this bush on the hillside.

911: Does he have a weapon?

Me: I don't know, but he won't stop staring at me and he's not going away.

911: We will send officers out right away.

In about five minutes two Orange County Sheriffs arrived above my house, where this bluff is located outside my window. They drew their weapons and flashed their lights into the bushes, and the entire time I was in my bedroom window pointing to the officers where the psycho killer was: "He's right there! He's fucking looking right at me—get him, please!"

The officers shining their lights into the correct bush reported, "There's no one here, sir."

I had officially lost my mind. There was no one out there—sober police officers verified this, but I couldn't be convinced otherwise. I was going through a full blown experience of cocaine psychosis, and the Oxys and morphine pills probably didn't help much.

The officers asked, "Sir, is it okay if we come and talk to you? We will be right down there."

"That's okay, officers. I appreciate your coming out here—it's my mistake," I nervously replied.

Had I opened up my home to those guys I would have been arrested for sure, what with all the drugs in the house and the fact I was completely insane. For whatever reason, they just left and didn't push the issue. This was not a time to be a wise ass or be funny. But then again, I had lost my sense of humor long ago, and nothing was funny to me anymore. I was just a very addicted and tortured human being.

Between the seed planted by my former classmate Cammie being in intensive care, the fact that the drugs were not doing the neat tricks they used to do, that both of my doctors had cut me off due to the Feds discovering all the doctors I was visiting, that I was barely alive and surviving on a respirator, and of course, that I had completely lost my fucking mind, this all equated to one thing...

I was officially done.

LAST CALL

My last drink was on Valentine's Day, February 14, 2007. I was throwing down Crown Royals with a splash of 7-Up, I must have had six triples. I was trying to induce sleep, and it wasn't working. Never will I forget being alone, watching the Red Hot Chili Peppers sing "Snow" at the Grammy Awards for winning the album of the year. (*To this very day, I listen to that great Chili Peppers song several times a week. For me, it represents so much: desperation, beauty, and a million other things all rolled into one.*)

Tears streamed down my face as I watched the band play this beautiful song with the audience smiling and cheering them on—I couldn't relate to any of it. The Chili Peppers had been heroes of mine back when Hillel Slovak was their guitarist, who would eventually die of a heroin overdose.

The decision was made to try to get clean one last time, and this was it. I had made the arrangements to try to keep my San Clemente home by renting it out to a guy I knew, as I was rapidly running out of money to keep it up anymore. My now fiancée and I had agreed it was best for me to move in with her after my stay at South Coast Hospital in Laguna Beach.

Moving all the things I owned in the state of mind I was in was impossible. I actually had a client in Long Beach called "Substance

Abuse Foundation"—how fitting for me. This organization helps provide housing for drug addicts and alcoholics in recovery. It's a wonderful place, and they have helped many people.

I knew this one gentleman there in recovery, Norman, and I asked if he and some of his friends could help me move my stuff into storage for some cash. He agreed, and to this day I owe Norman a huge "thank you" for many reasons; not only did he and his friends work their asses off to help me move my things as I could barely function, but he was very kind to me and he told me this about drug addicts and alcoholics—"There are only three places guys like us end up, and that is jails, institutions, or the cemetery."

Norman had been sober for a little over a year when he told me that, and it was really profound to me. That made sense to me in a world where absolutely nothing made any sense. Norman and his guys helped me pile up stuff for donations, and I must have donated half of my things to charity because I was too sick to have a garage sale. Are you kidding me? Can you imagine me holding a garage sale? "How much for this lamp, sir?" "Ummmmm, bllllurraaraahhhh... just take it."

I couldn't haggle with people about household items—you could just take it, I didn't give a shit, I had a life to save and that was my own. All I cared about were a few things I put into those "pods" that they pick up at your house.

I will never forget all the drugs and bottles of pills I found in drawers. I must have thrown away several hundred pills worth thousands on the streets, and vials upon vials of coke that were filled with the powder. That's how "done" I was—all the drugs I still had left could have kept the Partridge Family high at Woodstock for a week, but I couldn't even look at the stuff anymore.

I was thinking how it had been Halloween just a couple of months earlier, and I was the only human pumpkin that I knew—I was all carved out and hollow inside, and if you put a candle inside me I wouldn't glow. My tattered soul would have blackened any light brought into me.

HELP ME

There would be no intervention for me. I had not yet been sent to jail or prison but I deserved to be, and there was no one else left in my life at that point—I was that isolated. Even though I had a fiancée who did want to see me get well, I felt we were on different planets, it was just me, and being "just me" was as lonely a place as you can imagine.

I was on an island of immeasurable desperation. I parked my car at South Coast Medical Center in South Laguna Beach, with a packed suitcase and an empty suit of skin that didn't even look like me anymore.

With tears running down my face, unable to speak, I managed to utter the words, "Please help me" on the fourth floor of the chemical dependency unit of South Coast Medical Center. I had called a few days earlier asking if they had any beds available, and I promised I would be there. This was on a Friday. I didn't care about my business or anything else anymore and how could I?

The intake person said, "We can't verify benefits on your health insurance."

I replied, "This is my Visa Card. You can keep it—I don't care... Please just help me."

I couldn't understand the payment plans the hospital was offering or what the minimum payment was, but they needed something to secure payment for my treatment. I wasn't a rich guy by any stretch of the imagination—I was a really sick guy—but luckily I still had a few credit cards that weren't yet maxed out.

It took them a long time to admit me, and it went down like this:

Intake: What are you here for, Mr. Zalkins?

Me: I am sick, and I am going to die if I don't get help.

Intake: Okay, we want to help, but why are you here?

Me: I can't stop taking the stuff, I can't sleep, and I want to give this thing a shot. (Tears began to stream down my face, the teardrops became bigger and bigger, and I was relieved in a way because I was out of ammunition. I could no longer fight this and I was putting up the white flag, surrendering for the first time in my life—honestly admitting I was defeated by my addiction. I hated to admit that, but there were no more lies to be told, only the truth, and that was refreshing to me.)

Intake: Give what a shot?

Me: To get clean.

Intake: Have you ever been here before?

Me: Yes, twice.

Intake: Did you stay the entire thirty days?

Me: Never.

Intake: Why not?

Me: I just wanted to get off of all the pills.

Intake: I guess it didn't work too well.

Me: You are funny and you must perform at the IMPROV soon. Will you let me know when you are there?

Intake: Okay, I wasn't trying to get you upset, Mr. Zalkins. Now what have you been taking?

Me: Oxycontin, Fentanyl, heroin, cocaine, Valium, Norcos, liquor, and some morphine.

Intake: For how long?

Me: Forever.

Intake: Can you define forever?

Me: I started drinking at a young age, maybe thirteen, and I started doing cocaine when I was fifteen or sixteen, but it's those goddamn pills, man. Those things are just a motherfucker.

Intake: It sounds like it's all of those things, Todd, not just the pills. Can you tell me how long you have been taking the pills?

Me: Yeah. 1990, after my back surgery.

Intake: 1990? Wow, you have been on them for a long time— you are lucky to be here.

Me: I don't feel very lucky right now.

Intake: What kind of pills were you taking, the amount, and for how long?

Me: That is a tough one to answer… I started with Vicodin and I was on those for a few years, then it went to Norco, and I am not sure when. Maybe in 1998 or 1999 I started on my hell ride with the devil.

Intake: What's the devil?

Me: Oh, I am sorry, I call Oxycontin the devil because it's satanic, man. It's the devil disguised in this little turquoise pill… that shit is a bitch.

Intake: You have taken the pain meds for almost seventeen years?

Me: That's correct. Only a few months off when I did a medical rapid detox or blood transfusion—I think I was off for three or four months, and other than that I have always been addicted.

Intake: You need to be here, Mr. Zalkins, and we can help you, but you need to promise us you will stay the thirty days this time.

Me: I will do anything you say… I swear.

The director of the facility at the time, Sherri, was an angel to me. During the intake process she held my hand like a mother would do with a sick child or infant. She had a huge box of Kleenex that she had to keep ripping through to help me mop up my broken, empty face, and she even shed tears of her own. Sherri had a way of empathizing with me and I needed that at the time; if she'd had a real militant manner, I would have been even more terrified.

The withdrawals were already kicking in and I could feel that all-too-familiar feeling of insects and rats nipping at my skin. I was all clammy and my mind was racing a million miles an hour; I couldn't think straight, and all I could think about was asking if they could put me under for thirty days and let me sleep through the fucking detox. I didn't ask such a silly question, but that's what I wanted for sure—not to feel any bit of what was ahead of me.

I can't ever forget that little intake room and all the sadness and desperation I was trying to let go of. In a way I was relieved because I was going to be safe for a while, but at the same time my nerves were petrified because I knew that there was going to be a lot of sickness just around the corner.

That's something that only those who have been addicted and have tried to get well would understand. Seeing someone go through it is one thing, but going through it is another. It's painful for anyone involved, but it's a new form of hell while going through the detoxification process from hardcore opiate pill abuse.

In my room about two hours after all that intake nonsense, I crashed on my bed and started to shake; I could almost hear my skin crawl, and I felt my heart race and the sweat running all over me. But, I thought, just maybe for the first time I was finally desperate enough to actually do something about my problem, and a problem it was indeed.

No one could ever have told me what was ahead of me for the next several months—no way in hell could anyone prepare me for it, or how bad it was really going to be… and "bad" would be a gross understatement for what my life would be like in the coming months.

Part Six
In Treatment

Sometime late Friday night on February 16, the nurse gave me a Subutex to stick under my tongue, and I got a very comforting feeling as a result. I had been given this before for my withdrawal symptoms with my failed attempt at a medical home detox, and it works within a few minutes.

Taking this was like making all the invisible spiders that were going to be crawling on me have to wait at the "border" to pass through to my skin. Eventually though, they would get through the border and play their game of spider hell all over me.

There was some really good news though; Dr. Headrick (the doctor in charge of the facility) told me I no longer had to wear the CPAP breathing apparatus! I was no longer Hannibal Lecter!! I had worn that damn machine for two and a half years. It suddenly dawned on me, "Why do I not have to wear this any longer?"

Dr. Headrick simply said, "Your drug addiction is what was shutting off your brain. You don't have sleep apnea—you were so intoxicated from the pills that your brain would tell you to stop breathing."

All those nights after snorting cocaine, at 3:00 or 4:00 in the morning I would put on that mask and push the "ON" button and feel like a character from a really bad psycho thriller. It was always so uncomfortable to wear, and trust me this was an unattractive device to be wearing. This was a really big deal to put that machine into retirement.

The next few days were about the most comfortable I would feel for many, many months, because the Subutex they gave me made me feel somewhat euphoric—but this would only be given for five days, and then the shit would officially hit the fan. After my last dose of Subutex wore off, it was like some spiritual figure entered me and said, "Hello, Todd. You have been a drug addict for a very long time. Welcome to hell—you have arrived." I had no idea what was in store for me psychologically, physically, or emotionally, and neither did the doctors or nursing staff of South Coast Hospital.

Before entering the hospital, I had had only very brief moments of sleep. I had not had a normal night's sleep in many years because of the totally sedated brain I had from the pills. One thing I learned is that the "tweakers" or meth addicts who stay up for days on their drugs end up sleeping very well when in rehab. Hell, they have been awake for most of their using career anyway, so I would hope that they fucking slept.

I was an opiate addict, and I had no problem sleeping until the last few months of my active addiction. Opiate addicts can fall asleep at a traffic light (yes, I managed to do that numerous times). There were moments I would inflict physical pain on myself to try and stay awake. It's called "nodding out," and under the influence of enough opiates, one can find oneself in a deep sleep that a hibernating bear would envy. The "nod" comes without warning, and if you are operating a motor vehicle you put yourself—and even worse, others—in a high risk game of Russian roulette.

There were many times on the 405 Freeway when I would slap the shit out of myself and even punch myself in the side of the head and scream, "Fucking wake up!" Often I would pull over at an off ramp, grab a Diet Coke or coffee, and try to carry on. I would also be scratching my face and arms incessantly. A true junkie will have marks from scratching themselves to the point of scarring, and I have a few of those as well.

One last comment on how quickly I could go to sleep. There was a period I believe from around 2002 to 2004 where I dated a few really sweet girls—I could still speak clearly for the most part at this time. At dinner, for example, I would often have a glass or two of red wine, and combined with the pills by the end of the date I was face first into a plate of pasta.

It was normal for me to have one of the girls I was dating grab my hand at the dinner table and walk me into a spare room where I would slobber and watch Forensic Files (if I was lucky) or just pass out.

These types of "scenes" often occurred while having dinner with the girl's parents, aunts and uncles, etc. It was a complete embarrassment, but I didn't give it much thought at the time because I didn't know any better.

LIVE THROUGH THIS

I t's bad enough that my skin was crawling and I would sweat profusely, but to be unable to get some true sleep in rehab was a nightmare, one I would be enduring night in and night out for a lot longer than I ever would have imagined.

The nurses gave me different medications every four hours or so; my body was so deficient in vitamins that they had me taking some form of vitamin supplement regularly. I just wanted to sleep, and at night they would give the patients who were having trouble sleeping 80 milligrams of Seroquel.

Keep in mind I said they would give patients 80 mg of Seroquel. I wasn't sleeping at all, and my stuttering and drooling was making me feel I should probably have some nice bibs made up for me to avoid getting my shirts messy. The doctor put me on 800 mg of Seroquel at night to get me to sleep. That's ten times the dosage on average, and I still couldn't sleep!

This was getting serious, because I already had not slept really at all for the past few months. Now I was trying to get well, and my brain couldn't effectively heal without quality sleep—you know, that deep REM sleep we all know and love so much.

I would take this 800 mg of Seroquel and just stumble around the hallways crashing into walls and doors, slobbering and crying, and begging for a decent night's sleep. At about four days, I was scared shitless because I now thought I was rendered mentally retarded as a result of my pill addiction and everything else.

I can remember wiggling on the floor outside the "medicine room" where they give you the pills, and I was all over the place yelling, "Fuck this! Please just shoot a needle in me with something to get me to sleep!" Then I would get back to my drooling festival and crawl back to my room. I am sure the nurses just loved taking care of me.

I was trying so hard to keep it together, but it's nearly impossible to keep yourself together when you are broken into a bunch of different pieces. I was so scattered, and as time wore on I made less and less sense. The head doctor and the nurses had a special meeting about my condition, and they were contemplating putting me on the second floor of the hospital, which is the psychiatric unit.

That probably sounds funny to many of you reading this, but trust me when I say it was the scariest thing I had ever experienced. I was completely losing my mind, and between the crawling skin, constant sweating, and lack of sleep I was very much steeped in a state of complete delusion.

Around the fourth or fifth day they asked me to start going to "group." I was thinking, "Yeah, I've got your group—it's located right below my waistline disguised in the shape of a dick and some balls."

Defiant would not even come close to my state of being. I was Sid Vicious, Marlon Brando, and James Dean all rolled into one, I was a complete anarchist and I hated being told what to do. So I started to go to these lame-ass group meetings where most of the other patients in rehab seemed to have it all going on, they were smiling, "Yeaaah, we're in rehab, and this is my new best friend Jenny—we are going to be friends forever and ever."

I would just mumble, "Hey Jenny, fuck you. Fuck you and your new best friend. I hope in the middle of the night a really horny elephant comes into your room after taking three big Viagras and bangs you with his five-foot-long elephant Viagra dick." And I meant it.

When you are in the state of misery I was in, it's difficult to be grateful that someone else is feeling happy like they are on some fucking winning streak. Everything around me seemed fake. No one made sense, and these little "groups" of patients who were all best friends now could all get in a special "best friends bus" and drive off a fucking cliff into the Grand Canyon. I would have gladly paid for the bus rental too.

I would have to be up by 6:30 to get down to the Twelve-Step recovery meeting at 7:00 a.m.—Oh boy, did that sound fun. Ahhh yes… a Twelve-Step meeting. That's all I want to hear—a bunch of assholes talk about how they used to drink and black out and now their lives are all wonderful now that they are sober.

The first thing that came into my head at the recovery meeting when I could actually conjure up a thought was, Listen to these fucking lying asshole criminals! They got sober before the drugs were even any good—drinking, that was your problem? My head would tell me anything to make me feel one of a kind, like no one understood my pain—I was this walking time bomb of negativity because most of what I saw or heard was positivity and I wasn't feeling it at all.

The 7:00 a.m. meeting consisted of several round tables and all the patients in rehab were required to attend. If you didn't attend meetings, you ran the serious risk of being released from the hospital for not complying with the rehab program. So I would crawl down there in the mornings in my jammies and slippers with my subliminal "Go Fuck Yourself" hat on.

These meetings didn't just have patients in attendance. They were open to other alcoholics and addicts. So I would have to hear and see all these lying, criminal, sober asshole people talking about how good their life had become.

Now at the time I was so deep in anger, fear, brokenness, sickness, and frailty that I could only go to work on judging others. I was just there to detox, damn it, and so let the judging of others begin! I did my best to get along with everyone, but inside I had this head of mine that would negotiate anything to get me back to the hell I was trying to get away from.

I have come to realize and understand that people in recovery are the same, we may have different stories, but our disease is of the same cloth. But at that time, I just referred to everyone as "Fucking, lying asshole criminals." Those were the thoughts of a very sick and frightened little boy, a little boy who was 6'3", 235 pounds, 39 years old, and scared to death of everyone and everything around him.

My drugs and alcohol were missing, and my protective shield was stripped from me. I was raw, an openly wounded man with no answers to my problems without my drugs.

After the morning recovery meeting I would go upstairs—or, I should say, "shuffle." I would shuffle upstairs for breakfast, and as much as I wasn't sleeping, I was making up for it in eating. I was packing the food away, and the food there at the hospital wasn't all that bad.

Hell, I hadn't eaten much in months, so an institutional piece of meatloaf almost made me feel like I was having a rib eye at my favorite steakhouse, Morton's. Okay, that's a stretch, but I was starving all the time and I was eating two or three meals at each sitting, so something good was happening. We could order our own stuff off the menu each day, so I ordered double of everything and then I would eat leftovers from some patients who offered.

The routine was very rigid. I would wake up, put on some rockin' pajamas with teddy bears on them, and go to the Twelve-Step recovery meeting downstairs and listen to lying criminal assholes share about how fun sobriety is. Okay, I will not refer to my fellows in recovery like that anymore, but maybe I have one more left in me.

Breakfast was at 8:00, and all of us patients would sit in this little dining area and I would overhear some of the biggest crocks of bullshit ever. All the ideas people had, and how great their lives were going to be just sounded like the result of attending some Tony Robbins motivational seminar.

However, people really did seem to care about each other, and I found myself caring a lot for my fellow sick-ass patients on the fourth floor.

Slowly, I was realizing that we were all just so sick and damaged, regardless of the circumstances we came in on and what we were addicted to. I didn't interact much in the TV room or socialize the first few weeks. Hiding out in my room and looking north toward Long Beach seemed to best fit my frame of mind.

There was this beautiful view outside of my room, and when it was clear I could see all the way up to Long Beach. I wasn't sleeping, so any time I had to myself I would daydream about being a kid, and if it was nighttime I would still daydream about when I had fun and when life was so wonderful—it just seemed like such a long time ago.

The rest of the morning consisted of bullshit group meetings that had no point to them… at least that is what I thought. I couldn't get my head around any of it, but why would I? I was going through a detox courtesy of Satan himself and I hadn't slept in ages.

But I would show up to these things and just whine like no other. I remember there was this one group meeting after breakfast each day, and the topic was, "Happy, sad, mad, or glad." No bullshit—we were supposed to go around the room and comment upon what we were feeling.

I would hear some chick say, "My name is Stacy, and I am an alcoholic and drug addict, and well… I'm kind of sad today because my boyfriend wants me at home soon, but I am glad because I will be seeing him in two weeks… yay!"

My head immediately said, "Stacy, your boyfriend doesn't give a shit about you coming home soon… However, he is praying to God that you somehow can be able to give the same epic blow jobs when you are sober that you used to administer while loaded."

Then I would hear, "My name is Dan... and I am an alcoholic and drug addict, and I am mad today... I am mad today because I just found out my wife is having an affair, and I am stuck in this hospital."

My head immediately said, "No shit Dan... really? Your wife had an affair? It probably has nothing to do with the fact that you are constantly fucking drunk and loaded out of your mind and probably fucking your babysitter. Oh, and one more thing Dan—I hope your wife had three orgasms last night, and this weekend there will be a neighborhood potluck gang-bang at your house, except you won't be there because your ass is stuck in fucking rehab."

When it was my time to share it would sound something like, "Ummmm, I, uhhhhhh, ummmmm, my name is T-T-T odd (start stuttering and crying). My name is Todd and I am an addict (I hadn't accepted I was an alcoholic yet). I am not sad, happy, mad, or glad—those words suck. I am sick as a motherfucker. I feel like I am retarded and I can't talk to people, I haven't slept in God knows how long... I can't stop using drugs, and I don't know how to stop, and I am fucked (start to slobber and cry, mixed in with some stuttering). And too many of you are too fucking happy, and I don't get it, and quite frankly I feel you are completely full of shit."

I may have whined a lot when I was in the hospital (and I would whine a lot more for the next eleven months too) but at least I was finally telling the truth about where I was at for the first time in my life. That was a big deal for me, because I never wanted to be honest about where I was at, nor did I want to find a rational way to deal with life. I react the way I do, which is generally insane, because I know of no other way, and I am conditioned to do whatever the hell it is that I want to do.

We would have lunch, and time for some "reading assignments" afterwards, then more group bullshit, and then a Yoga class. Yeah, Yoga—you should have seen me in Yoga class. I would slobber on the mats, my right hand and leg shaking constantly from detoxifying, and then try to stretch with this drop-dead gorgeous Yoga instructor.

Todd A. Zalkins

Her name was Emily, and I know for certain she was the best part of many of the patients' long days in rehab. She was a wonderful human being, gentle, kind, loving, and very pretty. I know Emily made being in rehab just a little more bearable. Wherever you are, Emily, I thank you for your kindness from the bottom of my heart.

So I would try to stretch, and I could do absolutely none of the crap in the class, but I liked it because I could lie down in a quiet environment and Emily would play some beautiful music, and at the end of the class she would do the most cool thing—she would pick up your feet ever so gently and shake your legs out and give you a stretch.

For those few moments I felt like everything in life had meaning, and that I was going to be okay, and that maybe one day I could have a beautiful woman like Emily in my life who would make me feel so special and loved.

Emily played some music that would just soothe you, and it would often transport me into a different time and place. She had this one CD where Jack Johnson sang, "Badfish," which is a cover from the originally written song performed by Brad Nowell and Sublime.

If you haven't heard that song, it's a must. I remember just lying on this hard floor on a half-inch yoga mat and following along with the words with these huge tears doing laps down my face. It's a great cover that Jack Johnson did, but no one did it like Sublime, and Brad's soulful sweet voice always had a way of putting my heart at ease and keeping my spirit intact. It's pretty cool that music can do that, as I had long forgotten how important and healing it can be.

There was almost a mourning period after Emily shook your feet and legs and moved on to the next patient—it felt that good, I wish I could have paid an extra $20 for her to shake the feet for an extra five minutes, I would have been at the ATM regularly in the hospital lobby to pay for that privilege.

We had dinner at around 5:00 or so, and then either an evening recovery meeting or some rehab group meeting. This would be my routine for 23 days... I would not stay the whole 30 days, but we will get to that.

On about my fifth day in treatment, I was having dinner by myself when I heard a voice—it sounded upbeat and all too familiar. It was my good friend Hazard, and we had a long history together as both friends and drug addicts, and our diseases had taken us our separate ways several months earlier.

I had no idea that he had been to rehab about 90 days before me. He seemed to have a spring in his step and was smiling ear to ear. The moment I saw him I gave him a big hug. He had no idea I was in the hospital, and I just started to bawl my eyes out.

This experience of seeing Hazard was another big piece of encouragement for me to want to try to get well. One of the biggest things in recovery for me was that if I couldn't relate or identify with others I would say to myself, "Well... screw this, and fuck that... it just can't work for me."

I was in dire need of proof that someone I knew—someone with a similar track record of using the way I did—could actually put up a fight against this disease.

A sense of hysterical relief washed over me when I saw Hazard. We both went into the "meditation room" where I let it all hang out. I cried until nothing else could come out. This was a combo cry, a cry of desperation, relief, and gratitude.

Seeing him looking healthier and hearing him talk about how he got through the hospital and what he was doing to stay sober was music to my ears. Even though I couldn't really understand a thing he was saying, I believed him because I could see it.

Let me share a quick story about Hazard and me that should paint a good picture of our drug-addicted friendship. Sometime in 1993 I had gone on a surf trip with my good buddy "G-Force" to a place in mainland Mexico called Playa Saladita.

This place is really fun to surf, the surf breaks really far outside, and it's a long left-hander and you take off out by this river mouth. It is a really bitchin' place in the middle of nowhere, about an hour and a half north of Ixtapa.

G-Force and I were the first paying customers there when this place was still being built, and nowadays surfers from all over the world go there to ride the 400-yard lefts (you can ride three different sections, and if you get the right wave it's four football fields long for sure). We would surf six hours a day until we couldn't move our arms, and it was just an unreal experience. My addiction wouldn't allow me that physical freedom after this trip.

Fast forward to 2005, and my friend Hazard and I thought it would be killer to dig out of San Clemente for a week and go to Playa Saladita. The difference between going in '97 versus '05 was night and day. Hazard and I had to be sure we had enough Oxys to cover us for the trip and that was the first thing I packed up for us. We flew all the way to paradise on earth and scored a beachfront, killer three-bedroom house, fully air conditioned right in front of the surf break.

We ended up snorting and chewing Oxys for the entire week, going into town to score all the ice cream sandwiches that the "mini supermercado" could sell us, and never once even paddled out to surf. The highlight of my day was buying all of the kids outside the store all the cookies and "Pinguinos" (just like Hostess Cup Cakes) they could eat.

There would be as many as twelve kids waiting for Hazard and me to walk out of the little market. We would give each kid two of whatever the hell we grabbed, and it felt good making someone else feel good when I couldn't even come close to feeling good about myself.

I do not want to know how much sugar we ingested on that trip—it would put dozens of diabetics into comas for sure. We traveled all that way to sit inside, watch movies on DVD, snort Oxys, and eat big grips of ice cream. We should have changed our first names on that trip to Ben and Jerry.

I could have been "Ben," and Hazard could have been "Jerry," because ice cream and Oxys dictated our every move, and we didn't move much.

I don't think Hazard and I even said much to each other the entire trip. Maybe something really important like, "Hey Z-man, do you have some more Oxys we can chop up?" or "Good morning, asshole, why did you eat all the ice cream sandwiches?"

I was also really paranoid. I had this fear that if I walked to the restaurant for a few more desserts that maybe Hazard would steal all the Oxys. Hell, after all the bullshit I put him through, I deserved it.

But he never did steal my grip of pills, probably because I hid them in a different place every time I left the house for a few minutes—and trust me, I was never gone long.

We paid a lot of money for a change of scenery, but no matter where I went I was right there with me. No matter how gorgeous and breathtaking the scenery was, it was never fully appreciated. It's tough to take in beauty when inside you are void of happiness. I couldn't comprehend brightness and good stuff around me, just darkness and the wanting of more pills.

I don't believe much of anything unless I can see it. When I met Hazard in rehab, I saw a guy who I knew had been really sick, and he was now turning his life around—the impact this had on me was tremendous. I am convinced that if it weren't for seeing Hazard that particular day, there would have been no proof for me that the program of recovery works and I would not have trusted or believed anyone.

There will always be a deep sense of gratitude and love in my heart for that particular encounter with Hazard, and there is no doubt in my mind that he saved my life by just showing up to the rehab kitchen area to grab a crappy soda from the fridge. Even though I was "shit nuts" and sick as a dog, I clung on to a little molecule of hope that my friend Hazard gave me. Today, we are better friends than we ever were in our addiction, and I would do anything in the world for that guy. I owe him…big time.

But seeing Hazard would not prove to keep me physically in the hospital. A few days later at around day eight of being in rehab,

Dr. Headrick (the chief rehab physician) was off for the weekend and there was a new doctor on call for him. I still had not slept, and I managed to convince the new doctor that I was fit to go home and I had just wanted to detox. What a fucking sham this was! I had no idea what I was thinking, I know I just wanted to get the fuck out of there as soon as possible and get home. My head was talking to me, and it wanted to get me alone and just say, "I can do this on my own." Now if that isn't insane, I have no idea what is.

I'm Outta Here

I had rented out my home in San Clemente and moved in with
my fiancée in Newport Coast right before going to rehab. So
I packed my stuff and drove on home. Yes, I am free!! Totally
insane, but I am free and out of rehab! I haven't slept and I can
barely talk, but I am off the pills again!

Something in my head once again told me that I could battle
this disease and handle it on my own. I had eight days of no sleep in
the hospital and was still shaking uncontrollably and very, very sick.

I made a go of it at home for two days, at which point Alison
(my fiancée at the time) said, "I just talked to Sherry at the hospital,
and you are going back tomorrow." I replied, "No fucking way—I
am not going back there! Please don't make me go there. I can do
this, I swear I will stay off the drugs!"

She wasn't buying it, and she demanded I go back to rehab on
Monday. I was so pissed about this, I never wanted to return and I
hated her for standing her ground. In hindsight, she did one of the
best things that have ever been done for me.

For this, Alison, I am forever grateful, and your insistence on
my returning to the hospital was a lifesaver for me. We ended up
splitting up after I was eight months sober, but I often think that
had she actually agreed with me to let me stay home, I would have
killed myself within weeks... it's an absolute certainty.

READMITTED

I have mentioned that I am a true anarchist and defiant to the very core. Here I was, eight days clean (more like eight days of tears and slobber) and I still felt I could do it on my own. I returned to the hospital on Monday morning where I was readmitted, with more blood drawn and all the stuff they needed to do so I could get that really neat white bracelet on my wrist identifying me as a sick person who needed to be hospitalized.

I didn't drink or use drugs when I left the hospital, which is what I had done the two previous times the moment I got out of detox. They did not believe that I hadn't used, and when the tests came back "clean" I felt this sense of, "I did something right for a change and for once and I didn't have to lie about it." I had made one little baby step toward something positive.

It was upon my return to rehab that I started to try my best to pay attention and give this a shot.

The problem was I still wasn't sleeping, and I was detoxing really hard. I soon had a conversation with Dr. Headrick that went something like this:

Dr. H: Your detox is going to last a while... and everything you're feeling is normal.

Me: But I don't feel normal—I feel like shit.

Dr. H: How long did you drink and use drugs for?

Me: Around 24 years.

Dr. H: And you expect to feel decent in ten days?

Me: I guess you are right.

Dr. H: Detoxing off of Oxycontin and all the things you are on could take a really long time. The worst of it will probably take months, but the brain will take a year to eighteen months to heal, maybe even longer.

I was in a state of shock, but at the same time I realized that this was not going to be a picnic and if I wanted to get well I had to be patient and ride it out. The problem is, I am not patient. In fact I am the most impatient person I know, and I know some pretty fucking impatient people. For me, even "now" is not soon enough—I want to feel good last week. Where is that little magic pill that I can pay $20,000 for to make all this misery disappear?

For the first time in my life the ugly truth was that I couldn't go around this, I couldn't go over this, I couldn't go under this— for the first time, I had to go through this. There would be no magic pills to take or shortcuts as an option. My entire existence was fabricated on the will to get shit done as quickly as possible, half-ass almost everything, and do anything possible to take the easy way out.

I was stuck. There were only a few things that were going to improve my circumstances: time and patience. And for the first time in my life it wouldn't be in my time, it would be in the hands of a force much, much bigger and completely foreign to me, and I guess that would be God and a natural process that scared me to death.

There were many patients who were now all "buddy buddy," and I couldn't understand it. The little games and politics that take place are just funnier than all hell. It was common to hear things like:

Lisa: I don't like that girl Michelle, she's a major bitch.

Me: Why don't you like her?

Lisa: She looked at me funny this morning and I can't stand her hair, she's a bitch.

Me: That sounds real logical to me... excuse me, I have to get back to my room and not sleep some more.

We are all just children inside of adult bodies, some more mature than others, and don't think for one moment that I am proclaiming myself the mature one—are you kidding? I was trying to fuck the doorknob in my own room, for goodness sake (more about being horny in the hospital later).

I Found a Friend

I met this older gentleman in there, whose name was Rick. This guy was very, very sick, and I liked him immediately. I say this because I was really sick too, and this was a guy I wanted to be around—he was in a wheelchair because he was too weak to walk. He was a straight alcoholic, and he was certainly near death had he not checked into the rehab center. He and I hit it off right away.

Rick couldn't carry his tray of food because he shook so badly, and even though I was shaking myself, I could still grab his tray and sit with him during our mealtimes. It took a few days before he could really talk, which again made me feel like this guy was "family" to me, because I was in a similar predicament. Sometimes we would just point at something and invent our own sign language because talking clearly was not in the cards for us at this early stage of the game.

There was a daily walk which was optional to take with this one counselor who was a real pain in the ass, but looking back I know that he meant well. This was really a pleasant sight to see, there would be about eight to twelve of us walking outside the hospital, led by "Hitler" the counselor, who was really pretty gnarly. He would take us through these streets behind the hospital, and if you have ever been to Laguna the streets are not flat—they are pretty damn steep, actually.

I was a very weak and empty walking-shell of a man. I talked my fellow patient and new-found friend Rick into going with me. If there was a video of us, it would for sure make it to some network show like "America's Most Ridiculous Patients in Rehab."

He and I walked at the back of the pack. When I say we "walked," that would be giving us too much credit. We hobbled along holding each other up, and crept up and down the streets like little frail, wounded soldiers having lost the war to drugs and alcohol.

The other patients, the ones walking strong and with vigor, I just hated. They seemed to be on that good old-fashioned winning streak, full of bubbly life, with an aura of, "Isn't life just fucking grand here in rehab?" I am telling you, if it were legal I would have buried all of them. I just could not understand how they were reeking of joy.

I was short of breath, and Rick and I were getting further and further behind. Counselor Hitler would yell at us to catch up. I was very close to saying, "Listen, you little cocksucker, this guy and I are a little weak and frail. We are patients in this fucking place and we are trying our best—yell at me one more time and you will fucking need this hospital for sure, most likely the emergency room." Somehow I refrained from saying what I truly felt, and both Rick and I did our best to catch up to the "energizer bunnies," I mean, happy-go-lucky patients.

The irony of all this is that to the best of my knowledge, Rick and I are the only ones who are still sober without relapsing, among the 28 patients we were in rehab with. I love Rick, he has his family back in his life and he's retired after working many years for a Fortune 500 company. I see him almost every Sunday at one of my recovery meetings, and he's such a quiet and calm soul, and a wonderful human being.

We both have a common thread that binds us forever. Both of us were on death's doorstep, and we have punched our way to the other side of it all. Our time together, my carrying his food trays and our struggling to take a walk will forever be special in my heart. Isn't it funny how something that was so pathetic and dire can be not only wonderful, but a link of a chain in a relationship that is forged as strong as steel.

SOMETHING CLICKED

At about day thirteen I still hadn't slept. I would spend my nights awake in my room crying uncontrollably and asking God, "Why? God, why is this so difficult? Why am I so sick? Will I ever be able to blend in comfortably with this world? Will I ever not be sick like this?" And lastly, "God damn it God... would you please let me get some fucking sleep?"

A few things came to me, as clear as the beautiful ocean water we have in Laguna Beach. I will take advantage of anything that is easily given to me in this life, and if it comes too easy for me, I will find a way to wreck it. Whether it's financial success, relationships, you name it—if it comes easy, I will dismantle it and find a way to screw it up six ways to Sunday. Which is why I'm 100% sure that God wanted to teach me a lesson and get the following through this thick skull of mine:

1. None of my detoxification would be easy.
2. I would not be given the gift of feeling good quickly like a lot of my fellow patients.
3. I would have to walk through a tremendous amount of pain and suffering, the type of which I had never felt before, in order to get to the other side of this hell.

4. If I drink or use drugs ever again, I am a dead man.

I know these things were true because if any of it came easy to me, I would destroy it and not come to cherish or place value on it. I would take it for granted and soon forget the sickness and despair I was experiencing in the hospital. This process needed to be very slow and very painful for me.

So, let's get back to the fun of rehab! While detoxing, I constantly felt like my skin was this massive pin cushion, and small pins and needles were being pushed into my skin all over. This coincided with muscle spasms, extreme weakness, sweating, shaking, and my insane mind bordering on mental retardation.

I had come into rehab with the following: severe dependency to prescription pain medications including Oxycontin, Norco, Vicodin, Fentanyl, and Valium, complete cocaine psychosis, sleep deprivation, and alcoholism (but I could not admit that quite yet, because alcoholics live under the bridge and drink out of bottles wrapped in paper sacks and never take showers, and I was just a binge drinker!!). I have now learned that one doesn't have to drink every day to be alcoholic, but my head will try to twist and turn things around to give me that one last "out," if you will.

My disease will negotiate deals in my head and justify that I can give up certain things, but others are okay. So I also have a chronic disease of perception and short-term memory. No matter how bad things get, something inside my head will try to corner me, and the pills, cocaine, or drink will say, "It's okay, this will make you feel better—we are friends, remember? Just pop a few of these, or snort a few of those, or drink some of this. You don't want to leave all of this behind, do you?"

I am trapped in this head that speaks to me in this manner and it can be very frightening.

One other thing I needed to get through this thick skull of mine was to acknowledge that alcohol is just as dangerous as the other shit I was taking. Once I drink, there's a hunger for cocaine, and that hunger has to be fed—this is non-negotiable.

I am the human version of Pavlov's dog, when you give me alcohol, this siren goes off indicating it is time to obtain a lot of cocaine, and I will not rest until that mission is accomplished. No matter how I sliced it, I had to admit to myself I was alcoholic, but that wouldn't happen for a few more weeks.

Talking to Myself

I was climbing the walls at around day fifteen, crying out loud to the nursing staff and anyone else who would listen to me, "I can't fucking sleep! Please help me get some sleep." Then my jaw would become loose and I would babble some other random complaints and gibberish, not to get attention but because I was coming undone inside and I was trying my best to let it out.

Sleep wasn't happening for me, so I would just sit in my rehab room and look out of my window toward Long Beach, where it all began for me. While the whole world was sleeping I lay in bed where minutes seemed like hours, and days seemed like weeks. I would close my eyes and talk to myself in a very low voice:

"I know there are people in Long Beach right now who are sleeping... who are happy people with families, who are responsible fathers and mothers, sons and daughters. I know people there who love their lives, and they can handle the stuff that life gives them without traveling the road I have traveled. I know that once upon a time I was a child in Long Beach who craved love and attention."

Crying harder, I mumbled aloud, "I know that I still have love in my heart, but it's been misplaced and hidden beneath the layers of addiction and emotional pain. I know that I need to grow up and I know I want to be loved. I know that I have been a child, immature for many years, absent the capacity to deal with life without drugs and alcohol. I know I miss my mom whom I love dearly and I feel I have lost my best friend. I know that I no longer want to hide anymore. I know I want to get through this and maybe have an opportunity to be decent. I know I no longer want to be a drug addict and I don't want to feel alone. I know I want to laugh again and find the love that has been lost... but I don't know how to do these things. Please tell me how I live this life without my crutch and my savior. I no longer want drugs and alcohol."

When I opened my eyes, my head told me I had been asleep and dreaming but the reality is I hadn't and my skin was burning, the pins that stuck me on my back and forearms were relentless, and there were spiders and other bugs having a field day with my body, and I could not shoo them away because they weren't really there. All of this because I was going through a detoxification that was nothing short of satanic.

My eyes were bloodshot, my face was pale, and my body was weak. But I was still feverishly eating and there was no sign of my appetite subsiding. "If I keep eating like this, I will make that fat guy Jared from Subway look anorexic... may I please have some more pie?" I thought to myself.

THE JOY OF SEX

Even though I was completely insane in the hospital, one thing slowly started to come back to life, and that was my libido. Jesus, I thought I was horny after coming down from cocaine those hundreds of times—I was masturbating so much in the hospital, I thought I was developing carpal tunnel syndrome in both wrists.

I was not the only one horny in treatment, by the way. The floor was loaded with people willing to shoot "Rehab Porno" at the drop of a hat. In fact, one day (I think I was on day twenty) there were two couples caught fucking each other's brains out, and all of them were discharged for misconduct.

Me, I was trying to fuck the doorknob in my room—you know, "normal" shit like that. Well, okay, having sex with a doorknob isn't really normal, but it was to me at the time. I would just be lying there in my room and I would think to myself, "I really like sex. I miss sex. I want to have sex right now—in fact, the door of my bathroom could be a really hot chick if I think hard enough, and that doorknob could be just one of her two fabulous steel tits."

I should have had some sort of anti-hard-on pill given to me because my head was playing tapes of wonderful girls I had had the privilege of being with in the past, and my obsessive head couldn't drop the issue.

It was official—my head had turned into its own Pussycat Theater showing quality adult films starring myself 24 hours a day and I really thought I was losing my mind. In looking back, I see I had done just that.

There was this beautiful psychiatrist who would spend a few minutes talking with us one-on-one, and here I was in my pajamas with race cars or teddy bears all over them, saying something like, "Say doc, when I leave this popsicle stand, what do you say you and I have a cup of coffee and discuss my treatment plan?"

She laughed at me and replied, "I don't think that would be a good idea… it's against the law for us to see patients outside the hospital."

For me, this opened the door for further comment, "Well, when I leave here I am no longer a patient of the hospital, and aren't laws sort of like rules… in that they were meant to be broken?"

Once again she laughed and just said, "Okay, Mr. Zalkins, that's enough of that."

"Excellent then, I will call you when I am out of here!" I said, laughing.

People fucking in rehab are as common as fat people shopping at Costco. Yes, people who shop at Costco for the most part average a daily caloric intake of 12,000 to 15,000. If you are thin and you shop at Costco, be grateful as you are part of a real small minority.

Where was I? Oh yes… fucking in rehab.

There was a girl named Laura in rehab with me and we shared the same sobriety date. She was very attractive and I'm pretty sure she was attracted to me. (I have no idea why—I didn't look very attractive. Slobbering, stuttering, and making zero sense aren't real attractive qualities in my estimation.)

Anyway, she was really hot, and although we didn't have sex in rehab, I am sure we both wanted to. In fact, I would have traded my doorknob in a heartbeat to sleep with Laura one night.

We all know I wasn't sleeping anyway, so we may as well have had a "Rehab Fuck Fest"! That's my insane head again, just wishfully thinking.

I had to start wearing two pairs of boxers under my sweats and pajamas due to the constant erections I was providing the hospital with. I was in one group meeting where I had sweats on and forgot my "anti-erection boxers," and what a surprise, everyone was leaving the meeting and I was just sitting there waiting for everyone to get out of there, which couldn't happen quickly enough. Laura said to me, "Come on, Todd, I'll walk up with you."

"Ummm, that's okay Laura, I think I am just going to sit here and try to figure some things out."

I was so embarrassed. It must have taken ten minutes for the diamond cutter, I mean my penis, to calm down so I could get to the dining area. I wouldn't forget those damned boxers again!

Sex would become a very intense and complex problem for me in recovery, and I will get to that in a little bit for sure.

LOST INTEREST

The opiates I was addicted to had slowly erased—I mean, eliminated—my sex drive. When I was actively in my addiction, I couldn't even masturbate. I remember one time out of the blue I said to myself, "I think it's a good time to jack off." After trying for about seventeen minutes I gave up because I could barely get a hard-on and it was pointless... I think my right wrist still bothers me from that failed attempt.

I consider myself to have a very healthy sex drive, and those who know me probably think my sex drive borders on the extreme when my libido is in check and healthy. How the woman I was engaged to put up with the lack of sex, I have no idea, there was about a solid year where I think we were physical once or twice. I had lost total interest in the act itself—in fact, all the beautiful things about love making were a total chore to me and not interesting in the least.

Everything in life that I either enjoyed or held in high regard was gone long before I entered rehab. My surfboards had gathered dust, my mountain bike hadn't been ridden forever, my running shoes hadn't been worn, my business hadn't been tended to, my friends hadn't been respected or reached out to—I had distanced myself from basically everything I had loved.

That's the power of addiction to me. It will slowly but surely take away and make you forget everything you have ever loved, until all that is left is the addiction and even then there comes a point where the drugs betray you, and you are on an island. That island is in the middle of fucking nowhere, and all you want to do is just be a part of death, because life is no longer interesting.

One other thing I need to stress is the loss of laughter and joy—I had lost them, and throughout my whole life laughter and joy were a cornerstone to my being. I always wanted to make others laugh, and it was something that seemed to come naturally to me. But as you hopefully have seen, things towards the latter part of my disease weren't funny and they sure as hell weren't filled with any type of joy.

That's what addiction also is to me—it's the ultimate eliminator of joy, love, fun, laughter, life, caring, respect, honesty, loyalty, one's personality, and on and on it goes.

When I was in my early teens, I told myself I never would be like my father, ever. What's ironic is that I would turn out to be even worse—he never touched drugs and he despised them, while I liked it all. How "non-prophetic" I was.

I don't think I really had a choice though, and if you are not an addict you won't understand this, the road I traveled is one I had to take, because the moment I discovered drugs and alcohol I found something that made me feel wonderful, and that was my answer for just about everything, it was absolutely impossible for me to turn off the switch of my addiction.

Had I have been able to simply turn the switch off and "just say no" to drugs and alcohol, I would have done so many years ago, but as long as it all worked "well" for me I had very little desire to change my circumstances.

Back to the rehab insanity and the "time of my life" (not)! There was no sleep to be found toward the end of my stay at South Coast Hospital. Dr. Headrick was giving serious consideration to placing me on the second floor (the psychiatric unit), which probably wouldn't have been a bad idea.

But my biggest fear was being put on some drug that would make me even more insane than I already was. My brain needed a chance to heal and to calm down, but when would that be?

Last Days in Rehab

The program at South Coast Hospital is thirty days. It's not that I didn't want to stay the full thirty, it's just that the final week is "family week" where all the relatives, spouses, kids, etc. get the opportunity to just unload on you and tell you how much of a sack of shit you really are, then they cry and say they still love you (I guess), and then you "coin out," like a little graduation from rehab.

I sat through one, and it was one of the biggest loads of bullshit I have ever seen. It was more of that stuff like, "I'm gonna miss you, Jenny. We are so close now—you are my best friend, and we will go to meetings together, and we will share family get togethers, blah blah fucking blah."

My head went straight to, "Jenny will not be your best friend... You were in rehab together—you are all so full of shit... the walls reek of your bullshit. You and Jenny will probably be sharing a fucking crack pipe in Santa Ana next week, and be participating in multi-ethnic gang bangs in hotels that charge by the hour... so don't give me this shit. None of us can stay sober!"

Again, that's just my insane thinking. Mix a radical detox, no sleep, and a sick guy like me and you are going to think the sick shit that I do. It's also a way for me to somehow get some relief, and at least make an attempt to humor myself. If I no longer have drugs and alcohol, what else is there? I had to find something to laugh at.

I was not involved with family week because I did not have the family around to participate in it. This is not a "poor me" story, it's just how it was for me. Participating in family week was uninteresting to me, and my fiancée wasn't joining in, so I became disengaged from the idea of staying the entire month of rehab.

Overall, my experience in rehab saved my life... there is no question about it. Even though I spent approximately twenty-three days there and didn't sleep, it gave me a safe and secure environment—and equally important, I found "hope."

That is one of the most beautiful words I have ever known, because for so long I had never known what hope was. For many years I was hopeless and helpless in my disease of addiction.

Hope would be discovered for me in many different forms, and one version of "hope" for me was seeing my friend Hazard in the dining room in rehab, which was paramount for me at the time.

Another profound dose of hope I heard was at the Tuesday night recovery meeting. It was one of these meetings while I was in the hospital, pajamas on, slobbering, shaking, and crying, but I heard a gentleman share something that just made me feel alive inside.

To this day I cannot remember what he said as I was so out of my mind, but when he said it, I literally chased him out of the meeting to talk with him during the break.

That man is a dear friend to me now, and he is an amazing example to me and a lot of other men in the program. I guess they call it "hearing the music." For me it was hearing something so strong and with honest conviction, it bled "hope."

See, that's all I ever wanted—a shot or a chance at living differently than the way I had. Now, I had to beat the ever-living shit out of myself to get to this point, but my feeling is that in order to want recovery I had to be "done"...and that's exactly what I was.

Anyone who stakes a claim to sobriety and lives it has to be beaten up enough to want it, and I have since learned that it isn't even about wanting it, it's about "doing it." Meaning, a program of recovery involves taking action, and unless I am taking the right action, I am not actively involved in my recovery. Just not drinking and/or using drugs isn't enough for me to be happy, I have to be "doing" what my program of recovery suggests.

So I heard "hope" in the form of a gentleman sharing at a Tuesday night meeting, sharing what is called in our Twelve-Step program his "experience, strength, and hope," and I am eternally grateful for that man speaking. He prompted me to think that maybe, just maybe, I stood a chance. My alternatives were minimal anyway, and I had nothing else to lose anymore.

At day twenty-three I was permitted to go home, and I had mixed emotions. I was still totally insane, and you are probably tired of hearing it, but I still hadn't slept yet and I was getting increasingly agitated and crazier.

Anyone else who was in the hospital with me just seemed so happy and excited, like it was some type of spa weekend with the girls, and it's all okay and time to go back to their normal lives of taking care of the kids and playing tennis.

My skin was still a big "pin cushion" and I felt like I was walking around with millions of pins sticking out of me—they were there but they were invisible.

I am very grateful for Dr. Daniel Headrick for being there for me, the sick man that I was, and for his taking the time to listen to me and sharing that my life would get better. Also the staff at South Coast Medical Center was gentle and kind to me when I really needed it, and they should get some type of medal for putting up with my 24/7 complaining ass.

I immediately started going to two or three recovery meetings a day. I don't want to share which program I am involved in, but there is Alcoholics Anonymous, Cocaine Anonymous, Pills Anonymous, Narcotics Anonymous, Marijuana Anonymous, Sex Anonymous,—Jeez, I think I could be a part of at least five of those for sure! But they are all effective, have all saved lives, and all base their spiritual program on the Twelve Steps.

My insurance business was already going straight to hell so I decided to give recovery my best shot and take a stab at saving my life and getting sober. I didn't even like that word either, "sober," that is for drunks!

I am special—I am a junkie, damn it, so call me an "addict." What a narrow-minded prick I was being, thank God I have now accepted the fact I am an alcoholic and whatever else you want to call me, it makes no difference in the world to me in the least.

"You Don't Have to...
Even if You Want to...."

I was coming up on a month sober when I heard something else that meant the world to me. It was after the Tuesday night men's meeting, and a few of us guys went to this beautiful spot by the ocean to meditate for a few minutes. I said to myself, "Oh sure, let's go meditate... Yeah right, I can't fucking sleep... maybe I will just mediate myself into the thought that I am well rested."

I knew nothing of meditation, other than it meant being quiet and still, both of which I wasn't any good at unless I was asleep. Oh, and by the way, at thirty days of sobriety I still hadn't slept yet (God's honest truth).

A gentleman, very large I might add and quite commanding with a deep voice, looked right into my eyes and calmly said, "You don't ever have to drink or use drugs again, even if you want to... and you don't ever have to be alone again either."

He was a gentle giant, and spoke with truth and conviction, and it shot right through that thick skull of mine. It was a verbal gun blast to me that penetrated my head like a hollow-point bullet.

I responded with something like, "Are you serious? I don't have to ever do that shit again? And I don't have to be alone anymore either?"

This was a really foreign concept for me. For whatever reason, hearing those words from another human being, someone who had peace in his life and love in his heart, meant everything to me. It's something I hope I will never ever forget, and this gentleman is now a dear friend and someone I consider family.

Since I had no business trying to speak, think, or write, I dove into going to Twelve-Step meetings of recovery. This became a safe place for me as I had zero faith in myself and trusting of self was at an all-time low. I was still detoxing very hard, my right hand and right leg shook constantly, and I thought they would never settle down or stop their wicked twitching.

Crying was something that came very easy to me. Confusion and feeling raw were at the head of my "feelings" list, not to mention scared and fearful. I would hear a song while driving and have to pull over because the words were so profound and beautiful that they moved me to tears. I was just starting to hear and see things differently, and I hadn't even gotten any sleep yet! Imagine how sweet that will be when I actually get some sleep!

I would try to share in a recovery meeting and I am really glad none of that shit is taped. I couldn't finish a sentence, and if I did, it made no sense whatsoever. It's called, "I was completely insane."

Most of us are pretty wacked out when we are brand new in recovery, it's totally normal not to understand one damn thing that a brand new person in recovery says. We are so twisted in the head and fragile that we don't have a lot of balance when speaking privately or publicly for that matter—I know I didn't. I do know that I scared the shit out of a lot of people, especially in my first six months of recovery.

I started to hear people with quality sober time tell me that I was helping to keep them sober. I thought to myself, Wow! I am an asset to someone—no way! How can I, with 33 days of sobriety, be helping someone with long-term sobriety?

Well, I now know it's because of one simple fact: when you hear someone new like me, come into recovery completely out of their fucking mind, making no sense, with major speech impediments and wanting to screw doorknobs in rehab, it makes other sober people feel really good. They were grateful beyond words they weren't in my shoes, and it reminds them what this disease does to us, and it makes them have a very stern understanding of not wanting to drink or use again, at least for that day.

Bottom line, I probably helped keep a lot of those guys sober because I was such a mess. Plus, I was really scary and uncomfortable to be around—my detox was so radical that a lot of guys joke to this day that they think I was actually loaded my first year of sobriety, and I tend to agree with that assessment.

Keeping Me From Harm

I said that the meetings helped me feel safe, and I sincerely mean that. So I would get out of bed each day, after lying there and not sleeping, and get to a meeting at 7:00 a.m., eat a gigantic breakfast, make some phone calls to some other guys in recovery and let them know how uncomfortable I was.

Then, I would go to a noon recovery meeting, eat a gigantic lunch, make some more calls to tell a bunch of guys and continue to share how uncomfortable I was, go home and lie down and try to remember what sleep was like, and then go to a recovery meeting in the evening.

That was my life, and it just had to be that way. My muscles, the ones I had left on my body, would ache constantly, and the sweating and clammy hands were a constant fixture of my existence. I had to keep going, though—I didn't want to be addicted anymore and I wanted a way out. A way was being shown to me but I couldn't process much of anything that was being said, because my head was so noisy inside.

This awareness of having a noisy head brought me back to when I was a young boy. I was always starving for exercise and something that would wear me out. I would be counting the minutes before school was let out so I could race to my bike, get home, and play football, baseball, hockey—anything that would tire me out. Never was I one to sit around the house and just watch cartoons all morning.

The kids I knew who did that were fucking tools, and I wanted nothing to do with them. Sometimes I would call three or four times in an hour to get a buddy to get his ass out of the house so we could go skateboarding, swimming, or whatever.

I would sleep pretty well after a long day of activity, and if I was sick, which was rare, I would be restless and dying to get outside to do something.

I was also starved for attention, and no matter how much I received it was never enough. It's only taken me 40+ years to realize this, and I didn't realize it on my own. I had to work the Twelve Steps of recovery to help me discover what the heck was really going on in that head of mine.

Upon having that first drink when I was young, everything slowed down for me. That was the magic. A drink or a pill or some powder ingested into my body would take things down a notch in this crazy head of mine. This had to be similar to a miner striking gold. That's what it was for me—alcohol and drugs were like striking into a goldmine, and it provided all the "good" that I needed and allowed me to step back and say, "All right, I am good right now and I can deal with things."

When I got a chip for "thirty days" of sobriety it wasn't that big a thing for me, which is not meant to demean the achievement, because I couldn't get thirty minutes of clean time before I came into recovery.

But what I wanted a chip for was "thirty days of continuous sleeping." I was now delusional, and I found myself with nervous twitches in the corners of my eyes, my right hand and leg wouldn't stop shaking, the corners of my mouth would nervously move, and I must have looked like I had Down Syndrome.

My mind was already gone. I was going to three meetings a day and I was listening to assholes in meetings say things like, "I am grateful to be sober today, and I am really lucky to be alive, and thank all of you."

My head was like, "You are so full of shit... If I was getting some sleep, I would pass off some lying bullshit like you just shared, you lying criminal." So there you have it—I was a disgruntled addict in recovery. I couldn't find the joy or comfort in anything, not yet at least.

SOME FUCKING SLEEP
WOULD BE NICE

I had checked into rehab on February 16, 2007... I did not sleep the rest of February, nor did I sleep the entire month of March. That's 44 days of no sleep, and I was very close to suicide—in sobriety, and this wouldn't be the last time I contemplated suicide, for real.

I would hear guys tell me, "No one ever died of lack of sleep." Which is a crock of bullshit, many people have died from lack of sleep. It's called being delusional and being driven to suicide. I locked myself into a safety net of recovery meetings two to three times a day, mostly three.

But that's a thing of the past. On April 1, 2007, I actually got some real sleep. It wasn't much, about three hours, but I got it. I cried like a baby at a recovery meeting the day after I got some sleep, and I think most of the guys in my recovery group were saying, "Thank God, now he might stop whining."

There was now a bit of light at the end of this dark tunnel. Trying to get clean and sober is the toughest thing I have ever tried to do, and when you mix in the sickness from withdrawal, muscle spasms, stomach aches, severe emotional twists, and sleep deprivation, it appeared to be like trying to climb Mt. Everest with no hands and no legs—just an impossibility for someone like myself.

The reason I wrote this book is to share with others who are dug so deep in the addiction to pain meds and other narcotics that it is possible. And you don't have to go to the depths I needed to go to get well and travel a new path.

The chief chemical dependency doctor at the rehab facility I was at in Laguna Beach, Dr. Headrick, told me the following, verbatim, about a year ago, "I have detoxed more than 12,000 patients, and yours is without question one of the worst if not the worst I have ever witnessed. We couldn't get you to sleep, no matter what we gave you, and I honestly thought it was very possible your brain would never heal or recover from all the abuse you put it through. It's a miracle you are sober, and I wasn't sure if you could get well."

That meant something to me when he said it. It was validation that one could go from "hopeless and helpless" to someone with hope and with a purpose in life, and that's a beautiful thing.

I started to eat healthier and exercise. Now, when I say exercise, it went something like this: I joined a gym in Laguna Canyon that has some real hardcore trainers and athletes, but I was not one of them at the time. I was so weak that I started out doing five or six minutes on a Stairmaster machine, and that was on very light resistance. Upon completing this "big workout," I would be out of breath and almost hallucinating.

The physical part of my recovery would change drastically over time, and is a critical aspect in my recovery today. Now I can't get enough physical activity, and I swim in the ocean two miles almost every day, along with surfing and mountain bike riding. But it took months and months to get stronger, while that thing called "life" was gradually being spoon-fed to me... and I wanted more of it.

I was buried completely into my meetings of recovery. I got a sponsor as they recommend, and I would call him each day whining like crazy, asking him, "When am I going to feel better?"

Hell, I would say that to anyone who would listen, like some other addict or alcoholic had this crystal ball that could dictate when I would feel better.

Then the same guy who told me, "You don't have to drink or use drugs ever again" had the audacity to tell me, "I don't give a shit how you feel—I care what you do."

That was unacceptable to me. "What do you mean you don't care how I feel? That's just mean, man, that's fucking mean." If he had been a bit smaller and not the bear of a man he is, I would have wanted to brawl, but thinking of being violent with this man was a losing situation no matter how I looked at it.

I have now learned that feelings are just that, feelings. Feelings always pass, and in recovery we aren't in the feelings business—we are in what is called the "action" business. I can't feel my way into right acting, but I can sure as hell act my way into the right feelings; that's what has been told to me numerous times.

This is something I don't want to try to dissect and explain, mostly because as I write this I have a little over two and half years of sobriety. I'm learning this new way of living a day at a time (and I didn't like hearing that, either, when I first came into recovery).

What I do know for sure is that when I start to help someone else out, either in the program or outside of it, I tend to feel a lot better about myself. The key for me is to "get outside of myself" and do the very best I can for someone else, whether it's my mother, a friend, a fellow addict in recovery, an elderly person needing help with their groceries, opening doors for others—anything that has to do with assisting others. This doesn't mean I will wash your fucking car for free, though. If fact, I hate washing cars, so don't ask me to do that, please.

They have all these wacky sayings in recovery meetings, things like, "Live and let live," "Easy does it," "Let Go and Let God." I sometimes can be in a groove of understanding these things now, but not when I was brand new, and the slobbering mess that I was.

One of the best things a gentleman told me was this: "Trust the process" and "Don't leave before the miracle happens." That's the stuff I needed to hear. All the other shit meant nothing to me, and it was generally said by some old codger with 59 years of sobriety who had gotten sober during the Ice Age before there were any good drugs available—see, there's my judgmental head going off on a tangent again! My head wanted to pass judgment and discredit the person who was sharing as much as possible.

I learned to put my trust in others, and I wanted to know a lot more about this thing called a "miracle." "What is that?" I would say to myself, and, "When is the miracle going to happen for me, damn it?"

Like I said, all the stuff I have learned and am continuing to learn in recovery has been given to me in little tiny pieces. This is a really good thing for me because as I mentioned earlier, if it's given to me at once or quickly I am going to take advantage of it. That's what I do.

In my second month of sobriety, I was like a baby learning to crawl again—forget about learning to walk. I was fresh out of the chute for this thing called life. Most of the people I was meeting who were new in recovery had a past of drinking and doing some blow and things like that. That was fine, but I could not really identify all the way, because I was a pill junkie for the last seventeen years and mixing coke and alcohol were merely frosting on the cake for me.

When I hear of someone getting clean and sober who had a similar affliction as me, it just warms me all over. I met a gentleman who had very long-term sobriety, and in fact at one point in his sobriety he had done "Twelfth Step work" with my friend Brad from Sublime (Twelfth Step work is basically carrying the message of recovery to those who still suffer, and doing this kind of stuff is a huge joy in my life today).

This gentleman, who now has more than twenty years of sobriety, was a hardcore heroin and cocaine addict and he was a mess his first year in getting clean—he shook and was uncomfortable like I was.

This was a breakthrough for me, because now I not only had Hazard back in my life with a few more months than me as a positive example, but I had my new friend who had more than twenty years of recovery, and his life was amazing after he endured a painful and uncomfortable first year of sobriety like I did. This gentleman is one of the biggest reasons I am clean today, and he is very special to me in many ways, which gave me glimmers of hope to hold on to. I tell him when we speak, "I love you, brother," and I mean it.

I was feeling miserable constantly, my back would break into these cold sweats without warning, and I was still detoxing very hard, what is called "Post Acute Withdrawal Syndrome." Well, isn't that a neat little term, I thought, now I have a "syndrome." Those around me seemed to be so happy about this newfound life of being sober, and it was just way too foreign a concept for me.

What I wanted was a little sleep each night, hopefully on par with what others in society have come to expect and love, that's all. The obsession for a good night of sleep was all consuming

But, sleep improved for me, but really slowly. I probably averaged anywhere from three to four hours for the next several months.

What I want to get into now was how different things around me seemed. In movies and television they often portray an addict or alcoholic going to rehab, and in 28 days when they get out, their life is just dandy and it's time to put on their "Kiss Me, I'm Sober" hat.

It's just not that easy, unfortunately, at least not for me. My feeling was that if I just got off of everything that life would be wonderful, and by not being enslaved by addiction I would just be a money-making machine, happy-go-lucky, and on my way to glorious things.

I cannot speak for anyone but myself, and for me the world outside addiction was a very different one. People around me seemed to have an air of confidence and a sense of purpose. I had been stripped of all the things I had relied upon to get through my days with pills, coke, and booze. Because I was no longer taking those things, I was left with really no idea of how to function in the world around me.

Running from Markets, Work, Movies, You Name It

I once went to this supermarket in Newport Coast and the lights inside were just blinding. With my right hand shaking nervously, I was attempting a new task in sobriety: going to the market. Most people do this like breathing in and out, they just do it and it's no big deal. Well, it was a major deal for me.

What would happen if you put a small child alone in a market? (I am exaggerating the point here a little, but stick with me.) If you put a five year old kid in a market to do some shopping, he or she will probably not be really effective with the task that's to be done. It's all new to the child, and that's my point.

I had a list of stuff to get, and then suddenly it just "rained" anxiety all over me. I couldn't focus, and people who were getting their shopping done seemed to be more capable people without a care in the world and without any sense of nervousness about them. For me, I couldn't find the fucking right type of bread to save my life, I had about three things in my cart, and I just left it there. I bailed. I could not handle it—I went out to my car, my right hand shaking wildly, and I just cried.

I hadn't experienced stuff like this without my thick coat of drug armor, not since I was a kid. I had gone through my entire life with some type of substance running through me to reassure me that everything was going to be okay. Everything I was doing was for the "first time" really. Paying bills was a complete debacle, forget about it. I could barely open up my American Express or Verizon bill for fear that the number on the bill would be something outlandish and I would never be able to handle it. My fear level was off the charts, and I always had this sense of impending doom like black clouds dancing around me.

Going to my office? Yeah, that was a real treat for me. I mentioned earlier how I thought I might have been rendered retarded from all my abuse. Well, throw me back into the wonderful world of commercial business insurance and what you had was a guy who could barely log onto his computer, and this is the guy who owned the damn insurance brokerage!

A day at my office was easy to sum up: I would go in after my morning recovery meeting, attempt to get something done, be scared to do it, and then leave in less than an hour.

Operating the fax machine was a challenge because I couldn't keep my detoxing trembling hands still. I would slump into my chair, my face in my hands, and unleash boatloads of tears due to my discomfort and this funny world around me that I could not identify with.

To even think that I was going to accomplish something in my office after rehab, while shaking, sweating, and scared out of my mind was absurd, and trying to handle the insurance of someone's business was a concept that might as well have been written in Chinese.

It was all too much for me, and I let many accounts switch to other brokers. Most of my clients couldn't get a hold of me anymore, either, so they just did business or renewed their policies with a different broker. I tried for a couple of months to work for a large brokerage in Newport Beach, but I would barely show up.

I was incapable of producing any new accounts, and the environment was just too intimidating for me.

That was fine by me, because all I wanted to do was be able to carry on a decent conversation with my fellow man without stuttering, crying, and slobbering. My brain was fried, and I would often wonder if God could help me out with this one and give me one more shot.

I had always loved going to the movies, but I hadn't been to the movies sober since I was a young kid, so I didn't know what to expect. My nerves and senses were really raw in my first year of sobriety. It didn't really appeal to me to go see *Grindhouse*, that double-feature film by Quentin Tarantino, but I thought what the heck, I could handle it.

I had to bail about thirty minutes in, I was scared shitless, like a little kid in way over his head. I raced into some G-rated cartoon movie, where I cried uncontrollably, and didn't calm down until about an hour later. I just wasn't adapted and ready for a movie that was out of control and violent, though if they are done right I really love that type of movie. It would take a year and half at least until I could invite myself to see a picture like that. In fact, I just saw *Inglorious Basterds* a few days ago, and I truly enjoyed it.

I often go to the movies alone, and consider it a good thing to do by myself. But no matter what theater I go to, and no matter how perfect a seat I score, I always get the random asshole coming in late with his fucking cell phone, texting and conversing with his "movie date" the entire time.

It's hard to digest when everyone else is being respectful and some donkey just thinks he's too important and the rules of common decency don't apply.

In sobriety, I am still capable of being insane, though not nearly as bad as when I was using. I have done the following to people text messaging during a film: I walk up and whisper, "Excuse me," and I now have their attention. I instantly go to my Joe Pesci attitude. "Tell you what, turn off that fucking phone and I won't break open your fucking head with it." Yes, I have done that, and maybe it wasn't the right thing to say, but he did turn it off and he did leave the theater, which I felt was a win-win.

This is not a common thing for me to do. I swear I am a lover of most people, only with the exception of verbally assaulting "Johnny Text Message Guy" at the movie theater.

There were several days in the first ten months of sobriety where I would have to lie in a fetal position on my bed and just let the tears flow from me. My interpretation of people and the world was too new and awkward, so in frustration, the best thing to do was to let my anger go in the form of a lot of tears.

Often the best part of my day was lying in my bed at night and eventually I would shut my eyes. That was bliss for me because eventually I would be asleep, and during that time my mind was turned off and I was safe from all the bad things in life.

During my active addiction I was doing well enough financially to buy my mom a home out in Green Valley Ranch (outside Las Vegas) and send her a little extra money each month. This was something I was proud of, and it made me feel good to help take care of my mom.

As a result of my addiction and inability to be financially productive, I had to ask my own mother to move out of the home I had bought for her and she had to fend for herself.

I had taken so much pride with being able assist her with the simple things in life, but there was no pride or self-esteem left by the time my addiction was through with me. Having put myself through hell is one thing, but adding my mother to the equation was devastating to say the least.

This was traumatic and heartbreaking for both my mom and me, and my biggest fear was that I would never again have the love and friendship I had for so long with her. The disease had dismantled everything in my life: financially, emotionally, physically, and mentally.

What's scary about it is that it happens gradually, not overnight, but then just like a tsunami hitting you—and it's just all gone.

I had about seven months of sobriety and I was trying to get my mom's house sold in Nevada, I was spracked out of my mind, meaning I couldn't think clearly, and as those of you who have bought or sold a home before know, it's not like buying milk and eggs at the store.

The market had taken a vicious turn, and in October of 2007 I was able to sell the house at a huge loss and I was basically broke, but I had a few retirement accounts left with a small amount of money, and that was it. They were sucked dry shortly thereafter. Had the drugs still worked for me, none of that money would have been there. I would have ridden the train as long as there was money around.

My losing the home I had bought for my mom can still eat at me to this day a little bit, but a lot of the guilt and shame has left me. There will come a time, I feel in my heart, when I will be able to buy her another one, and this time I won't lose it due to my selfish addictions.

This new "life" thing wasn't agreeing with me at all. But I was so sick and miserable that this sober thing was still worth trying. I just wanted to sleep normally and feel normal. But how in the hell do I know what any of that stuff is? I have never slept normally, and feeling normal? It's impossible! For I am a sick-ass pill junkie, cocaine-addicted alcoholic. How in God's name would I know a thing about normal?

Change of Heart

A t around six months sober I realized something that may make not one bit of sense, but it is my truth. As sick and confused as I was at that time, it was crystal clear to me that I was not "in love" with my fiancée. The reason I was not "in love" with her was that I didn't even know who I was.

That may sound foreign to some of you, but if you are an addict like me there's a good chance you have no fucking idea who you really truly are. There are so many layers of emotional items we must address when getting sober, and I will get to that later on.

But that same gentle giant I mentioned earlier who had said, "You don't have to drink again" and "I don't give a shit how you feel" also told me something that made me burn up inside, "You don't even know who you are." I was in shock. I replied, "What the fuck do you mean? I know who I am... I know exactly who I am!"

His response was one word, and he is known for this. He simply said, "Riiiiigggghhhht!"

I was so perplexed and pissed off at the same time. How dare that son of a bitch tell me I don't know who I am! The fact is, he was right, and I had a hard time admitting it at the time.

I had no idea who I was and I am still getting there, but things are getting much clearer. However, breaking up with a woman, especially my fiancée, is something I had zero experience doing sober. I don't do anything sober, remember? The normal thing for me when I was "done" with a girlfriend was to do one of the two things:

    A) Not tell the truth with how I feel and just ignore her.

or

    B) Not tell the truth, ignore her, not say anything, and get really loaded for days on end until she says, "I am sick of it—we are done."

Now that's pure music to my ears. To have the girl break up with me takes all the pressure off, and makes her look like the villain. You see, I am not emotionally mature enough to just say, "Hey, this isn't working for me. It's not going to work for me, and I am sorry."

Saying that would sure as hell be hurtful, but isn't being honest the best possible thing? I was incapable of being honest in my active disease, so this thing of living honestly was going to take some work while living sober—a lot of work.

But I did it. I broke off the engagement and did the best I could with explaining my sincere position at where I was in my life. It was devastating to her, and it tore me up inside to see that. I don't like to hurt anyone, and to see the pain on her face was just brutal. However, being in my shoes it was the best thing to do, and to this day it's one of the best things I have ever done.

I didn't want to get married to someone I was uncertain about being with, and to always question if I was capable of being the right partner for her, so I did what a man should do—I was honest about it. This I had to be taught, because I was just going to do what I usually did in my disease, and that is run. I run from everything.

As much as this was painful for both of us, I know I did the right thing. I had so much growing up to do, and I still do. I cannot be the quality partner I want to be for a woman unless I am sure of myself and of my intentions, and that I have healed as much as I can. I have been a destroyer of so many relationships that I can't count them. I want to be involved in a healthy relationship with a woman, and be honest, truthful, loving, and kind. How do I do this? I need to change.

I Need to Change

A gentleman I met in recovery told me when I was about three
months sober that "the same man will drink or get loaded
again." It took me a while to figure out what he was saying, but
for me it is the absolute gospel. If Todd doesn't change his attitudes,
behavior, and way of living, Todd will drink or get loaded.

That scared me, a lot. So I had to ask, "How do I change?"

He replied, "Work the steps in order, with your sponsor, and
outside of changing everything in your life I wouldn't change a
thing."

"Well, okay, damn it. That's what I want to hear." I had already
started to work the steps with my sponsor, and I don't want to get
too involved with dissecting all of that for those reading. But I have
to also change everything in my life, too?

Yes, I had to change where I went, who I saw, the things I did,
and the list goes on and on. I didn't think it was possible, but now
I understand it a bit more, and doing the things this man suggested
has made a huge difference with the quality of my life.

What I can say with complete conviction and 100% positivity
is this: The Twelve Steps of recovery have saved my life.

This is a process that an addict or alcoholic goes through with
a sponsor. My sponsor and my recovery program have taught me

that I must also have three things that are completely necessary in order to recover: to be honest, open-minded, and willing. When all of that is put together, something incredible happens that I cannot quite explain because it's such a miracle.

There's a sense of beauty and freedom that I personally received from taking the direction of another man and walking through the steps. However, it was a very, very painful experience for me. It was a type of emotional discomfort that was completely foreign. The Twelve Steps has been a way to look at myself, and uncover what is really going on inside of me. It allows me to find a God that I understand, and it allows me to make amends to people I have harmed.

They say you can have a "spiritual awakening" as a result of working the steps of recovery. I am not sure if I can testify to that. What I can say, is that as a result of working the steps and continuing to do so on a daily basis, my life is absolutely incredible and I am changing as a man.

It's not that I have fireworks blasting out my ass 24/7 because I'm so happy. There's a certain peace I get to have (for the most part) that is something I always used to try to obtain with drugs and alcohol.

So, I did the work as the men in my group asked that I do. I started to clean some stuff up that was referred to as "wreckage," and I was starting to sleep a little bit more each month—not perfectly, but I was starting to heal, and that was the best gift I could have ever hoped for.

Suicide in Sobriety?

At around ten months sober, I was still fighting with a low level depression that would just rip right through me. I would be up and down, up and down. I was going to lots of recovery meetings, sponsoring a guy, and "being of service" to other human beings inside and outside my recovery program.

Being of service is hands down the key for me, because the key for me is to not be thinking of myself. I have been taught that my disease is one of selfishness to the extreme; any time I can help anyone, it makes me feel better in return, and my life improves as a result.

My disease wants to isolate me and get me alone so badly, sometimes it's just ruthless. They say it is "cunning, baffling, and powerful," and I agree without question.

I was still detoxing at this stage. Most people don't understand this but it's the truth. Oxycontin is like synthetic heroin, and it's much tougher to get off of than heroin. I'm not saying that heroin isn't a bitch to get off of, it is. But there's something about detoxing off of Oxycontin, morphine, Fentanyl, and stuff like that. Picture Satan on steroids: It gets into your bone marrow and deep muscle tissue, and it also really messes with your brain and central nervous system.

I had worked the steps of recovery and benefitted from doing them tremendously. Yet I was struggling emotionally as well as with what is referred to as PAWS (Post Acute Withdrawal Syndrome). This can last up to eighteen months, from what I was told, and in my case, I was under the impression that it probably would.

The back sweats had gone away for the most part and the right hand and leg shaking had slowed, but not completely; it was this sense of darkness within me that I couldn't seem to shake.

Seventeen years of taking this stuff I believe qualifies me for some serious ups and downs, raging depression, uncertainty, and the darkest of thoughts—suicide. Yes, suicide. So I made an honest deal with myself. I would try my best to be happy and fake being happy if I had to, and if I was still experiencing these things at one year of sobriety, I was going to buy a 9 mm handgun and blow my fucking head off… I am not kidding around.

I have heard stories about people with both short-term and long-term sobriety who have taken their lives. I have a huge lust for life—most people who know me I think would agree with this.

Given a choice between suicide and relapse, some people go back to using drugs and alcohol. If someone said to me, "You can choose the Oxycontin, coke, and alcohol… or you can choose the handgun," I would grab the gun, stick it against my head, and pull the trigger. Now please don't take this as my being suicidal, because I am not—at least not today.

However, returning to the life I lived before is so scary, so frightening, and so devoid of joy and glory that I would simply rather go six feet under for the permanent dirt nap.

The thought of returning to the addiction, sickness, and constant chase for drugs is not appealing to me whatsoever, but this doesn't make me immune from going back out to using—let's get that perfectly straight. All I have are the 24 hours in a day, and if I stick with that I have a shot of living.

So I sealed the agreement in my head between me and God: If I didn't turn the corner on this depression thing, I was going to take the dirt nap. Pretty insane when I now think about it, but I am being honest with you, and that's where I was, up until February of 2008 when I would be getting my first year of sobriety... if I was lucky.

I don't have too many photos of my father. This one he's sporting a beard, in the mid 1980's.

Dad

There had been some communication by phone between my father and me in recent months, and this was something that made me feel really good because there hadn't been much of a relationship between us, and I was willing to give it a shot.

When I was growing up, my father didn't attend any of the sporting events I often participated in, or anything else for that matter, so there was severe detachment between father and son. I attended one football game in my life with my dad. It was around 1975 or 1976, and it was the Los Angeles Rams vs. the Kansas City Chiefs, when they were still playing in the Coliseum in Los Angeles where USC plays their home games.

I remember my dad had to stop at his factory that was located in the City of Industry, or Commerce, I forget which one. We went to look at some women's swimsuit samples and he had a few beers while we were there, and when we left to drive to the Rams game, he stopped at a liquor store for some more beers.

I don't ever remember my dad without a beer, glass of wine, or some other type of alcohol in his possession. I think it would have been weird if I didn't see my dad drinking, and it would have been a complete foreign concept to see him as a sober man. My memories of my father were of him being either very drunk, or terribly hung over. Only a handful of times did I see him not in a state of alcoholic disaster.

My dad had always been a very hard drinker, but he also had a disdain for drugs of any kind. Alcohol was the key to my dad's existence, from what I could tell, and he had struggled with his alcoholism for many years. He had gone to the Betty Ford Clinic in Palm Desert back in the 80s to make an attempt at getting sober.

I remember my stepmom Jean, stepsister Jill, and myself going to the clinic for some type of family meeting. We went out there, and my dad just cried for hours as he was losing his "best friend" in alcohol like I later lost mine with drugs.

Things did not go well with our "ultra dysfunctional" family rolling to Betty Ford. I think I said something that pissed off my dad and he replied, "What do you guys want from me?" That was one of his favorite things to say, and I think this was one of his defense responses when he could not "man up" or be accountable to what was really going on.

My dad had once been a successful businessman and had owned a chain of swimwear and lingerie stores. This had all gone away with his drinking, as did his marriage to Jean, and in my early sobriety he was living in a rented home and driving a car that didn't run very well.

The days of brand new Mercedes and Cadillacs were gone, but he still maintained a good character about him. When sober my dad was a fun guy to be around—the problem is, those moments were very few and far between.

He would go on these prolific drinking and gambling sprees, and when he got either broke or too sick from the alcohol he would throw in the towel. He was always lying to my brother and telling us he was sober, but who am I to judge? I have absolutely no room to judge anybody. I just wanted my dad to have a chance of living life differently, like I was trying to do.

In recovery we have a ninth step that states, "Make amends wherever possible except when to do so would injure them or others." Making amends to my father was a painstaking ordeal for me.

Because making an amends is not saying you are "sorry"—hell I said I was sorry thousands of times, and it was always meaningless. This process basically involves my owning up to my being wrong with my past actions and behaviors, and determining if there is anything I can do to fix it.

I set up a meeting to see my father who was still living out in Palm Desert, in the third week in January of 2008, one month away from my first year in sobriety. I was excited and scared at the same time, because there were so many different degrees of emotions and discomfort.

Being in recovery has taught me that I must be free of anger, resentment, and self-pity—this is so true, for me at least. If I have any of those three things, I am an emotional wreck, and if not addressed right away it could lead me to use drugs, drink, or both, and with me it's both for sure.

So I drove out to Palm Desert to see my dad. I was gripped with anticipation, but I also knew from having done many amends before this that there would ultimately be a huge weight lifted from my heart and shoulders.

We agreed to have breakfast together, and I picked him up at the very modest home he was renting. This was a far cry from the gorgeous home he had owned at PGA West for many years. I arrived early and he was ready. Dad had a very consistent regimen that he had learned from his Marine Corps days, and he was not one to sleep in ever, nor was he lazy.

Dad was a "doer" and he believed that people earn their way in life, as he was never given a thing (we both had that in common as well). He would be up at 5:30 or earlier each day, and he would make his bed just like they taught him in the service.

He was also very clean, and he couldn't stand a mess, so the kitchen and his living space were always nice and tidy. I liked that a lot—I can't stand a mess either, so the apple didn't fall too far from the tree in that regard, but I am pretty sure both my father and I knew what it was like to be a mess on the inside.

When I picked him up that day, I couldn't believe my eyes. He looked so old and weak—I wouldn't say frail, but alcohol abuse had weakened him and he appeared so much thinner. His face was leathered, which wasn't uncommon because he always loved being in the sun, but there was something missing and to me it registered loud and clear: he was just absent in the eyes, almost as though I could see right through him.

We immediately went to a local coffee shop and ordered up breakfast. I said how good it was to see him, and he said the same thing. Then I explained what the purpose of this visit was. When I started to get into the heart of the matter, his eyes began to water on the edges, and mine too. I had to wait a second before continuing on, as I was feeling all those years of torture that I had sustained, but also the emotional torture I had administered to others.

This wasn't about telling my dad I was pissed about him not being around, or sharing the trauma of what happened when he got physical with me. This was about my owning up to the wrongs I had caused at the household when I lived with him, and believe me, I caused major chaos.

My dad suddenly stopped me and said, "It's my fault you are an alcoholic, all my fault... I gave you my genes."

I told him, "None of this is your fault... I am proud to be your son (with tears streaming down my face). I am also proud of you for being my dad."

We both just hugged each other and cried enough tears to fill a few soup bowls. As much as this was emotionally totally draining, there was a sense of warmth and goodness that resulted from this encounter. All those years of detesting my father, all those years of being angry with him for not doing more for my brother Eric and me, all those weekends of disappointment from him not showing up to take us for the weekend—all that stuff that haunted me was suddenly gone.

Now, I cannot explain this because years of bullshit therapy when I was younger could never fix this or make me feel better.

Now I was 40 years old, an infant in recovery and really proud I was just around the corner from my first year of sobriety. The relief that was given to me was like a really heavy weight being lifted from my soul, and it's an experience that I consider to be one of the greatest gifts I have ever received. This is something that was gift wrapped and delivered by God himself, so thank you, God.

Never would I have dreamed that this would be possible, that the troubled water and extreme turmoil of our father-son relationship could be healed. So I looked across the table at my alcoholic father and softly said, "I love you, Dad."

He replied, "I have always loved you, Todd... I was just never very good at showing it."

After this exchange of honesty for the first time between us we stood up and hugged each other as father and son really for the first time. I felt his warmth as my father, and I felt the strength of his hug because he meant it, and I did too. We were two fairly large men in the middle of a restaurant embracing each other, and it didn't bother me in the least because the world stood still at that moment.

I drove him home and I had to get back to Laguna Beach. My eyes were swollen and my entire body was drained of all energy, but there was this sense of goodness and right. As I pulled away from Dad's driveway I can never forget what I saw. My father was standing in the driveway watching me drive like a cowboy riding off into the sunset in an old Western film.

Tears were streaming down his face and for the first time in my life I felt that my dad was proud of me. I examined him in my rearview mirror the entire time until I had to make my turn to the highway. He stood there until I was well out of sight.

Was the corner being turned for me emotionally? The deep depression seemed to lift over the next few days, and I made another pact with myself, it was time to grow up and be a man for the very first time in my life. I was taking ownership of the mistakes I had made and trying my best to fix things I had broken with people, places, and things.

There would be no chicken-shit suicide, even though I was serious with the first pact I had made with myself, it just seemed not to be an option. It was another way of acting irrational and immature as a result of my not feeling good when I wanted to.

I was rounding the corner and coming up on my first year of sobriety, which would be February 17, 2008. I was stoked, good things were starting to happen, and I was feeling free for the first time in my life.

A BAD DAY

I t was a beautiful day in Laguna Beach on February 14, 2008, and it's a day I will never forget. I had finished a mountain bike ride in Laguna Canyon, one of my favorite activities. I am pretty sure it was a Thursday. I returned to my North Laguna apartment and was putting my bike gear away when my cell phone rang with the area code of "760" appearing, which I believe is Riverside County. I rarely pick up a number I don't recognize, but I did in this instance.

The call went something like this:

Me: Hello?

760: Hello, may I please speak with Mr. Todd Zalkins?

Me: This is him. May I help you?

760: This is Detective Johnson form the Riverside County Sheriff's Department... Are you related to a Mr. Robert Zalkins?

Me: (My heart instantly started sinking) Yes, I am his son... What's going on?

760: I am sorry to report this to you but your father has died, and it appears to be as a result of suicide.

Me: Oh no, please tell me this is a joke. There's no way... please... no.

760: I'm sorry, Mr. Zalkins. I would like to give you the information for the County Coroner along with a report number, so you can claim him.

Just like that, I had been told that my dad had committed suicide and I get to "claim him" like I would a fucking coat in a restaurant. It sounded so cold, but the guy was just doing his job. I was numb, I was crying, and I was angry. I was shaking violently as I tried to phone some of my brothers in recovery and none of them were answering.

My level of discomfort cannot be explained correctly—my first thought was, "Fuck it, I am going to get loaded. I cannot handle feeling this way—I can't do this anymore."

Then something else popped into my head, "Just keep dialing the numbers of your brothers in recovery, and don't stop." And I didn't stop. I got a hold of some guys and told them what had happened, I could barely speak and I was inconsolable.

I wanted to feel different, immediately. I asked God why this was happening. After all this sickness I have endured, after all the shaking, insanity, sleep deprivation, all of this shit, for this? I thought things were supposed to be getting better?

I finally got a hold of one of my most trusted men in my group of recovery. He has a beautiful wife and family, and on Valentine's Day he received a call from a despondent individual (me) and I shared with him what had happened with my father.

On an evening he should have been spending with his wife, he immediately rushed to my place in North Laguna, and the sight of him showing up may very well have saved my life. I couldn't stop crying, and he just held me in his arms and said, "It's going to be okay, it's going to be okay."

He's one of those guys that always tell it like it is, and giving me sound advice as to how to handle the situation, he calmly said, "Todd, I know this is fucked up. I can't imagine how you feel right now, and this is probably going to feel fucked up for a little while, but you don't have to go through it alone."

That was one of the biggest doses of comfort I have ever been fed, and it didn't come from a pill, a line of coke, or a drink. This relief came in the form of one man helping another cope with a situation that normally is addressed with lots of drugs and alcohol. This gentleman is a huge part of my life today, and he helps many others on a daily basis. He is like a brother to me.

Life dishes up stuff we don't always like. The fact is my life was already improving, I just didn't realize it at times because everything was so new. But now I had to call my brother Eric to tell him that Dad was gone.

My dad was Eric's hero, and they were closer than my dad and I ever were. This was going to be difficult. I made the call, and Eric surprisingly handled it okay (for the moment, the shock would wear off and he would really be affected later).

My father was a very depressed and sad alcoholic. He had lost everything and he couldn't get sober. He wrote a note that simply said, "I cannot go on living like this anymore. I am sorry. I love you, Dad."

What he did was drink a large bottle of vodka, go into the garage, and start his car, and he never woke up. He died from the toxic car exhaust fumes. A couple of days later I drove out with a brother of mine in recovery to Palm Desert to check out my dad's place; my brother Eric was meeting us there as well.

I mentioned how my father was a proud former Marine, and he was always very clean and neat. His bed was always made perfectly, with his clothing and things like that always put away in meticulous fashion.

The scene was heartbreaking. His room was a total mess, and nothing was in order. My brother and I held each other and cried—without having to say a word we knew what the other was thinking. "Look at this—dad was a broken man. He was a sad, depressed, and lonely alcoholic, and he was a lost soul."

Not one word was mentioned about the condition of the house. Just seeing it spoke a thousand volumes. I had separated my body from my mind, and my body helped my brother Eric be strong and we cleaned the place up. Later I told Eric how much Dad loved him, and how proud Dad was of him. The empty look on my brother's face is one I shall never forget. He couldn't talk because his heart was broken and he was sad—we both were.

We then drove over to the county coroner's office. I walked in with Eric, but he lost it and turned around saying, "I can't fucking do this." I totally understood.

My brother and I didn't get along well as kids, but this was a time for us to come together and be strong, and we both did just that in different forms. Eric would later on deal with some very difficult people that I couldn't handle, and I addressed some other things. Eric "manned up" and did the best he could.

I proceeded to "check in" with the clerk at the front of the coroner's office and they walked me back to a room where a detective met with me. The detective asked things like, "Was I aware of anyone who may have wanted to harm my dad?" Or, "What had his behavior been like lately?"

I answered the questions as best I could and finally just said, "Can I please see my dad?" as tears rolled down my face. I was anxious to get this over with and go check on my brother and hold him and tell him I loved him.

The detective walked me over to the area where the bodies were, and I watched as he unzipped the body bag. There was my dad, looking at peace for the first time. I asked the detective to give me a second alone, which he did.

This gave me the opportunity to say my last goodbye. I said, "I love you, dad. I am so glad I had the chance to see you a few weeks ago... You are my father... and you are Eric's father... and we both love you a lot. I hope you are no longer in pain, and no longer suffering."

It went just like that. My body was numb, I couldn't believe I didn't want to drink or take a drug, and I don't get any credit for that. My belief is that God wanted me to be there for my heartbroken brother, my brother who had lost his hero.

Had I not been sober I would not have been there to love my brother. Or if I was loaded and I made it out to see my brother, there would have been a huge brawl both verbal and physical, and nothing would have been accomplished.

Being sober for this tragedy was actually a gift that I now realize. There were people in my life who helped me cope, and I didn't drink or use. This was unfamiliar to me as I don't grieve—I get loaded and stuff whatever it is I am feeling down in this garbage disposal known as "Todd."

There are some things I learned from this heartbreaking loss of my father. The best thing I learned is really quite simple, but I needed to hear it, and that was, "Your dad did the best he could with what he had."

That's exactly right too. For so many years in my addiction I was quick to blame the bad things that happened on an irresponsible father and his incapability of being a real father. This just isn't true, my father had love somewhere deep within, he was just a very sick alcoholic, and it's hard to reveal genuine love when alcohol is blocking it all out.

I was having my first sober birthday, and I had just been to the coroner to see my father who had taken his own life. I had a funeral to plan, a brother to look after, and strangers to contact whom I didn't want to call. I did all of this, but I did not drink or use drugs.

The fact I didn't get loaded after my dad committed suicide was a big deal for me, and it's a big deal for anyone who has ever gone through it. Something was tattooed in the forefront of my mind, "I just don't want to return to the way I was living... I just don't."

All of this came with a very heavy emotional price tag though, and there were many times in the months to come when tears would come out of nowhere. This was sadness I was experiencing from the loss of my father, and of my hope of building some type of loving relationship with him.

There is a beautiful part to this though, and that is the fact he and I spent some time together loving one another with no anger or bitterness. Just love—and for me, that's good enough, even if it was just for a few minutes in some cheesy coffee shop.

People die in the disease of alcoholism and addiction, unnecessarily. There are car crashes, overdoses, shootings, suicides—all that stuff happens, but it doesn't have to. I have experienced the loss of persons I have loved in every one of those scenarios. What they have taught me is how lucky I am to be free and to be breathing the salty air where I live.

I now have a chance to share love with others, without condition. I now have a chance to be a man, and cease being that child who could never grow up. I believe having some childlike qualities can be a good thing, but not 24/7, and that's what I was for so very long.

Shortest of Fuses

My brother and I held my father's funeral service at a military cemetery in Riverside. There weren't many people there, but the ones who were remembered how well my dad could run a company and how hard he worked. The former CEO was there from New York—this is the same guy whose limo ride home I ruined during the Christmas holidays by getting loaded with his driver. He had long forgotten this incident I believe... or maybe not.

My dad died with $1,142 dollars in his checking account and had no retirement fund or stock portfolios. There were no lawyers to visit or a big estate to fight over, and I am actually grateful for that.

My brother and I were fragile enough as it was. I took the death certificate to a branch of my dad's bank to close out his account, and I was already a gigantic walking stick of dynamite and raw nerves unwinding and waiting to go off.

It went down just like this:

Teller: Hi, how may I help you today sir?

Me: I am fine, thank you... I am here to close out my father's checking account... he passed away recently.

Teller: I am sorry to hear that, sir.

Me: Thank you....I have the death certificate here and several pieces of my own identification. There was no written will or estate to speak of.

Teller: Thank you, Mr. Zalkins... In order to process your request I will need a JGT-50 Form.

Me: Well, okay... May I please have one of these forms to complete?

(The teller turns around and looks around for a second, then turns back to face me.)

Teller: I am sorry but I don't have this form right now. But you can go to one of our other branch offices to take care of this.

Me: No, I don't think I would like to do that... Please excuse me, but it's been a rough couple of weeks. Can you please contact one of the other branches and have it faxed or emailed so I can take care of it right here?

Teller: I am sorry, I cannot do that. There are people waiting behind you.

(This is where the spirit of Joe Pesci instantly runs through my veins and I am now making an appearance in *Casino* right alongside Pesci.)

Me: Waiting behind me? I will tell you what, you cunt-faced rodent, if you don't close out this fucking account right now, I am going to grab you by that gay-ass fucking tie you are wearing and drag you over the fucking counter and I will break open your fucking head in front of everyone here, and I fucking mean it.

Teller: Sir, you don't have to talk to me like that... and I am going to call the police.

Me: Forget the police you cocksucker, you better call the fucking paramedics!!

I can tell you with 100% certainty that I was homicidal at that time. I didn't grab the "little rodent with the lame tie" and beat him, but I wanted to. Just because I am sober doesn't mean I don't have moments of horrible overreaction—granted they are rare, but they do occur.

Especially with the way this guy talked to me, as he arrogantly said, "No, there are people behind you."

That's all it took, and my "fuck you" switch was turned on. If it were the old times of the Wild West, I would have taken out my revolver and shot him in the face, then dragged him down the main dirt street behind my horse for all the townsfolk to see.

I was so upset, I was trembling, and the first thing I thought of was a drink and a few pills—yes, that will take care of this shitty feeling, and, "Fuck that guy in the bank, I will show him!" That's the type of rationale that will kill me, and anger is not something I can carry around like a little tote bag. I have to be free of anger any way possible.

The next day I went back to the bank and apologized to the little shit, I mean bank teller. I didn't want to, but I did feel bad that he almost crapped his pants. Plus, after sharing this with my sponsor it was suggested that I go and see the teller and make an amends. I really hated doing it, but I am glad I did.

When I walked into the bank, you should have seen his face—it was like Armageddon rising or something. I cannot tell you how much I wanted to say, "Remember me, you fucking little prick? I am here to make your life miserable." But the conversation didn't go like that, it went more like this:

Me: Excuse me sir, do you remember me from yesterday?

Teller: Of course I do. I barely slept last night because of it.

Me: Well, I am apologizing for my behavior yesterday, and I need to tell you that... And there was a time when this conversation would not be taking place, but it is.

Teller: You scared me yesterday.

Me: I know, and you pissed me off yesterday. I just want you to know that I'm sorry, and I hope you have a great day.

Teller: Thank you for saying that. I was already having a bad day before you came in.

Me: A bad day? I can relate to that. I had several bad days in a row before I came into the bank, but that's all done now. Have a good week.

Teller: Thank you, and you do the same.

This was a most unlikely thing for me to do because I can harbor anger for a long time when I am on drugs; when sober I simply cannot function while angry, and I need to channel it and find a way to quiet that "angry storm" that can twist around in my head.

For me, going to apologize to this bank teller was the most contrary type of action I could imagine doing. I only did it because my sponsor told me to, and it turned out to be the right thing for me to do.

Sex Addict?

Once my head got a little clearer and my sex drive started returning, I couldn't get enough of it. I mentioned earlier how I find a woman's orgasm to be one of the most beautiful things I have ever experienced, and I still believe that.

However, having affairs with women in sobriety has done nothing for me but fill that void I had, that used to be filled with drugs and alcohol.

The physical part of sex became a complete obsession with me, to a point where I thought I might have to go to some "sex addict hospital," if that exists. Having a loving and meaningful relationship is something that is very important to me, but also very foreign. I had to uncover what was going on behind my obsessive sexual drives.

Getting a woman off became a new addiction for me, and it's something that's no more or less twisted than the man who used to chase prescription medications for a living. At the end of the day, I am still left feeling empty and alone—that had to be addressed.

Deep down I have come to understand that I have a tremendous fear of my partner leaving me. That's what I did to others in my disease, and I would force others to do that to me. I am conditioned to let someone in only to a certain extent, and that's because it will end up being hurtful—and I don't do hurt, remember?

All of these things are new to me, and when drugs and alcohol protected me I didn't fear losing so much. Temporary sex partners no longer satisfy me. I had to travel a path of having meaningless sex in order to reach yet another "bottom." It's similar from an emotional standpoint to the bottom I reached from my addictions, but nothing could ever compare to the pain I went through getting sober, no way.

Life is going to happen and things don't always work out the way we want them to. If I can get through all of the things I experienced in my first year of sobriety, I can get through anything with the support of others, of course, and staying connected to God and my program of recovery, but trying to handle everything on my own is a frightening proposition, and not a good idea.

Sometimes I will see a beautiful couple and I will say, "That's what I want. That's how it should be for me," and I have absolutely no clue or idea about the persons I am admiring—hell, this could be the gentleman's mistress and not his wife, or vice versa.

I still have a disease of perception, and it's right in my head. It will tell me, Wow, I want that person! Or Look at her, isn't she amazing? I would do this without having any knowledge about the quality of the person's insides. I can find outer beauty in thousands of women, but how do I have any clue as to how the person is on the inside?

The outsides give me the immediate impression of, "Oh yes, she is smoking hot, and she is perfect for me." That's just my selfish desire to have her physically, and she could be the biggest nightmare of all time. Women are no longer "targets" to me, persons just to get it on with and detach from when things get out of line or unattractive for me.

I am now looking for something more, and it involves being able to hold and respect that person, to be there when she has a good day or a bad one, and to love without condition. Growing up can be painful for me, and definitely not comfortable, but when I get to the other side of some pain I get the chance to grow just a little bit, which is totally new.

When I was addicted, there was no chance I could be there for someone else—I couldn't even take care of myself. I am walking through this "exercise of life" now, and it's pretty cool to be a participant in life, instead of a spectator, where before I wasn't even in the stadium.

NOW

It's Labor Day, 2009 as I write this. I am looking out from my apartment and I see the tranquil, blue water. It's days like this when the colors are so richly blue that I have cried because for the first time in my life I can actually see and appreciate the beauty around me. There is so much out there—so much to see, and so much more to learn.

Never was I capable of being a student before, now I just want to absorb information, as much as possible. I also want to listen, and listen closely.

I want to turn the cell phone off and just breathe, and not be so caught up in the insanity of how life can often be. I can now fully acknowledge that I am both a drug addict and an alcoholic. The cool thing is, I am a recovering drug addict and alcoholic.

There are days where I am uncomfortable, but those days are few and far between. It's a blessing to not want to have to rip off my skin to stop it from hurting, and it's a relief for me to not want to wish I was someone else, or something else.

I can be myself for the first time in my life. I can learn to love others, and love with conviction, without condition, and without expecting anything else in return.

I don't chase doctors from city to city, and I don't lie to them anymore because I don't have to. I don't forge prescriptions or call pharmacies with fraudulent prescription refills, nor do I carry around sacks of white powdered cocaine in my vehicles.

I sleep like a baby every night, and I regularly call my mom to tell her I love her. I tell my friends I care about them, and it's the truth, not an empty-drunken bullshit, "I love you, man."

For so many years I hated being addicted to all of those pills, and for so many years they gave me something special. But all of that all changed, and even when it changed for the worse I still carried on. I continued in my disease because each time I tried to get off of the pills on my own I simply couldn't do it, and I tried so many things to get well.

Pill junkies go through a long process of hell with their recovery, and how quickly you feel good has a lot to do I think with your age and how long you used. For me, I used pills solidly for almost seventeen fucking years—that's thousands and thousands of pills. We all bounce back differently, and for me it had to be brutal and painful.

People do recover, though—they really do. There were two things that in looking back were the most important for me. First, was just getting some physical sobriety, which I knew nothing about.

Second, was seeing "recovery" work for someone else who had been addicted to the same stuff I was.

When I saw my friend Hazard in the hospital, and when I met another gentleman in recovery with a heavy opiate addiction who had been clean for many years, that closed the deal for me. After that it was like, "Okay, tell me what it is that I have to do in order to get well."

I want to make it perfectly clear to those who are suffering and wanting to get clean and sober that it can be done, even though your head tells you otherwise. If you love someone who is slipping away in this horrendous disease of prescription drug addiction, they can get well.

It's a fact, because never would I have thought it was possible for a guy like me to get clean, but I am.

Turning the Tide

Earlier I mentioned how in my addiction all of my surfboards had collected dust, mountain bikes were no longer used, and all that stuff. Today is a complete different story—the surfboards are used regularly and I take these unreal mountain bike rides in the canyons of Laguna Beach that can test every fiber in your body and really kick your ass.

I live just across the street from this gorgeous little beach called Tablerock, and almost every morning I swim down to the Montage Hotel which is about a mile away, and there's nothing like it. I have had schools of dolphins swimming next to me, and I often say to myself, "This isn't me, but it is me now and it's all because of getting clean and sober."

The best part of this swim, though, is that I get to talk to my dad at the 1-mile mark when I turn around to swim home.

I spread my father's ashes in front of the Montage Hotel, and it's a ritual for me to stop in the water and say a few words to him. Sometimes it's just a simple, "Hi Dad, how are you today?" or a quick, "I love you." There are moments where I can really go deep and literally have a conversation with him that is reinforcing on many levels.

Experiences like this are so important to me now because I am stripped down totally from an emotional perspective, with no walls to hide behind, and nothing is serving as that buffer that drugs and alcohol once did.

All these activities have been a very important part of my recovery, along with eating healthy and getting plenty of sleep. Never would I have thought I would be able to experience all of these beautiful things again—for the first time, I am clear enough to take in and truly appreciate the scenery around me. I see things differently, and I smell things differently, and it's just a joy to have my senses really alive for the first time since I was a kid.

My senses were numbed and non-existent for 24 years or so, and that's long enough, I believe. It wasn't too long ago that the most exercise I got was going to the kitchen for more yogurt and granola, or putting on pajamas and slippers to go meet my dealer in Long Beach.

I had lost sight of everything with beauty and meaning, now they are within reach on a daily basis and all I have to do is stay sober to continue to experience these things.

It's funny in a weird way, that I actually like not having any idea what's going to happen tomorrow. In all the years of my perpetuating addiction I knew what was around the corner, meaning I knew I had to get more drugs to stay loaded or "well," and I knew that I was going to feel crummy and lethargic in the morning, or I knew I was going to feel like committing suicide—the "knowns" were obvious and a certainty.

Now what's a revelation for me is that I have no idea what the next day will bring. I have days where I am on cloud nine, and I have days sometimes where I am grateful just to have gotten through the day with some form of dignity and respect and more importantly, to have been kind and respectful of others.

I had plenty of moments when being respectful of others was the least of my concerns, and my crazy mind was fixated on one thing—that fast relief that drugs and alcohol provided which would eradicate my fears and protect my fragility.

It's nice to be able to open up and look others in the eyes and speak with truth, as I have absolutely nothing to hide anymore. I don't have to. That is something that I now know, but that was an unknown for many years while I was terribly addicted.

DESPERATION TO HOPE

ebster's online dictionary defines "desperate" as: "Having lost hope, a spirit crying for relief."

If there is one word that could best explain my emotional status it was "desperation." That's exactly what I was, a sick guy crying for relief and having no hope. Nothing is worse to me than when someone has lost hope. I love that word today, but before I got clean I was uninterested in its meaning.

The definition of "hope": "To cherish a desire with anticipation."

That gentleman who shared at a Tuesday night meeting of recovery gave me "hope." It was life-changing for me, and it makes me warm inside when I think of that man giving me some feeling that I too could have hope.

I don't know of any drug addict who says, "I dig being a drug addict—this is the life and I wouldn't change a thing."

Show me a junkie and I will show you a very miserable human being. I never intended to become a junkie. On "Career Day" in sixth grade when people were sharing that they wanted to be a fireman, teacher, or the president of the United States, I didn't chime in with, "I want to be a hopeless pill junkie, cocaine addict, and alcoholic."

As a kid I dreamed a lot, and I had a lot of joy and wonderment, but all of that changed for me with my dad leaving when I was seven. Once I had a real, true drunk experience with my friend George, the stage was all set. I know a lot of people who after throwing up and blacking out after drinking either never drank again or drank only very sparingly.

Not me—I am an alcoholic, and I am going to chase that feeling I get from drink and drugs so long as it gives me what I need, and even when the wheels have come off and I am insane, I will still try to keep going.

I made my choices, and I have to be in recovery for the rest of my life if am going to have the life I have this very day. Love has been let back into my heart along with the joy of being free from the pain of addiction that has left me, and it is hands down the greatest gift I have ever received. There is no material possession that could take the place of what I now have inside. For me, it's the insides that now count most.

What means everything to me is waking up to breathe another day without a machine attached to my face pumping air into me so I don't overdose. What means even more is being able to reach out and hold somebody at a meeting, look him in the eye and tell him, "It's going to be okay," and mean it.

That's the payoff for all the shit that I went through—the payoff is being able to pass on "hope" to some other guy wanting to change his life, just like the gentleman did for me in Laguna Beach on a Tuesday night in 2007.

WHAT CHRONIC PAIN?

Before I got sober I was really concerned I would have all of this chronic pain come racing back through my body because I was no longer medicated with pills. For those of you reading this who have these issues or fears, let me tell you what happened with me. As you know, I had some heavy surgeries in my life, some that were needed and some that weren't. Something in my head told me I had to have these drugs because I had legitimate chronic pain.

But how would I know how much pain I was really in without being off all the narcotics to begin with? My brain and addicted mind demanded that I have more pills—I needed this stuff to get by, and there was no way I could be talked out of that way of thinking.

From what I have learned, my brain demanded more drugs because my head was simply playing tricks on me. I had to "feed the tiger," and that meant a lot more pills. My brain wasn't in a natural state and it was unable to gauge anything, like pain, but the drug-filled brain knew for sure that I needed more and more pills for my worsening pain.

It was just the addiction.

After the first couple weeks of being in rehab, I wasn't in that much pain related to my surgeries. I was going through the horrific detox and emotional pains of getting sober. It's been two and half years as I write this and I still go through emotional stuff, but I do it differently today. I can process things differently, and hopefully not overreact to things that are out of my control.

I have some physical discomfort at times, but nothing that an Advil or an Aleve can't help me with, and I never would have dreamed I would even be saying those words… "Advil or Aleve, are you kidding… That shit doesn't help my pain! I need drugs."

The truth is, those over the counter things work for me just fine when I am uncomfortable, and what a blessing that is.

If you're reading this and you are addicted with a surgical history, I hope you can relate. And if you are just simply addicted or alcoholic, I hope you can relate as well.

Only a few things can really happen to addicts like myself: You can either get clean and have an amazing and beautiful life, or you can carry on in the misery of addiction and hopefully reach that level of desperation that I experienced so you can make a change, or you can simply die from an overdose, car crash, or suicide.

The options start to get really thin as far as I am concerned, and when that road narrows it simply comes down to "Change or Die." That may sound harsh, but it's also the reality of this disease. Once the drugs had truly stopped working, and I was completely insane, I had to make that decision.

The drug companies aren't going anywhere, pharmacies will continue to thrive and new ones pop up all the time. In addition, there is the Internet now to get drugs and doctors who will prescribe drugs freely—the epidemic of prescription pain killer abuse isn't getting any better, that's for sure.

Another sure thing is that there will always be a lot more people addicted to this crap than people getting off of this crap. Why would you want to get off of something that works so well? If the pills still worked for me, I wouldn't be writing this story of recovery. But the fact is my addiction progressed to a point where everything in my life was gone, and I had lost my mind.

That's the choice we must make for ourselves. No individual can make me get sober. I can get help from others, but unless I possess a willingness to get well, I will never get clean, it's just that simple.

NUDIST NO MORE

I took great pride in being a lunatic since I was a little kid, starting with running around Naples Island naked for free fireworks, graduating to naked bridge jumping, surfing naked behind boats, and let's not forget the need to cram my dick into the mashed potatoes at holiday parties.

These were all forms of my garnering attention, and I still think some of it is funny, but I haven't jumped off any bridges lately—not naked at least—and I swear I am safe to bring to any holiday party. All guests can be confident the mashed potatoes haven't been visited by my private parts.

However, there are instances where nudity presents itself in a good way, and that's more of a private matter, and it's important to know that it doesn't involve any doorknobs either.

THESE DAYS

I show up when I say I am going to show up, and excuses and cancellations don't rule my life. If I say it, I mean it, and I do what I say I am going to do.

I get to surf and take long ocean swims and appreciate all the beauty that God and a strong program of recovery have given me. I get to see the beauty in other people, when I could see none for so very long.

I get to spend time with my beautiful mother, who is back in my life only because I am sober. Addiction took away and destroyed our relationship; now I can't wait to hear her voice and tell her I love her. My mom and I have both concluded that as much as we know each other as mother and son, there is so much we don't know about each other.

At first I was hurt when we discussed that and I heard my mom say, "There's so much we don't know about each other." It stung like bees in my skin to hear that, but there is so much freedom in being honest. I view it as such a wonderful opportunity to learn more about my own mother, as well as learn more about myself.

I used to think that the most important thing that defines a human being was his or her financial accomplishments or social status—all I knew was how badly I wanted to earn more and more, and be something I just wasn't. The thing that really matters to me now is relationships with other human beings, honest relationships that have substance and meaning.

I still love to laugh and I want to have fun, but I also want to grow up. Laughter is still the greatest healer to me, and when I laugh now it's just better, pure and real.

Yet I have so much further to go. I just finished a long swim in the ocean where I live in South Laguna Beach, and I am laughing at myself. I opened my wallet, and there are two dollars and a free movie pass, but I have never felt so rich and abundant inside, that is something I always wanted.

I am just learning to live this thing called life, and the fact is I wholeheartedly love my life today but it wasn't that way for a very long time.

My wish for you is that if you or someone you know is suffering, this book will help you realize that there is a way to get out of this addiction and to start something new, something you can embrace, like a new life.

This memoir is dedicated to the addict or alcoholic who thinks they are forever stuck and can't get out. I swear you can do it, I promise.

What's really cool is that I am finally getting to know who I really am after 42 years. The man that I was would despise the man that I am today, and the man I am today never wants to forget the man I was.

Oh, and one last thing, remember that woman I gave CPR to in Little Saigon? She gave birth to a beautiful, healthy baby girl, and her name is Vi.

A little infant will get to grow up and experience life, and maybe even get the chance to be a mom herself one day, all because a former insane, drug addicted guy like me got clean and sober... and I think that's pretty cool and probably the neatest gift I have ever received.

THE END

Selected Journal Entries from Sobriety

2-27-07 (Sober 11 days)
"No way can I live like this. It's impossible for me, I am so scared. I am so fucking sick, and everything hurts and I can't sleep. Everyone around me seems fake, and I don't understand. I want to fly away, somewhere where there's no one else, and I am not sick. That would be okay with me."

3-15-07 (Sober 29 days)
"My skin is crawling and I constantly sweat. I can't fucking sleep and I am trying everything. I am stuttering all the time and I cry in frustration. Take off this uncomfortable skin please, I am losing my mind. Please God, I don't know what to do and I am barely hanging on."

3-26-07 (Sober 40 days)
"I'm at the end of my fucking rope, I can't stand this. I'm going to all of these meetings, I don't understand a thing and I can't speak clearly. I think I might be retarded from all of my drug use and that's scaring the shit out of me. I'm scared and I don't think I can hang on much longer. Some asshole said, "no one ever died from lack of sleep," and I wanted to grab that cocksucker and say, "Oh yeah, really? When was the last time you fucking didn't sleep for 39 or 40 days, or however long it's fucking been, you big sober asshole?" If I hear one more guy say he has two weeks sober and he loves his life, I am going to kill him in front of the entire meeting. How in the fuck can anyone be happy after being sober for two weeks? It's impossible. I think he's a lying asshole criminal."
"P.S.: My name is still Todd, I believe, and I am just completely fucking insane. I hope to God I don't ever have to read any of this shit that I am writing down because I don't make one bit of sense."

4-1-07 (Sober 44 days)
"I can't believe I fucking slept, I think I actually slept for three hours! Maybe I can sleep again tonight."

10-19-07 (Sober 8 months & 2 days)
"I want to remember. I don't ever want to forget where I was, how dark my addiction was, and how sick I was. Never do I want to forget how alone I was, the isolation and nonexistent soul, the empty heart, the broken mind, and the horrific withdrawal, just void of life. The fact I am not addicted today is just a miracle. To not be a slave to the drugs, to not have to chase doctors and dealers all over the place—I never have to go back there."

10-29-07 Sober 8 Months & 12 Days
"I have a total fear of financial insecurity. It's all been drained away in front of my eyes. I can't stop the fear I have at this moment, and it's causing a lot of pain. I had to let everything go to get well. I should be grateful I had a few bucks left to get by while I am getting well—that should be my focus, gratitude. But I am often so uncomfortable in my skin that I think sometimes about saying "screw it," but I have done that my entire life. I'm not sure why I am so miserable, but I am not going to use today. They tell me God will remove my fears. It's just not working today for me, God, but what the hell, I am alive..."

11-12-07 (Sober 9 months & 22 days)
"Any serenity I may have had went straight to outright anger and rage as I could not find my fucking iPod and my computer isn't fucking working. I completely flipped out and I was irate—jeez, this isn't normal behavior, I am so fucking sick, and I have so much work to do on myself it's ridiculous."

12-13-07 (Sober 10 months & 26 days)
"I had a pretty killer day today, but low level depression and hopelessness hit me at about 1:00 PM. It subsided though, and it's all okay. It's going to be okay."

2-14-08 (Sober 11 months & 27 days)
"Today my father took his own life, and it hurts. It hurts a lot. I'm
certain he was a tortured soul, in every facet. His inner sadness
far outweighed his capacity for joy. I pray that he is now at peace
within, and that God is now protecting his tormented soul. I will
always love him, and he did love me. I'm just sad this is the way it's
going to be: "my father died of suicide." I need to stay strong and
stay sober no matter what."

2-17-08 (Sober one year)
"Today I celebrated one year of sobriety at the Canyon Club. The
support and love has been very encouraging. I am grateful to be
alive and to not be addicted. It's a really big deal for me. I don't
know how I ever got away from the addiction—it had to be God
intervening. All I want is love in my life, no more anger, just peace.
In my troubled soul, it's a big deal to have some peace."

11-25-08 (Sober 1 year, 9 months, & 8 days)
"I love my life now. I love the storm that is upon us here in Southern
California because it's not within me. For so long I had to fight and
struggle with my addiction. It's not that way now—people mean
something to me again, life means something to me again. Tonight
I get to speak at Charlie Street [an indigent detox house], and for
me that's huge. I have been going there every week to read with
other alcoholics and share with them that they can get well. I was
so sick early on when I went there, and I would wonder if I would
ever feel comfort and joy again. I am pretty comfortable mostly
these days. I am going through some growing pains with my new
business, but it seems to be just a conflict with my ego. So many
things I have no control over."

11-27-08 (Sober 1 year, 9 months, & 10 days)
"Today marks my 2nd sober Thanksgiving as an adult. I spent it
with Hazard's family, and they were wonderful. I couldn't take my
eyes off of this little baby girl named Skyler, 11 months old. Just

precious. My comfort level today was far greater than last year, no comparison really at all to the year prior. I have some fears, but nothing God won't help me with, right?"

4-15-09 (Sober 2 years, 1 month, & 28 days)
"I awoke today with my head racing a bit, as it frequently does. The best thing for me is to get busy, do something physical to calm things down. There's so much to be grateful for; to recover from what was a hopeless state of mind and body is such a miracle. For that I bleed with gratitude—the storm of constant addiction has left and now there is unrivaled beauty. I pray to live in God's grace. I crave love, affection, and joy. Gone is bitterness and despair and that is so beautiful. It warms a heart that was dark and lonely for so long. Isolation has left and sunlight has crept in, not quickly mind you. The war is over. Now it's about maintaining a spiritual condition that will ensure my sobriety and well being. I love being alive."

Made in the USA
San Bernardino, CA
16 February 2013